Destructive Poetics

# Destructive Poetics

## Heidegger and Modern American Poetry

# Paul A. Bové

Columbia University Press · New York · 1980

# 63214

The Andrew W. Mellon Foundation, through a special grant, has
assisted the Press in publishing this volume.


Library of Congress Cataloging in Publication Data

Bové, Paul A          1949–
  Destructive poetics.

  Includes bibliographical references and index.
  1. American poetry—History and criticism—
Theory, etc.   2. Influence (Literary, artistic,
etc.)   3. Heidegger, Martin, 1889–1976.
4. Criticism—United States.   5. Whitman, Walt,
1819–1892—Criticism and interpretation.
6. Stevens, Wallace, 1879–1955—Criticism and
interpretation.   7. Olson, Charles, 1910–1970—
Criticism and interpretation.   8. Phenomenology.
9. Hermeneutics.   10. Poetics.   I. Title.
PS78.B57          801'.951          79–24917
ISBN 0-231-04690-1




Columbia University Press
New York          Guildford, Surrey

for Carol

# Contents

# Preface

You must become an ignorant man again
And see the sun again with an ignorant eye
And see it clearly in the idea of it
                    —Wallace Stevens

The literary history of Modern and Postmodern American poetry is being rewritten in the 1970s because much of this poetry
throws into doubt the very language which Anglo-American
critics normally use to write such histories. Furthermore, Modern poetry provides a more adequate, because less rigid, sense of
poetic "tradition" upon which authentic literary history must
"rest." The "history" of Modern and Postmodern poetry is
largely the work of New Critics and academicians trained in the
New Criticism. Although there have recently been many attempts to deal with Modern poetry from non-New Critical
standpoints, I do not think they have succeeded in escaping fully
the New Criticism's influence. Indeed, a deconstruction of the
rhetoric of the New Critics and of some of its antagonists such as
Harold Bloom, Walter Jackson Bate, Northrop Frye, and Roy
Harvey Pearce to mention only a few, reveals that many of the
recent alternatives to the New Criticism are really not substan-
tially different from it at all. A destructive reading of Bate,
Bloom, Cleanth Brooks, and to a lesser extent Paul de Man,
shows that they all are caught within essentially the same metaphysical critical tradition. To varying degrees all of these critics'
works—consciously or not—nostalgically reify an aesthetically

ordered, often humanistic, tradition as an alternative to the radical flux, disorder, alienation and death which characterizes the Postmodern world. The purpose of this book is to demonstrate the underlying antihistorical critical motives defending this "tradition," as well as to suggest the inevitable resultant misreading of this poetry as the agency of this reification.

Although the book seemingly has two successive parts—a critical destruction of the Modern critical mind, and a destructive reading of the poetry of Whitman, Stevens, and Olson—the structure of the argument presented here is "actually" circular. For the most part, the condition for the possibility of performing the destruction of the traditional critical rhetorics in chapters one through three is an awareness of the nature of the poetry of "interpretation" or "destruction" which makes up the second part. In other words, experientially, the second half of this interpretation must have occurred first. The readings of the poems do not grow out of the "method" derived in the first chapters; rather, the awareness that the critical tradition needs to be destroyed emerges from my understanding that a great portion of Modern and Postmodern poetry refuses to be coerced into the concrete universals and aesthetic monads of Modernist criticism. The Modernist critical tradition begins to crack under a close reading of Wallace Stevens' poems, and it "breaks down" completely when it is brought into contact with the poetry of Whitman and Olson.

This book is, therefore, a record of a hermeneutic situation. When habitual modes of perception and expectation fail, authentic doubt and the sense of the *"Ab-grund,"* of the "abyss," of the *mise en abîme,* which Modern critical rhetorics of "presence" obscure, deny the reader a secure unified perspective and cast the critic into the free play of interpretation. The traditionally privileged critical process based for so long upon both the myth of the objective analysis of autotelic texts and the stability of the self obscures the radical play of reading. The weakening of Modernist habits of reading which are based on critical theories of aesthetic distance and disinterest makes the Postmodern reader aware of the potential for violence and novelty in every act of reading or interpretation, indeed, in every nonhabitual use of language.

Beyond being the record of a hermeneutic situation, this book might demonstrate that Postmodern criticism should always be hermeneutic if it intends to be authentic. In fact, the second half of this text argues that Modern poetry, in its relation to the accumulated past, destroys the language, forms, tropes, and poems of the "tradition" projected by Modernist criticism. Confronted by a poetry which refuses an ideology of poetic disinterest projected by the Kantian New Criticism and some of its structuralist descendents, Postmodern critics can only turn to an equally hermeneutic, destructive, interpretive process of literary analysis and history.

Ultimately, Modern and Postmodern poetry destroys the very notion of the "tradition," as long as that term means a reified aesthetic set of interrelations among texts. Indeed, the critique of the concept of Modernism's nostalgia for "tradition" can be extended beyond the limited sphere of literary history and analysis to the broader range of historical, philosophical, and discursive inquiry. As Charles Olson's *Maximus Poems* make eminently clear, the idea of "tradition" as defined above has no claim to privilege or priority: all particular "traditions" are historical, ideological fictions, i.e., unacknowledged myths, the creations of mystified minds. Modernist critical notions of "the tradition" disguise alienation, history, and absence.

For the most part, the destruction of the Modern critical tradition in the first three chapters reveals that both the New Criticism and its antagonists can be called Gnostics "interested" in establishing the priority of word over world, presence over absence. Both Bate and Bloom, for example, create theories of poetic interrelationships which protect the "existence" of a sacrosanct "tradition" that is continuous and unchanging. The New Critics and their adherents likewise insist upon a poetics of "unmastered" irony which allows the individual poem, as artifact, to interpose itself as Image between the reader-poet-critic and the

Preface

world. And, as my analysis of the specific New Critical evaluation of American poetry in the later chapters reveals, Brooks, Tate, Ransom, Wimsatt, and all the rest also insist upon a continuous, unchanging tradition maintained by the exclusive definition of poetry as ironic, closed form.

Bate and Bloom are both intent upon establishing an ahistorical "psychological" model of belatedness and anxiety as more primordial than the linguistic model as a basis for understanding not only one poet's relation to his past, but also our critical relationships to the past and present. Yet the "psychological" model and its defining rhetoric of continuity and genealogy becomes in their work a way of disguising the Postmodern "dis-ease" caused by the historical uncertainty of our point of view in the act of reading. Bate and Bloom build their structures upon a centered language of presence, of absolute beginnings and ends. A hermeneutic analysis of their works not only reveals their mystification about the way in which their language brings along with it the entire logocentric or onto-theological "tradition," but it also discloses the truth of precisely what they attempt to deny: the past imposes itself as a burden upon the present not because of the psychological inadequacy of Modern writers but because the language itself is historical—used-up, reified, habitualized by the nostalgic metaphysical "tradition."

Just as many literary histories maintain habitual aesthetic constructs as defenses against the potential for disorder which exists in the relationship among texts, so the New Critics in their insistence upon closed, ironic form create verbal monads which distance the poet and critic from the chaotic nothingness overlaid by demystified "fiction." Indeed, it is precisely at that point where the "traditional" insistence of Modernist critics upon a continuous "tradition" and the New Critics' demand for closed, ironic form intersect that my destruction comes to bear. Both literary histories and literary interpretations which are defined by closing off aesthetic forms—"tradition," or "concrete universal," or "competency"—from change and the world, are antithetical to the destructive process of Modern and Postmodern poetry.

Preface

The poetry of Whitman, Stevens, and Olson is marked by its historical openness to the world and by its hermeneuticly subversive orientation toward the language and forms of the past.

Demystified literary history and literary interpretation is marked by an awareness that all genuine uses of language are destructive, that is, that they stand oriented towards the future in a discontinuous, nonimitative relation to the verbal events of the past. Paul de Man approximates such a literary theory, but he remains blind in his claim for the absolute demystification of every poet. In fact, I would claim in opposition to de Man, not only critical discourse is marked by the blindness-insight structure he identifies, but *every* use of language. Therefore, to expose what lies hidden in blindness, language must be historically destructive. This fact discloses to the critic a complex interrelationship among literary texts, literary interpretations, and the poetic destructions of "natural" or "normal" interpretations of earlier texts.

The "tradition" as an unchanging, idealized order in which writer and reader must be competent is upset when close attention is paid to the destabilizing potential of language to disclose and to cover-over. A critic who is aware of the complex interactions among texts does not stand in any simple relationship to one closed "object" which he can describe. Rather, through intertextuality, i.e., the open form of the destructive language event which is the poem, the critic is placed into a historical relation with earlier readings of the poem and with those traditional uses of language which the poem, to the degree that it is authentic, is questioning. The New Critical aesthetic monad is broken down in this context as well as the genealogical, Bloomian model of a continuous post-Miltonic tradition. In the place of these traditional aesthetic units which cut man off from the world and time, there emerges an ever-changing set of relationships in which neither the poem nor the critic can function as a determined or determinable center.

In *Being and Time*, Martin Heidegger develops an ontological and existential theory of human being, understanding, and language which indicates precisely the simultaneously dual potential of all language to tell the truth and to lie. On the one hand, poetry can be reified into a "tradition" obscuring the original discoveries sedimented in language. And, on the other hand, poetry can reopen the site of the past, to examine the historical sedimentation and to make possible discoveries. Although Heidegger explains how the nature of Dasein's understanding (*Verständnis*) can reify as well as dis-cover, he develops a way of approaching the past in which the potentiality for authentic disclosure can be actualized and itself stand revealed. Heidegger's own project is to destroy the history of metaphysics in order to show how it has covered-over the Being-question and Man's basic temporality. To do this, he needs to reveal how the habitual use of language in metaphysics leads philosophers to ignore Being as such (and temporality as the ground of Dasein's Being) to attend only to beings. Heidegger, thus, regains from past texts, like Kant's *Critique of Pure Reason,* the dis-closures about Being that philosophers "wanted" to make but were unable to because of their historical position within the language of "tradition."

The poetry of Whitman, Stevens, and Olson stands in a relation to the poetic past which is similar to Heidegger's stance toward the metaphysical tradition; each of these poets tries in some way to break open the impediment which traditional continuous genetic models have become to the founding of new "traditions," to the future. Although he remains blind to the language of Emersonian idealism, Whitman, in *Leaves of Grass,* is extensively destructive. Stevens is more aware of the habits of past language than Whitman is and turns the major dualistic and quest metaphors of the Romantic tradition against themselves to reveal that they "disclose" the "nothing" which is at the "heart of utterance." Charles Olson, in *The Maximus Poems,* also subverts the traditional language of abstract concepts and ironic symbols to displace not only the continuous linearity of the Western onto-theological tradition, but to discover that the very notions both of "tradition" as a centered canon and of "history"

are Western *myths* used to defend the aesthetic, distanced, disinterested privilege of antihistorical metaphysics.

The broken, temporal, "open" forms of the poetry of these
writers resist New Critical and structural attempts to impose
upon them the teleological, ironic, atemporal, distanced structures of the reifying West. The historicity of these poets lies in
their insistence upon a poetics of "dis-closure," of opening up
the horizon of meaning which habitual expectations and forms
close off. Whitman and Olson are radically open in their forms.
That is, the works of both can be epitomized in the figure of the
voyager who reenacts his discoveries as he makes them, and not
afterward in a moment of recollection. While Stevens is admittedly less "spontaneous" than Whitman and Olson, nonetheless,
particularly in his long poems and late lyrics, he abruptly shifts
from topic to topic and perception to perception in his destructive "play" among the various "fictions" which "present" themselves. Whitman and Olson project a "figure of outward" who
journeys unendingly through the "Penetralium"; Stevens' equivalent encounter with "mystery" lies in the constant penetration to
nothingness which his various texts make in their testing of the
traditional forms and tropes of poetry. Perhaps, ultimately, this
text should suggest how the range and complexity of the interpretive interaction established by one poem's destructive relation to
the tradition prohibits any privileged or "complete" reading of a
text. Indeed, it prevents any "reading" which is not always itself
fluctuating in some relationship between the "truth" and "error"
of the poem which is being "misread" and the interpretation's
own dual potential for simultaneously disclosing and reifying.

Thus, no certainty should arise or should be *felt* to arise in
any reading of a poem or any reading of an interpretation of a
poem. Indeed, the very possibility of distilling the "purpose" and
"goals" of this text into a prefatory statement threatens to *fix* in
some way, in schematic or outline form, the very uncertain,
changing patterns of relations which might emerge. The lack of
any methodologically or thematically "prior" chapter or statement allows a series of "inter-actions" to emerge from the ele-

ments of the discussion. The destructive *wandering* through the "traditional" critical assumptions of genetic, dialectical, New Critical, and structural *methods* often requires, as in an Olson poem, that I touch certain spots in my trip several times. Thus, for example, the critique of the New Criticism is not restricted beforehand to the third chapter on Brooks. As the poetry of Whitman, Stevens, and Olson reveals different, *particular* aspects of the *general* truth about the New Criticism's static metaphysics, the destruction of the New Criticism expands, pushing back the horizon of meaning as more of the mystification of the New Criticism comes to consciousness in this repetition.

Because of the necessarily "process-ional" nature of the text any "pre-face" must inevitably be a lie. A "pre-face" suggests a well-organized, thought-out-in-advance series of analyses which are written to satisfy the program's "intention." It is precisely such intellectual and formal priority which Whitman, Stevens, and Olson attack in literature and Heidegger in philosophy. A "pre-face" expresses a commitment to a methodological, rhetorical, and ultimately metaphysical stance. Precisely how to destroy the presence of *this* "Preface" presents a unique problem for the destructive approach: "destruction" founders when it must be turned back upon itself.

Destructive reading always presupposes as part of the hermeneutical situation the closure of a historical period, a breakdown within the traditional language being examined, and the discovery of contradiction. A destructive misreading must, therefore, emerge from a *partially* "privileged" position, an incomplete understanding of what the mystified rhetoric of another discourse is covering-over. When, however, the opening up of the horizon of meaning involves destroying one's own rhetorical stance, the destructive process is brought up short by the necessary "error" or "blindness" of one's own position. The historical "cover-up" of one's own destructive rhetoric is not available for destruction until the time when that rhetoric has itself been displaced. As Kierkegaard's model of the "stages on life's way" points out, "repetition," i.e., a destructive rereading of one's

Preface

own stance, cannot be successfully accomplished until the prior position is no longer seen to "work," when it "fails" as a means of discovery, that is, when "history passes." At that time, a new incomplete understanding emerges from the previous rhetoric or model and a "repetition" with a difference of the "same" problems and materials becomes possible and necessary. Until the point where one's own period is "closed," when one's own rhetoric no longer "works," the destruction of one's own rhetoric is partially impossible and, to some extent, one's own language and program tend to solidify and misrepresent.

Rhetorically, the presence of a "pre-face" to an interpretation demands of its reader, as well as of its writer, an immediate attempt to subvert it, to disclose the possible limitations which its own "program" necessitates. The formal structure of a text cannot be assumed to be linear and progressive. Therefore, the potential *priority* of a "pre-face" must be thrown instantaneously into doubt by its very fictional existence as a "beginning." Even though *this particular "pre-face" is being written after the act of composing the book* and, in effect, continues it, its rhetorical function as a "preface" creates the illusion of a beginning. Potentially, all prefatory and concluding statements threaten to mislead the reader into an inauthentic encounter with the text. Prefaces cover-over the disclosing, process-ional nature of the critical act and can obscure the very nature of reading as a dangerous, fluctuating event. By their very *presence,* "pre-faces" invite the reader to perform a destruction to reveal what the schematization of the pursuant process covers-up. It demands a hermeneutical misreading of what follows in order to preserve the misreading from reification.

# Acknowledgments

During the time I have spent working on this book, I have incurred innumerable intellectual and personal debts. To Robert Kroetsch and Gerald Gillespie, I am thankful for limitless time and generosity in the early stages of this project. I am also grateful to those many colleagues at Columbia University's Department of English and Comparative Literature whose openness and support made revisions and improvements possible. I would like especially to thank those who have taken the time to read and comment on various sections of this book: George Stade, Joseph Mazzeo, Karl Kroeber, Steven Marcus, Michael Wood, and Edward W. Said. The lucid critical eye of my dear friend Michael Hays has been a support far beyond the limits of this book. Friends and colleagues in other places have been helpful in similar ways. It was a great pleasure and help to have had the detailed reading of the manuscript which Joseph Riddel so graciously provided. Very little, fortunately, slips past his eye. Ute Castleman gave freely of her friendship and typing. To my dear friend, Dan O'Hara—our lives have touched so often—I owe much of what education and feeling I have. To my parents, I owe the joy of the desire to learn and to think. For that incomparable gift, I cannot give thanks. My brother, Mark, knows what love I owe him for his presence.

To William V. Spanos, who as my teacher, for five years constantly made me see and hear anew, I can truly offer no proper thanks. What he has given and still continues to give far exceeds—as it does for all great teachers—even that of which he is aware. I hope someday I can reciprocate this to this man who "can't get away from the old measure of care."

[xix]

## Acknowledgments

It would normally be the greatest joy for me to thank Carol for her intellectual, emotional, and practical support through the long years of this project. But her concern that in doing so I would fall into the worst of clichés prohibits my doing so. As usual she is right. The love and debts I owe to her as meager exchange remain properly where they belong, closed off in our own silence.

For permission to reprint parts of chapters one and three, I want to thank the editors of *Union Seminary Quarterly Review* and *boundary 2*. I wish to thank Alfred A. Knopf, Inc., for permission to quote from Wallace Stevens' *Opus Posthumous,* ed. Samuel French Morse, © 1957; and *The Palm at the End of the Mind,* ed. Holly Stevens, © 1967, 1969, 1971 by Holly Stevens. I also want to thank Jargon/Corinth Books for permission to cite Charles Olson's *The Maximus Poems,* © 1960 by Charles Olson.

Destructive Poetics

Chapter One

# Literary History and
# Literary Interpretation:
# Toward a Theory
# of Poetic Destruction

I

Since 1970 there has been a renewal of critical interest in the nature of poetic interrelationships, in problems of influence, and generally in the theory and practice of literary history. Contemporary criticism has grown dissatisfied with Modern formalist— and even "Postmodern" structuralist—impulses which have periodized literature into static "worldviews"[1] and ignored the problems of poetic interrelationships in their commitment to the autotelic poetic structure.

Among those who have tried to confront these issues in the United States are Walter Jackson Bate in *The Burden of the Past*, Harold Bloom in *The Anxiety of Influence* and *A Map of Misreading*, and Paul de Man in *Blindness and Insight* and his essays on Nietzsche.[2] All of these texts begin from the position that the New Criticism is unsatisfactory as a critical approach to these problems—even though the nature of its insufficiency is not fully developed—and, in their diverse ways, each of these writers tries to return an awareness of "history" and of poetic inheritance not only to literary history but to literary interpretation as well. In fact, to different degrees they all deny the possibility of separating history and interpretation. Although they all debunk the New Critical "periodization" of literature into static pictures,

[1]

Poetic Destruction

they do not all present similar or even adequate ideas of history on their own. Yet, they all recognize the necessary interrelationship between literary interpretation and the methodological possibilities of doing literary history. A survey of their approaches to this relationship not only suggests some of the reasons for its necessity, but also points toward the failure of traditional positivistic histories to treat adequately literary language.

Bate's book is certainly the simplest introduction into the entire area since it is so traditional in approach. It begins by posing the problem of the existence of poetic predecessors and by defining it as one of the hallmarks of "modern" art:

> I have often wondered whether we could find any more comprehensive way of taking up the whole of English poetry during the last three centuries—or for that matter the modern history of the arts in general—than by exploring the effects of this accumulating anxiety and the question it so directly presents to the poet or artist: *What is there left to do?* (*BP,* 3)

Bate's theme, then, is the mental or psychological anguish which results from the mere accumulation of the past, of the "traditional" in art and poetry. His method is to proceed historiographically, not merely to record the facts of this accumulating anxiety, but to examine the responses of various burdened generations of poets to their own historical situation. However, Bate's intent is not only to examine this anxiety and these poets' own interpretive responses to it, but also to show that these responses are inadequate because they shy away from the most likely and most painful explanation, i.e., David Hume's theory that it "is the writer's loss of self-confidence as he compares what he feels able to do with the rich heritage of past art and literature" which leads inevitably to poetic decline (*BP,* 7; cf. pp. 80–85).

This "heritage" continually expands and accretes, closing off possibilities as it develops. The "moderns' " confrontation with this achieved tradition—which they have been trained to admire (*BP,* 107)—can lead to neuroses and stagnation:

[2]

> the essential problem—the real anxiety—. . . . is [the artist's]
> nakedness and embarrassment (with the inevitable temptations
> to paralysis and routine imitation, to retrenchment or mere fit-
> ful rebellion) before the amplitude of what two thousand years
> or more of an art had already been able to achieve. And mean-
> while, with every generation, our sense of that amplitude—its
> variety in subject, in approach, in power or ingenuity of ex-
> pression—has been further increasing as (justifiably, commend-
> ably) we continue to explore that heritage and extend our un-
> derstanding of it. (BP, 95)

Ongoing exploration and development, according to Bate,
requires "distinction" or "difference," that is, a marking off of
the works of one generation or of one poet from its or his immediate predecessor. However, the problem of the past results from
its accumulation into a *continuously* existing, ever-present colloca-
tion of an almost exhausted elaboration of variety. Thus, tradition for Bate is essentially defined, despite his emphasis on "difference" and its suggestion of discontinuity, by a *continuity* of
achievement which, as it were, crowds out "new" achievement,
that is, other variations within the essential tradition. He epitomizes the problem as he sees it in this question: "Does not the essence of our heritage in the humanities and the arts involve the
preservation of the best that has been so gradually, and against
such odds, attained in the past?" (BP, 90).

Bate "diagnose[s]" (BP, pp. 52–53; passim) the cause of the
decline of the arts as the inability of "modern" poets to overcome their own "psychological complexities" (BP, 7). After dis-
counting all of the 18th century's poets' theories as to why they
could produce no epics or Shakespeares as evasions of their own
freedom and responsibility to stand "boldly" (BP, 132f) in the
face of the tradition, he offers this set of rhetorical questions:

> Was it, after all, a case of simple psychological inhibition
> . . . ? Could this widespread feeling that the "advance" (or
> complication) of what we call civilization was unpropitious to
> poetry—that it seriously hampered the poet and would in time
> seriously hamper the artist generally—be explained more sim-

[3]

Poetic Destruction

> ply, and most truthfully, by psychological factors, by the universal human hope to make a genuine contribution and the fact that in the past so much had already been done so well that it seemed impossible to compete in the same way? Was the mere existence of the past beginning to exert an enormous pressure on poetry and forcing it into less promising directions? (*BP*, 80)

Bate's avowed purpose in this text

> is twofold: to pose for us, in general, this central problem—to express the hope that we can pluck it out into the open and try to see it for what it is—and, second, to help us reground ourselves, to get a clearer idea of our bearings, by looking back with a fresh eye to the beginning drama of what we ourselves are now living with and feel so deep a need to bring into perspective. (*BP*, 13)

In other words, Bate is not only offering a diagnosis for the disease, but he is also prescribing a cure. Once we become aware that our sense of being latecomers, as Harold Bloom calls us, is merely an illusion, a result of our own neurosis which has been obscured until now by our ideational explanations of the decline of the West and the exhaustion of language, we can take proper steps to "demystify" ourselves and presumably halt the actual decline in the arts which results unnecessarily from our illusion.

Bate points to the Romantics' temporary victory over the weight of their predecessors as a temporary halt in the steady movement downward in the arts begun at the Renaissance. The Romantics derive their strength from the 18th century's ideas of genius and greatness which, of course, for Neo-Classical doctrine, have their roots in Longinus (*BP*, 114–34). "Greatness" provides the 18th century with a "bedrock" of possible "value" (*BP*, 128); it teaches that "we need not be the passive victims of what we deterministically call 'circumstances,' . . . but that . . . with the *great* we can become freer . . ." (*BP*, 129). The ideal of "greatness"—which culminates, of course, in the 19th century's "hero-worship cult"—inspires "boldness" so that the artist can get beyond what he feels as the limitations of his past to seize

[4]

"opportunities and create new ones" (*BP,* 127). Ultimately, to overcome the burden, as the Romantics were able to do, is not only a matter of aesthetics, of art, but of "the freedom of man (that freedom so indispensable to achievement) to follow openly and directly what he most values . . ." (*BP,* 133).

Having achieved this diagnosis and having cured ourselves, we can establish a normative relationship to our predecessors and our tradition. We can continue to develop it by adding simply another possible variation to an already achieved series of permutations. Freed of needless anxiety, then, and assured of our ability to get beyond our place on the temporal horizon of creativity, we confront our past with boldness, that is, "directly facing up to what we admire and then trying to be like it . . ." (*BP,* 132).

The seductiveness of Bate's prose and the appealing simplicity of his diagnosis and cure tempts one into accepting his analysis of the "moderns' " relationship to their predecessors. However, a closer look at the rhetorical structures of his study shows that it proceeds from an unacceptable linguistic and methodological basis which he assumes unselfconsciously, naturally, as it were. Not all of the possible objections which could be made against Bate's rhetoric are relevant here, except to show the degree to which he leaves his language unexamined and in need of destruction. One rhetorical pattern is of primary importance, though, because it defines and structures, limits and confines, his method and insight: the privileged, i.e., unexamined and "central" metaphor of growth–decay.

Like all interpretation, Bate's proceeds in a circle.[3] His method and his theme complement each other so that he must necessarily "prove" his contentions and at the same time remain unaware of alternatives. It is neither to the point nor is it possible to say if his method precedes his theme or vice-versa. Priority itself is an issue for the method and theme of the text Bate creates.

He uncritically assumes a genetic model for the problem he is discussing: a beginning of the burden of the past, its growth into a middle of paralysis, and its end or death in an awareness that the entire problem is a neurotic illusion. Some of the com-

[5]

mon variants of this model involve the rhetoric of the Fall from some unburdened perfection in the past and the language of nostalgia and loss, of longing to return to that mythic, nonneurotic origin. As a result of these rhetorics and controlling metaphors, his narrative is not only historical, but historiographical as well; that is, it assumes and, in fact, requires the continuity of the subject being "historicized," i.e., the tradition; it makes possible both the cure of "boldness" into which the modern poet must grow and also the disease into which he *first fell* with Dryden and Descartes (*BP,* vii, 31).

Because Bate's language is not self-conscious, that is, because it does not reflect back upon itself in its own terms and question its own rhetoric, it creates the "myth"[4] of the burden of the past, *sui generis,* and provides a cure for a disease which is invented only so that the cure could be effective. Because the past, the tradition, is a continuous whole, it is ever-present to the mind of the modern. There seems to be no escape from it—the diseased illusion is that escape is valuable or needed—despite the attempts at originality which dominate modern art. It leaves the latecomer less and less imaginative space as it grows monolithically. Paralysis results from this confrontation with the past which seems to have entrapped us and determined the possibilities of our creation. This illusion fades after it is recognized as such and the poet is once again able, in an imaginative renewal, to be like what comes before, to draw upon the accumulated past which is constantly present before him. In this way, the poet achieves freedom from time as history, from any undesirable restraints which being a poet with a national, linguistic, and cultural past might impose. Yet the poet is not cut adrift; he can never get beyond the tradition because the tradition is a continuous unit which can be explored and modified, but not disrupted without "degenerating" "into the various forms of anti-art," (*BP,* 10) which for those still caught in the illusion seems to be the only, but barren, future.

Thus, Bate's genetic model, which he hopes to provide to Modern poets and readers, provides him with the exact release from anxiety stemming from an uncomfortable historical relation with the past. He remains, as Paul de Man would say, blind to his own insight. Not only does he not see how his own "explanation" and "cure" is no less an evasion of the burden of the past and the lessons of temporality than those he claims the 18th century devised to free itself from admitting its own weaknesses. In fact, he seems unaware of the "real" subject of his text: the burden of the past is not psychological illusion but unexamined, habitual, linguistic assumptions, rhetoric, and analogues such as the genetic model. Bate "proves" precisely that which he sets out to disprove: the accumulated past's usurpation of language pressures the Modern. The past reifies language into fixed patterns which seem self-evident but are, in fact, only unexamined and therefore habitual (*BP,* 87).

## II

Although in *The Anxiety of Influence* and *A Map of Misreading* Harold Bloom develops a more extended and sophisticated version of the psychological model of poetic interrelationships than Bate, he nonetheless can be accused of falling into similar rhetorical patterns. But any attempt to question Bloom cannot proceed from empirical refutations of his specific readings. Rather, his texts must be deconstructed to reveal in two of his early theoretical works, the unprivileged nature of his rhetoric, and perhaps more importantly, the relation to the world at stake in viewing literature and criticism from his idiosyncratic but influential perspective.

    *The Anxiety of Influence* contains many undestroyed tropes which structure Bloom's thesis and reflect his concerns and prejudices, the habits of his mind and writing. *A Map of Misreading* crystallizes the importance of two of these tropes: first, the genetic metaphor and its variants—the myth of the Fall, the idea of origins, the language of loss and nostalgia, and the ultimate death of poetry; second, the rhetoric of dualism and its transformations—the Cartesian isolation of the self, the quest to escape nature and time, the Gnostic desire for godhead, and the melancholy insistence on the priority of mind over matter.

Bloom's analysis of the life cycle of the poet as poet introduces the genetic pattern of birth, growth, and death (*AI*, 8). He immediately extends it to the larger scale of literary history, which he tropes as a "family romance," a metaphor which generates itself from the initial scene of the poetic selection of Oedipus (*AI*, 10), which grows into a "family" of poets in the tradition, and which dies out in the funereal poetry of Modern and Postmodern writers (*AI*, 8, 10, 56–57). In other words, the structure of genealogy lies behind both Bloom's description of the psychological processes within one poet anxiously confronting the past and also his more "historical" attempt to describe a "truer" literary history based upon poetic melancholy. As an implicit rhetorical structure, genealogy, the genetic pattern, provides an unquestioned base for Bloom's entire enterprise. As in Bate's *The Burden of the Past,* it guarantees the "results" of the investigation. It prejudices the discussion of all the issues, and it acts as the linguistic matrix which "generates" meaning and understanding. There is no semantic value in Bloom's work beyond this rhetorical pattern.

Simultaneously and intrinsically intertwined with the genetic pattern is the theme and rhetoric of dualism. Like Bate, Bloom discovers the "origin" of anxiety in the dualism which arises in Descartes' separation of the intensive *cogito* and the *res extensa* (*AI*, 33–34). The "Covering Cherub" is, in fact, made possible as a metaphor only by the Cartesian extensiveness which separates objects in space and events in time (*AI*, 38). It is this Cartesian dualism which is the defining characteristic of Modern poetry (*AI*, 39). Unlike Pauline dualism, it produces melancholy, not moral obligation.

The rhetorics of dualism and genealogy intersect in the theme of birth and priority. The argument of *The Anxiety of Influence* is that all strong poets, like Wordsworth in "Ode: Intimations of Immortality," try to overcome the priority of nature and

[8]

time and necessarily fail (*AI,* 9–10). The independently existing
"external" world claims priority over the poetic mind and restricts its freedom and comfort: "For every poet begins (however
'unconsciously') by rebelling more strongly against the consciousness of death's necessity than all other men and women
do" (*AI,* 10). Of course, according to Bloom, the acute anxiety
of the poet emerges from a fear of two deaths: the physical death
of the human being threatens the absolute freedom and priority
of the *"cogito,"*and the inhibiting temporal struggle with the poetic precursors promises "poetic" death. Thus, the poet's quest is
for temporal priority over his fathers as well as for hierarchical
priority or authority over nature. The poet's desire is to be not
only his own father and to displace his "real" father, but to be
the parent of those who give birth to him in what Bloom, echoing Freud, calls the "Primal Scene of Instruction," the moment
of "Election-Love" when the poet is called and answers (*MM,*
54).

Bloom sees the entire poetic enterprise encapsulated in this
"revisionist" relationship between poet and precursors and poet
and nature. In order to make imaginative space for himself and to
avoid being smothered by the precursor, every poet misreads his
father: "To revise the precursor is to lie, not against being, but
against time, and *askesis* is peculiarly a lie against the truth of
time, the time in which the ephebe hoped to attain an autonomy
already tainted by time, ravaged by otherness" (*AI,* 130). Temporality which insists upon a past violates the poet's desired authority, but duality which isolates the ephebe from the "outside"
also separates him from the work of his precursor. In the moment of his birth as a poet, then, he is instantaneously violated in
his integrity and self-sufficiency because the texts and poets
which elect him are not immediate, but "other." Bloom must be
quoted at length to clarify his use of the rhetoric of birth and its
intersection with the language of dualism:

> How do men become poets, or to adopt an older phrasing,
> how is the poetic character incarnated? When a potential poet

first discovers (or is discovered by) the dialectic of influence, first discovers poetry as being both external and internal to himself, he begins a process that will end only when he has no more poetry within him, long after he has the power (or desire) to discover it outside himself again. Though all such discovery is a self-recognition, indeed, a Second Birth, and ought, in the pure good of theory, be accomplished in a perfect solipsism, it is an act never complete in itself. Poetic influence is the sense— amazing, agonizing, delighting—of *other poets,* as felt in the depths of the all-but-perfect solipsist, the potentially strong poet. For the poet is condemned to learn his profoundest yearnings through an awareness of *other selves.* The poem is *within* him, yet he experiences the shame and splendor of *being found by* poems—great poems—*outside* him. To lose freedom in this center is never to forgive, and to learn the dread of threatened autonomy forever. (*AI,* 25–26)

The violation of this poetic "center" of autonomy is the pivot of Bloom's criticism as well as of his claim that all poems are of this origin or birth (*MM,* 54, 62). This passage also clarifies the central issue for Bloom and, he would argue, for all post-Cartesian poets. Temporality and dualism—the past and the other—create an anxiety which is not existential, but which is analogous to the threat which many of Kierkegaard's "aesthetic" authors feel when their absolute freedom to transcend the actual is in any way restricted by time or nature.[5] The poetic enterprise, then, must be an attempt to reachieve the priority lost in the Fall into Cartesian time and dualism.

Bloom's interest in the Primal Scene of Instruction in *A Map of Misreading* fills out the genetic structure of *The Anxiety of Influence.* In the sixth and final section of his analysis of the Primal Scene the critical act returns the poem of the son successfully to the beginning, i.e., to the moment he is called to be a poet. This return is a "source" both of the "revisionism" of the poem in general as it swerves away from its predecessors and of the possibility of the practical act of criticism which, like Bloom's own work in these two books, proceeds from this moment as a firm "ground." The fifth phase of the Primal Scene only establishes that each poem is "a total interpretation or *lidrosh* [the term comes from Lurianic Kabbalism] of the poem or poetry of origins" (*MM*, 54). However, neither the critic nor the poet can rest in this mere interpretation of a text about the birth of the poet in the prior moment of selection: "In this phase, all of Blake or of Wordsworth becomes a reading or interpretation of Milton" (*MM*, 54). The poet and critic must push back further beyond the verbal articulation or interpretation of "origin" as it appears in the precursor's poetry. The successful quest needs to be complete and to establish its priority and autonomy: "The sixth and final phase of our Primal Scene is revisionism proper, where origins are re-created, or at least a re-creation is attempted, and it is in this phase that a newer practical criticism can begin, at several levels, including the rhetorical" (*MM*, 54).

For Bloom, repetition is the means of achieving this return to origins. Basing his argument upon a misreading of Kierkegaard—he identifies Kierkegaard's "repetition" with Hegel's "mediation"[6]—Bloom concludes that repetition's "aesthetic displacement would re-affirm dialectically the continued possibility of becoming a great poet" (*MM*, 58). It would be a means of alleviating anxiety caused by the seeming irreversibility of time and the priority of the father. The splendor of being a great poet only "can be reached through the mediation of repetition, by a return to origins and the incommensurable Election-Love that the Primal Scene of Instruction can bestow, there at the point of origin" (*MM*, 58–59).

Bloom's unquestioning evaluation of the "origin" and, therefore, of the entire genealogical quest implicit in his rhetoric lies in the establishment of poet, and knowing critic, as godhead, as the One capable of transcending time, its consequences, and the dependency upon the "other" of the Cartesian dualism: "The compulsion to repeat the precursor's patterns is . . . an attempt to recover the prestige of origins, the oral authority of a prior Instruction" (*MM*, 59). A fuller sense of the aspiration to divinity emerges from this admission: "Poetic repetition quests, despite itself, for the mediated vision of the fathers, since such mediation holds open the perpetual possibility of one's own sublimity, one's election to the realm of the true Instructors" (*MM,* 59). Bloom's misreading of Kierkegaard's repetition as a concern for possibility, is in fact typical of those who, according to Kierkegaard, cannot make the movement of repetition, but remain caught in the aesthetic stasis of recollection, i.e., of a mythic attempt to transcend time, to refuse the limitations of actuality in favor of the "perpetual possibility" open only to those who are not of the world and flesh.[7]

The dualistic language of inner and outer worlds, of higher and lower, and of world and spirit compels Bloom to this movement out of time. For Kierkegaard, of course, Spirit and World are absurdly combined by virtue of the paradox of the Incarnation. For the post–Cartesian and, we might say, pre-existential Bloom, the inherence of the "two" worlds is an impossibility forbidden by his rhetoric and his own aspiration to sublimity. In *The Anxiety of Influence,* he insists upon the necessity of dualism to critic and poet (*AI,* 33, 34, 38–39, 40, 71–72). Dualism is not only the "source" of poetic anxiety, but it is a fiction necessary to Bloom's claims that all poets and critics of strength must be Gnostics (*AI,* 84–85, 130). The rhetoric of dualism and of origins compels the conclusion that poets quest for a way out of time and the world and not merely for some imaginative space not filled by their predecessors. The movement out of the world and time can only be justified if the "world," the "other" is Gnostically devalued and thus seen as inhibiting the creation of poetry itself.

The metaphor of the "end" or "conclusion" is of complementary importance in Bloom and it also results in the suspension of time and of the priority of the world over the mind. In the state of *apophrades,* the last of six phases of poetic misinterpretation outlined in *The Anxiety of Influence,* the end of the poet's growth marks his victory over time and his predecessors. It is the completion of the movement of "repetition." The tone

Poetic Destruction

and wording of Bloom's description of this final phase are of importance in understanding its significance for poet and critic:

> The *apophrades,* the dismal or unlucky days upon which the dead return to inhabit their former houses, come to the strongest poets, but with the very strongest there is a *grand* and *final* revisionary movement that *purifies* even this last influx. Yeats and Stevens, the strongest poets of our century, and Browning and Dickinson, the strongest of the later nineteenth century, can give us vivid instances of this most cunning of revisionary ratios. For all of them achieve a style that captures and oddly retains *priority* over their precursors, so that *the tyranny of time almost is overturned,* and one can believe, for startled moments, that they are being *imitated by their ancestors.* (*AI,* 141; all italics but the last are mine.)

The undestroyed language which Bloom uses leads to the sacredness of origins and ends. In the practical criticism of an individual poem or poet, according to this scheme, there is no value attached to time or history or to the place or position of the poem in the world. Poetic value, for Bloom, lies not in the *process* of getting to the end or in the events occurring along the way—except insofar as they share in the importance of the end—but only in the achieved return to origins and victory over time and the world. In fact, all of the stages along the way are hindrances; they restrict the poet–critic's freedom and autonomy; they interfere with attempts to do away with the journey, the actual and historical, and to "arrive" at the *telos* of divinity and timelessness.

On the scale of literary history, "tradition" becomes the timeless order of strong poets, who, since the Renaissance, have been engaged in forging this order of poetic interrelationships by establishing their own priority to time and matter. The problem of "tradition" is a complicated one in Bloom and it is perhaps the one issue upon which his attempt founders more than any other. However, before this critique can be undertaken, another aspect of his critical machinery, i.e., the "trope," must be introduced.

[13]

Poetic Destruction

Strong poets feel threatened by the entire complex of phenomena we have been describing, but most centrally by time, the separate world, and death. Literary figures, tropes, are, according to Bloom, defense mechanisms employed by those poets against these pressures (*MM*, 75). When the poetic father stands between the poet and the moment of his poetic origin as a block threatening to isolate the son from the sources of poetic vitality, the son must necessarily swerve to avoid the father. While this difficult task is underway—and only the strongest poets can ever return to the moment of their calling when they were solipsistically complete—the son, the ephebe, must protect himself from the anxiety of possible poetic death which the blocking father, the Covering Cherub, threatens. To avoid the pain of the temporal priority of father and of the poetic need for the Other, Nature, or earlier poetical texts, the poet, and even the critic, "tropes" earlier texts as a way of turning them aside and freeing the road to the origins. Wordsworth in *Tintern Abbey,* for example, presents "a defensive interpretation of the invocations to Books III and VII" of *Paradise Lost* (*MM*, 61). Bloom is quite specific, however, in naming what is behind the practical goal of using Wordsworth to explicate Milton and vice versa, as well as in clearing up what is fundamentally at stake in the exercise of these tropes: "A defense . . . is a psychic operation or process directed against *change,* change that might disturb the ego as a stable entity" (*MM*, 92). In literary terms, this definition is refined to mean that each trope is, in relation to the precursor, a defense against an earlier trope. As a result, literary history, according to Bloom, is the continuous record of these attempts to protect the self from external and internal pressures. Ultimately, in achieving the origin and the end, these tropes succeed in their "lie against time and nature" (*AI*, 130) which is needed to protect the poet's autonomy and priority. The impulse upon which literary history is centered then is an attempt to detemporalize the poetic act and poetic existence. Critically, the goal is the recognition or reestablishment of an order of poets which is continuous and which safeguards the self—now the critical as well as

[14]

the poetic self—from the chaos of why poems are written and how they are read.

In Bloom's idea of "revisionism" we find an emphasis, as in Bate, on the poetic *difference* from one's forebears. Such difference can, of course, take any number of forms, six phases of which are described in *The Anxiety of Influence*. We find, however, that, just as in Bate, Bloom's idea of "difference" is carefully designed not to allow for any radical break from the tradition and, therefore, for real discontinuity—if such is possible—but merely for "swerves" away from the immediate predecessor at a certain point of his achievement. In other words, tradition, in Bloom's work, is marked by continuity and not by disruption, inversion, or radical difference. Any break in the unified tradition might introduce change as a threat to the stable identity of the ego or to the narcissistic will.

Just as the trope functions as a defense for the ego of the poet, tradition functions for the critics as a defense against chaos: "if tradition cannot establish its own centrality, it becomes something other than the liberation from time's chaos it implicitly promises to be" (*MM*, 28). Critically, and poetically, then, tradition must be defined by stable continuity and it must be so strongly impressed upon the latecomers that it becomes a habit:

> Though each generation of critics rightly reaffirms the aesthetic supremacy of Homer, he is so much a part of the aesthetic *given* for them (and us) that the re-affirmation is a redundancy. What we call "literature" is inescapably connected to education by a continuity of twenty-five hundred years, a continuity that began in the sixth century B.C. when Homer first became a schoolbook for the Greeks. (*MM*, 33–34)

Bloom's articulation of the reduction of the tradition to habit is completely accurate, as far as it goes. He sees the tradition as a necessary context—or intertext—in which all creativity must act and from which it must be generated. The tradition is a closed system from which escape or divergence is futile: "If you will not have one instructor or another, then precisely by rejecting all instructors you will condemn yourself to the earliest Scene of Instruction that imposed itself upon you." The only creative stance in the face of tradition which will produce difference and continuity is repetitive and circular: "The clearest analogue is Oedipal; reject your parents vehemently enough, and you will become a belated version of them, but compound with their reality, and you may partly free yourself" (*MM, 38*). The repetitive movement of imitating the precursors' patterns within a continuous tradition and then swerving away to provide variety or difference leads to the reclaimed origins of the Scene of Instruction and the final inversion of time in *apophrades*. Inscribed within this scheme, Bloom must argue that all strong poets and critics are Gnostics.

Throughout his work, Bloom offers his theory as an alternative to what he calls Spiritualists and deconstructive critics. It is quite ironic, of course, that his insistence upon Gnosticism is as "spiritualistic" a type of criticism as any within the tradition. He has not "swerved" as much as he hopes. The value which he places upon escaping the earth into the "perpetual possibility" of inverted priority is the necessary conclusion of adopting the rhetoric of genealogy and dualism so unquestioningly.

Furthermore, much of *A Map of Misreading* is motivated by Bloom's disagreement with Paul de Man's deconstructive insistence upon the "priority" of the linguistic to the psychological model (*MM, 76*). The motives for Bloom's faith in the psychic model can be found in his general attempt to offer his theory of revisionism as an alternative to the tradition of deconstruction which he sees epitomized in the work of Nietzsche, Heidegger, and Derrida.

According to Bloom, deconstruction does not complete the movement of interpretation which *restores* value to the text after "breaking it apart" (*MM, 5–6*). He identifies the essence of deconstructive reading with only the second phase of revisionism which he calls "substitution," that is, the exchange of forms and images in one text for those in an earlier. The final phase of revisionism, "representation," is "the antithetical restoration . . . of whatever valid poetry we have left or may yet receive" (*MM,* 5). This phase gains its ideational priority, its conclusive centrality, in Bloom from his misconception that "There are no longer any archetypes left to displace" (*MM,* 31). That genetic and dualistic archetypes dominate Bloom's own work certainly undercuts this claim that deconstructive thought is no longer necessary; also, to whatever degree his readings of various poetic texts may "correctly" discover these unquestioned tropes, criticism still has a valid role in demystifying them and allowing what they obscure to be revealed.

For example, on this very issue of the preference of revisionism to deconstruction, Bloom's language is structured by the nostalgic myth of the Fall. To speak of "restoring" value to a text, and of "re-turning" to origins, as well as, in the final phase of revision, "re-presenting" or "re-esteeming" a text is to imply uncritically the possibility of an unfallen state which exists in what Eliade calls *in illo tempore.*[8] A critique of Bloom's use of this myth, in the context of the previous discussion of "ends" and "origins" would reveal his desire, his nostalgia, for a nontemporal, nonworldly, nonactual *presence* which would act as "center" for his construction of a practical *critical* myth.

This insistence upon the continuity of tradition as protection against chaos is a variant of the defense mechanism in the individual poet. Were this idea of tradition to be deconstructed further, it would become clear that it is also a variant of the myth of the Fall. The poet, Satan, expelled from paradise, "falls" into the temporal state, and doing the best with what he has (*AI,* 33), tries to return to that paradise through his life as a poet. He reaches for his origin as a poet and fails. But many poets, following the same impossible quest, constitute a tradition which itself becomes a bulwark against the chaos into which man is thrown upon his expulsion from the original paradise.

Thus, Bloom insists, the fundamental orientation toward the tradition must be mimetic:

> do we choose a tradition or does it choose us, and why is it
> necessary that a choosing take place, or a being chosen? What
> happens if one tries to write, or to teach, or to think, or even to
> read without the sense of tradition?
>
> Why, nothing at all happens, just nothing. You cannot
> write or teach or think or even read without imitation, and
> what you imitate is what another person has done, that per-
> son's writing or teaching or thinking or reading. Your relation
> to what informs that person *is* tradition, for tradition is influ-
> ence that extends past one generation, a carrying-over of influ-
> ence. (*MM,* 32)

It is with this argument that we approach the dark area in
Bloom's poetics, but a darkness about which he has obviously
thought a great deal. He goes on in this section of *A Map of
Misreading,* "The Dialectics of Poetic Tradition," to define "tradition," beginning with its etymology, in order to explain the
value of imitation:

> Tradition, the Latin *traditio,* is etymologically a handing-over,
> or a giving-over, a delivery, a giving-up and so even a surren-
> der or a betrayal. *Traditio* in our sense is Latin only in language;
> the concept deeply derives from the Hebraic *Mishnah,* an oral
> handing-over, or transmission of oral precedents, of what has
> been found to work, of what has been instructed successfully.
> (*MM,* 32)

"Tradition" in this sense is what is meaningful, permanent, and
because continuous, unchanging. It is the poetic "center" to
which all writers must return as a source, as a beginning for poetic life. It is a mythic paradigm. Tradition contains those spiri-
tually valuable events which must be recollected and it provides a
sublime order of instruction which, ironically, comforts the poet
burdened by the anxiety of his predecessors' achievements. Release from the melancholy of influence cannot come about by escaping the tradition since nothing meaningful or creative happens
except within it. The proper stance in the face of the past is recollection of this meaningful order and an attempt to join it through

mimetic "repetition." Complete breaks from the past are not only not a "cure," but they are not possible without sterility. Such discontinuity would mark a second Fall away from retrieved order into a world of futility.

In his intricate comparison of criticism and poetic misreading to the Kabbalah and Lurianic interpretation, Bloom advises that we "Remind [ourselves] that Kabbalah literally means 'tradition,' that which has been received" (*MM*, 31). This identification is important because of the parallel which exists between poetic/critical interpretation and Kabbalistic misreading, two variants of restorative revisionism. Kabbalistic texts and literary texts both interpret the "tradition." This analogy transfers from Kabbalah to literature exactly the kind of centrality, spirituality, constancy, value, and timeless security which I have argued must result from the rhetorical patterns of origin and dualism Bloom uses throughout: "All Kabbalistic texts [for this read literary texts as well] are interpretive . . . and what they interpret is a central text that perpetually possesses authority, priority, and strength, or that indeed can be regarded as *text itself*" (*MM*, 4). Tradition becomes a sacred text by means of this identification. It is rediscovered in the return to the origin of the Primal Scene of Instruction, and it is the goal or "end" of the revisionary poetic quest.

Tradition is a trope, a defense mechanism, not only because it is a center of a world inhabited by those Bloomian poets and critics among us. But moreover, it is the rhetorical center upon which the entire Bloomian critical structure depends in its *circular* effort to *demonstrate* the absolute necessity and value of *tradition as center*. This is the classic example of the vicious circle: critical language turns back upon itself, against the author's intent, to reveal its own blindness and unexamined rhetoric. Tradition turns upon itself to reveal, in this case, Bloom's attempt to justify it as a *Logos*. More critical analyses show that the game is biased by its rhetoric and that Bloom is "wrong" in his arguments for revisionism and imitation as opposed to deconstruction: language must be turned *consciously* and rhetorically against itself to see

[19]

what "results" its figures have predetermined, to understand what meaning or value they have excluded because of their unexamined, habitual, and privileged status.

At the same time that Bloom's rhetoric argues for and against the logocentricity of "tradition," he tries to maintain an anthropocentric universe for poetry.[9] He argues against de Man's and Derrida's valuation of writing as prior to oral language, not only because such an idea would "de-center" the tradition as Kabbalah, but also because it moves man himself out from the center of creation:

The first use then of a Scene of Instruction is to

> remind us of the humanistic loss we sustain if we yield up the authority of oral tradition to partisans of *writing* [Derrida's "l'écriture"], to those like Derrida and Foucault who imply for all language what Goethe erroneously asserted for Homer's language, that language by itself writes the poems and thinks. The human writes, the human thinks, and always following after and defending against another human, however fantasized that human becomes in the strong imaginings of those who arrive late upon the scene. (*MM,* 60)

Beyond the nostalgic idea of "loss" which emerges from the myth of the Fall and generally from the rhetorics of both genetics and dualism, this text, like those others on tradition, crucially establishes Bloom's need for a center, for something which cannot be brought into doubt, which must be kept out of play. Bloom defends the primacy of two crucial religious centers—the divine text, a source of inspiration, and the *reason* for that divine message, man—from the demythologizing and deconstruction which would destroy the self and the *logos* as privileged, safe positions.

Bloom attacks Modern and Postmodern writers, especially Thomas Pynchon, for marking the death of poetry because they threaten not only his centers, but the very idea of center. Pynchon's sacrilegious relation to the tradition not only makes Bloom anxious, but reveals the basic limitations of his theories on the relation of writers to the past:

[20]

Poetic Destruction

> For us creative emulation of literary tradition leads to images of
> inversion, incest, sado-masochistic parody, of which the great,
> gloriously self-defeating master is Pynchon, whose *Gravity's
> Rainbow* is a perfect text for the sixties, Age of Frye and
> Borges, but already deliberately belated for the seventies. (*MM*,
> 31)

Bloom's genetic rhetoric brings him to the necessary "conclusion": a tradition which has a beginning, and develops, must also
have an end. When *Gravity's Rainbow* and, one might add, *V*, as
well as the works of Beckett, are seen as emulators of a great
tradition, they must appear as decadent texts, as evidence of a
fatal decline. The problem is that Bloom presumes a stable intention among all writers which does not allow them to find a creative relation to the past which is not mimetic or anxious. More
accurately, his rhetoric does not let him discover any other possible relation because it restricts meaning to the genetic-mimetic
paradigm. Continuing in this dualistic rhetoric Bloom arrives at
an intolerable dilemma as critic and teacher in the age of Pynchon:

> If [the teacher of literature] evades his burden [to teach the
> presentness of the past] by attempting to teach only the sup-
> posed presence of the present, he will find himself teaching
> only some simplistic, partial reduction that wholly obliterates
> the present in the name of one or another historicizing formula,
> or past injustice, or dead faith, whether secular or not. Yet how
> is he to teach a tradition now grown so wealthy and so heavy
> that to accommodate it demands more strength than any single
> consciousness can provide, short of the parodistic Kabbalism of
> a Pynchon? (*MM*, 39)

The alternatives, then, are to accommodate oneself to the tradition as a whole or to "die" imaginatively as in Pynchon's paro-
distic sacrilege of the tradition. Bloom's dualistic rhetoric will
not admit any third possibility. His need for a center, for ontological security, cannot conceive the living in a productive but
unaccommodated relationship with the past. It cannot imagine

[21]

that the tradition no longer "works," that it no longer is *mishnah.*

Of course, I cannot attempt to deal with Pynchon here, although I think it is clear from his novels that for him the past no longer contains successful instruction. The same impulse which Bloom dismisses in deconstruction, i.e., the demystification of archetypes, of the *logos,* is behind much of his art. Also, in a way which foreshadows what I will argue about Heidegger, I would extend the destructive impulse to a "retrieve," as I believe Pynchon and other Modern and Postmodern writers do, of what is obscured by the hardening of the tradition into habit.

Not only does Bloom's commitment to the unquestioned rhetoric of genetics and dualism and total faith in the necessity of the tradition as *logos* blind him to possible, nonfunereal ways of reading the relation of Modern and Postmodern writers to the tradition, but his own work "proves" the invalidity of the "revisionary" approach and of the genetic and dualistic grammars. His texts show that all uncritical uses of traditional language are sterile and self-defeating. Like Bate, therefore, he has proven what he set out, in opposition to Nietzsche, Derrida, and de Man, to disprove. The anxiety of influence is necessarily a linguistic structure because the unexamined pressures of what Heidegger calls the ontotheological and Derrida the logocentric language of tradition bring him to demonstrate, unwittingly, the fact that to some extent, it is language which thinks, reads, and writes.

It would seem that Bloom's later writings, especially *Poetry and Repression* and *Wallace Stevens* would make it difficult for me to defend my view of Bloom as a somewhat mystified victim of his own original key ideas of anxiety, genealogy, and family romance. The almost endless play of substitution of signs, of metaphors for reading, in the Bloomian apparatus suggests that Bloom recognizes the metaphoricity of *all* language while at the same time his self-confessed Gnostic dualism seems to do away with all privileged origins by suggesting that "at the beginning" there is always difference and violence. Moreover, Bloom's studies in revisionism and his full-length analysis of Stevens' poetry have so demystified the notion of influence as an innocent and neutral transference of strength and tradition that to accuse him of being a conservative defender of the central pattern of Modernist critical action is apparently absurd.

Yet I would suggest that not only are all of these claims defensible, but that it is indeed possible to find in Bloom's work the major contemporary continuation of the ironic, aesthetic vision classically located in the New Criticism. I argue in my third chapter that for the New Critics poetry is essentially a defensive troping against time, pursuing critical power as a means to absolute freedom. Of course, there are important differences in technique and vision between Bloom and Cleanth Brooks, whom I take to be paradigmatic of New Criticism. For Bloom, a text is a dialectical interplay of rhetorical surface and psychological depth, of trope and intention, of ethos and pathos, while for Brooks a text is only a surface of analogical intersections weaving a tapestry of meaning. And, of course, the New Critics stand rigorously opposed to all notions of intention as a critical fallacy. Nonetheless, one could argue that the New Critics' explications do indeed frequently raise psychological figures to understand the continuous play of tropes in a text. But even so, the important parallel between Bloom and the New Critics is not to be located here but on a more abstract level in a consideration of their analogous desires to create machines or models or metaphors for reading which trope against time by playfully substituting a variety of figures within a well-controlled, unquestioned, powerful theoretical and practical critical apparatus. In fact, one can go even further and assert that, as I show in my chapter on Brooks, this freeplay within fixed boundaries, which represents an aspiration to power conceived as "absolute freedom," reveals itself as a subjective projection which ends in a critical self-parody revealing the deathly stillness of ironic play.

Bloom and the New Critics are alike in this. For even though the New Critics notoriously refuse to elaborate a systematic procedure for criticism, their rhetoric and their operations upon texts create, *de facto,* a powerful set of communicable

[23]

terms, concepts, and procedures which effectively constitute a method of reading. While Bloom has the apparent advantage of generating out of himself a seemingly endless number of signs and concepts for his revisionist idea of reading the shifts within and between texts—indeed, at times it seems as if he is capable of substituting entire systems of tropes for each other—it is clear that, in their variety, they are anchored in the one central utterance of Bloom's critical will—the recognition, projection, and elaboration of the figure of "anxiety of influence." Many of Bloom's elaborations are, admittedly, significant developments in his and our theory of poetry. Yet, despite the enlargement and refinement these developments bring about, and despite their utility, they do not ever put into question the authority of the central enabling device of the Bloomian juggernaut. Bloom's work shows that the "anxiety of influence" is a powerful mechanism for unlocking the mysteries of post-enlightenment poetry and criticism. But as powerful and at times persuasive as it is, especially in providing some of the most subtle readings of texts, it is not demonstrative, and cannot be. Of course, Bloom acknowledges that all reading is misreading and he exemplifies this by revising his own misprision of the figure of "misprision" (WS, 394).

This sort of destabilizing play, coupled with Bloom's recognition of the omnipresence of tropes and the absence of proper meaning, allows for a theoretical defense of Bloom's machine: poetry is an infinite process of willed lies troping defensively upon other tropes, disrupted within by the discontinuous relationships between the ratios of the psyche or the topoi of the tradition. Meaning emerges from the also willed healing act of the dance of the poet's intention. Criticism must be able to reproduce, indeed, endlessly to discover this dance not only to reveal it in a twisted confrontation with or misprision of each poem but also to provide a student-reader with an apparatus which will enable him or her to see the hitherto-invisible movement of tropes. The apparatus resulting from free substitution

[24]

effectively prevents the deconstructive movement into the *aporia;* meaning is restored to criticism and poetry.

Bloom gives a more eloquent version of his vision:

> The function of criticism at the present time, as I conceive it, is to find a middle way between the paths of demystification of meaning, and of recollection or restoration of meaning, or between limitation and representation. But the only aesthetic path between limitation and representation is substitution, and so all that criticism can hope to teach, whether to the common reader or to the poet, is a series of stronger modes of substitution. Substitution, in this sense, is a mode of creation-through-catastrophe. The vessels or fixed forms break in every act of reading or of writing, but *how* they break is to a considerable extent in the power of each reader and of each writer. Yet there are patterns in the breaking that resist the power, however strong, of any reader and of every writer. These patterns —evident as sequences of images, or of tropes, or of psychic defenses—are as definite as those of any dance, and as varied as there are various dances. But poets do not invent the dances they dance, and we *can tell* the dancer from the dance. The stronger poet not only performs the dance more skillfully than the weaker poet, but he modifies it as well, and yet it does remain the same dance. I am afraid that there does tend to be one fairly definite dance pattern in post-Enlightenment poetry, which can be altered by strong substitution, but still it does remain the same dance. (*PR,* 270)

This is an important moment in Bloom. Its echoes of Eliot, Yeats, and the New Critics as well as its obvious attempt to mark Bloom off from the deconstructors and their concern with the cognitive ethos of poetry—these echoes place Bloom's criticism in a field of competitors for critical authority and prominence. His insistence upon the inevitability of certain patterns to the poetic breaking of misprision is a curious adoption and inversion of a New Critical principle which asserts that there are certain irreducible figures in the carpet of a poem resistant to the acid-bath of the most powerful critics' desires. As I suggest in

[25]

my third chapter, for the New Critic there is a recognizable, repeated pattern of ironic, analogic structuring in poetry producing an allegory of the poem's fullness which, paradoxically, emerges, as in *The Waste Land,* from its own constant assertion of emptiness.

In a way which is typical of Modern criticism, and perhaps of all the human sciences, we see that the patterning of the poem or of the poetic "tradition" which assures their fullness is the result of the interpretive power of the privileged critical terms of the reading project itself—no matter whether that project is canonical or revisionist. In other words, the semiotic value of the poem—or tradition or inter-poem—is a product of the syntax and grammar of the critical method, of the enabling figure and its emanations. It is only the greatest irony that the insistence by the critic—Bloom, Brooks, Bate—that there is an irreducible poetic residue or structure beyond the reach of either the poet's or the critic's revisionist will is *itself* an assertion, in reality, of the power and authority of that critic's misprision as it is theoretically and practically elaborated. In other words, while Bloom claims to have discovered the essential choreography of the post-Enlightenment poem and, correspondingly, the inadequacy of New Critical and deconstructive projects to that choreography, I claim that at this very moment he stares most directly into a mirror and sees his own reflection. This is not to accuse Bloom of narcissism or solipsism. Although I do want to suggest an alignment between the way he sees himself everywhere he turns within the canon and the similar New Critical process of projection which reduces all poetry to irony and paradox, I also want to make clear that Bloom's self-reflection in projection is only a being-true to his Gnostic heritage.

I would like to transfer Bloom's comment about poets to critics (whenever Bloom talks generally about poets and poetry he is usually talking about himself, and since he is so powerful, he is, more importantly, talking about almost all modern critics): "But poets do not invent the dances they dance, and we *can tell* the dancer from the dance." The dance modern critics seem to repeat has to do with stepping along from an initial strong perception—which is often only a fearful vision of the self and its place in time—through a combative elaboration extending the insight to other poems and absorbing other critics, to self-parodic echoes of the original insight as its schematic outline becomes clear and often predictable—when, to put it another way, the machinelike nature of the critical operation becomes evident in its worst senses. When individual strong critics pass through each phase is hard to determine and varies with the strength of the one who reads them. But one thing seems certain: at moments when the critic's authority allows him to claim the truth of his perception as the excuse for his method—when, that is to say, he so powerfully projects his own method's syntax and grammar upon poetry *and thinks he has not*—at that moment when he no longer recognizes the shadow of his own desire and does not know that the method has become his master, then, certainly, the deathly limitation of literary criticism as a Gnostic preoccupation with subjectivity becomes apparent.

It is important to remember that *despite* Bloom's claims for the universality of troping, substitution, and misprision, and *despite* his frequent explicit application of these weapons to the stability of his own project, his critical project is not dissolved. Rather, it grows in strength by becoming a more massive and powerful archive of readings, metaphors, and absorptions. Even these aphoristic plays on his own terms—such as revising his notion of misprision—all carry the voiceprint of "Bloom," of an unavoidable power or presence in so many fields of literary scholarship. Indeed, one comes to expect these playful moves from "Bloom," and while they are often dazzling, exorbitant, or outlandish they are not really surprising. For example, in "Coda: Poetic Crossing," Bloom makes a daring attempt to recoup a repositioned *logos:*

> Theology and a system of tropes are an *ethos;* belief and persuasion are a *pathos.* The *logos* of meaning is generated either by the repressive passage (representation) from *ethos* to *pathos* or

by the sublimating passage (limitation) from *pathos* to *ethos*. The dynamism of the substituting process is the *logos,* which tells us that meaning in a poem is itself liminal, transgressive, a breaking as much as a making. (*WS,* 401)

This figure appears toward the end of a programmatic passage defending against Paul de Man's notion of rhetoric: "Just here," Bloom writes, "though it is rather late to be attempting fundamental definitions, I am compelled to explain the vision of rhetoric that my enterprise has taken as a starting point" (*WS,* 393).

The compulsion to explain forces Bloom to an overt figuration of his original critical desire, the restoration of the *logos:* the multitude of previous Freudian, romantic, Kabbalistic, Emersonian, etc. figures which position Bloom between recuperative, humanistic criticism and the deconstructors' preoccupation with demystifying *ethos*—all of these figures have yielded to their common metaphysical ancestor, the figure of *logos* itself. While Bloom has admittedly moved the *logos* away from a notion of full presence outside play into a new "dynamism" of troping, he has done so only by repositioning it in a discursive space opened-up by his own earlier critical work and that of his competitors in advanced criticism. This space between recuperative humanism and deconstructive demystification becomes visible in his announcement that "The function of criticism . . . is to find a middle way between the paths of demystification of meaning, and of recollection or restoration of meaning . . ." (*PR,* 270).

It is the ambition and power of Bloom's repositioning of the *logos* which makes his dance interesting. He does this sort of thing better than others who follow after or who compete with him. He leaps higher,.whirls more rapidly, and always maintains proper form. His dance can be conceived either as an ongoing Baroque encrustation or as a Ballanchine-like reduction to line, speed, and purity; one need only choose to read him globally or locally. But, more importantly, one must recognize that the

[28]

dance always remains the same because the original ground, the initial act of perception which announces Bloom as a "strong critic," the idea of the "anxiety of influence," is never and can never be questioned. It always remains out-of-play as the law of gravity which makes possible the moves straining against their own enabling condition. While there is no doubt about the achievement emerging from and defending this first idea, there should be some doubt if the constant need to reimagine the first idea, while always being careful not to displace it, has not finally brought Bloom to a position of poverty, to the melancholy halls of a parodic prominence purchased at the cost of his own strength.

Bloom is perhaps the most brilliant critic the American academy has produced in this century and certainly worthy of a more sustained, detailed, and dialectical study than I can provide here, within the hermeneutical restrictions of my project. I have dealt with Bloom's major writings—and will return to them in later chapters—because of the power and authority of his position, which always requires that one must differentiate oneself from him on these matters. Since I would like to indicate that Modern American poetry can benefit from a reading which attends to its openness to time and history, I have tried to suggest why the New Critical and Bloomian conceptions of poetry as a lie against time result from the limitations, needs, and glories of their critical stances. Bloom prefers the Valentinian speculation to the Heideggerean as a metaphor for poetic theory because he accepts "the Valentinian misprision condemning time as a lie" (*PR,* 12–13). As I have already suggested, Bloom, like Bate and the New Critics, develops a series of metaphors to stabilize "tradition" as a defense against time. In fact, this stabilization results in the gamble of projecting one's own strength in this series of figures against the perceived threat of time. I hope to suggest that accepting the Heideggerean metaphor for truth as *aletheia* provides a temporal poetics and historical sense of tradition. Moreover, the critical act no longer conceives its own interests to lie in troping against time, but in accepting the historical nature of hermeneutics and the comparative powerlessness of critical secondariness. The Heideggerean metaphor allows for an "optimistic" conception of history free of the defensive anxiety against impending death.

Moreover, Heidegger's development of *aletheia* provides a space for "truth" in poetics which even Bloom's revisionism does not: "Kaballah, as a Gnosis, starts with the rival assumption, which is that all distinction between proper and figurative meaning in language has been totally lost since the catastrophe of creation" (*WS*, 394). In line with this Vichian insight, Bloom substitutes the problem of meaning for the question of "truth." This is a substitution which all Modern fetishists of language have made. For Heidegger, "truth," gained in a destructive phenomenological hermeneutics, exists beyond the restrictions of the linguistically determined inside-outside metaphor implied by the dualistic Gnostic concern with subjectivity (*PR*, 11). And, a correlate of this Gnosticism is Bloom's insistence upon the priority of the will in poetics, a priority so certain that, for Bloom, both the tropes of action and desire on the one hand and the distinctions between them on the other are all themselves tropes of the will (*WS*, 393).

For Bloom, the will is dominant because he understands that in the internalized Gnostic world of romantic poetry which he describes, cognition must be a secondary function: "Where the will predominates, even in its own despite, how much is there left to know?" (*WS*, 387). But phenomenological hermeneutics destroys the assumptions of the internalized quest romance (and its critical equivalent, the endless quest for new metaphors for reading [*PR*, 14]) and reintroduces the cognitive aspects of a "World"-oriented, temporal poetry and criticism. This means, in effect, that the critical and poetic will, what Bloom calls a "stance" (*PR*, 1; *WS*, 11, 395ff), although essential in breaking down the inherited lies which separate time and poetry, are restricted in their self-loving (and perhaps self-destroying) freeplay by the generosity of a phenomenological hermeneutics concerned with "truth," not the authority of subjectivity and will.

Perhaps most importantly, I would like to suggest that for those poets I discuss in this volume, and for others like William Carlos Williams, Robert Creeley, A.R. Ammons, and Gary Snyder, the anxiety of influence is not an adequate trope for their poems' temporality and historicity. In what I take to be one of those thematically revealing but reductive moments of self-parody endemic to all strong critics, Bloom writes:

> I find useful enough Paul Ricoeur's summary of primal repression, as meaning "that we are always in the mediate, in the already expressed, the already said," for this is the traumatic predicament that results in what I have termed "the anxiety of influence," the awareness that what might be called, analogically, the infantile needs of the beginning imagination had to be met by the primal fixation of a Scene of Instruction. (PR, 232)

Without reprocessing my objections to Bloom's genealogical metaphors or reasserting my sense of the sameness of his project, I want to offer for consideration the idea that certain strong poets exist in the mediate without experiencing the trauma he describes. Or rather, their response to the "trauma" is not a defensive lie against time, a mastering of anxiety by an act of the deceitful will, but an open and projective poetry. These poets, like Whitman, reside openly in the mediate, look toward the future, and are open to the weight of the past. But these poets prospect in the past, hoping to renew the future out of the past. They do not unwillingly extend the decayed and decaying dance of the revisionist to the death of poetry itself.

## III

Paul de Man's speculations about the relationship of literature to literary history are negatively useful. His deconstructions of the traditional genetic forms of history—positivistic, organic, and dialectical—set in bold relief the absolute need for a more adequate theory of literary history and its interaction with the prac-

[31]

Poetic Destruction

tice of literary interpretation than those I have already discussed. Essentially, my treatment of de Man has two parts: first, I will follow through his deconstructions of traditional forms of history which show their inadequacy to the complexities of literary language; second, de Man's own simplifying blindness, that is, his claim that all poetic language is already demystified and not in need of destruction, emerges as an unexamined presupposition which some of his own rather oblique statements on the interrelationship of poetic texts actually calls into doubt. In other words, I intend to follow de Man's work to the point where it suggests the need for a theory which goes beyond what he himself claims is literary history, a succession of critical misreadings, into the region where poems themselves begin to appear as interpretations, as misreadings, of other poems. It is precisely out of this ongoing process of poetic misreading that a fuller literary history can emerge.

There are two strategies in de Man's work which are of interest here. By examining the structure of blindness-insight which appears in all the critical texts he treats, de Man reveals that literary language and literary texts are inimicable to extrinsic or objective theories of language and criticism:

> A literary text is not a phenomenal event that can be granted any form of positive existence, whether as a fact of nature or as an act of the mind. It leads to no transcendental perception, intuition, or knowledge but merely solicits an understanding that has to remain immanent because it poses the problem of its intelligibility in its own terms. This area of immanence is necessarily part of all critical discourse. (*BI*, 107)

The nonscientific status of the literary "event," the "text," prevents the application of any pseudoscientific or extrinsic models of criticism. Furthermore, the required immanental or intrinsic nature of interpretation—that is, the fact that a text needs interpretation, needs to be engaged hermeneutically and not merely described "scientifically"—makes all traditional forms of literary history inadequate because they themselves rest upon a concep-

[32]

tion of literary language which mistakes a "text" for an object existing independently "out-there" in space and time and amenable, like a rock, to objective "explanation." Until the point where I depart from de Man by deconstructing his own blind claim for an absolutely demystified literary or poetic language, his complex deconstructions of naive theories for reading and historicizing poetic texts move my own argument for a fuller literary interpretation and literary history toward its own statement drawn from the hermeneutic destruction (*Destruktion*) performed by Martin Heidegger in *Being and Time*. The programmatic use which I make of de Man often results in a blurring of point of view in the next section of this essay. Necessarily my attempt to think hermeneutically through these deconstructions with de Man requires the identification of our view-points, until his own blindness becomes the "subject" of the deconstructive process and compels me to abandon the immanental identity.

Traditional forms of literary history—this includes Bloom as well as Bate—rest on an unexamined language of continuity, privilege, and nonliterary models. De Man's deconstructions of critical texts throw all of these into doubt. Because critics are self-conscious readers, their texts reveal the problems of reading—which necessarily means interpreting—a text (*BI,* viii). These "problems" emerge from the essential nature of all literary language, according to de Man, and show why literature is contrary, fundamentally, to the rhetorical presuppositions upon which standard histories of literature rest.

Since I have already suggested some of the fallacies inherent in the language of continuity and privilege in my discussion of Bloom and Bate, I will begin here with de Man's deconstruction of the idea that literary criticism, and therefore literary history, can be based upon a nonliterary or extrinsic model. This deconstruction leads him to his attack on the genetic model—the basis of continuity—and the possibility of privilege itself.

Scientific or extrinsic models for literary criticism begin, according to de Man, from a naive understanding of the act of reading. When Tsvetan Todorov calls for a structuralist system to deal with the literariness of a text, he mistakenly assumes that a text can be analytically treated as a phenomenon and described in and of itself.[10] "The problem," however, "has not always been correctly perceived, partly because the model for the act of interpretation is being constantly oversimplified" (*BI*, 107). Todorov objects to all "immanental" methods of interpretation, i.e., to all hermeneutic processes, because a "description" carried out in such a way "would make the description into a mere word-for-word repetition of the work itself . . .' " (*BI*, 108). The fallacy of his argument, as de Man quite rightly perceives, is that in the criticism of a text, which is an intentional event, not a sensual object occupying space, there can be no strict, scientific description. Rather, the text can only be understood—again Heidegger is relevant here—and thus criticism can only rightly be called a description of this act of understanding.[11] Criticism is a hermeneutic, an interpretation. It is indeed legitimately a "repetition," a temporal process, akin to the hermeneutic circle, involved in the temporal process of understanding. The interpretation, the new text, cannot, therefore, be itself an object of description, but only a heuristic phenomenon which can trigger further interpretation and attempts at understanding.

The scientific or, in this case, the structuralist model, is bothered by the indefiniteness of the act of interpretation, which cannot be made into an "exact science." Todorov objects that no interpretation is faithful to or leaves unchanged the original text: " 'From the moment there is writing and no longer mere reading, the critic is saying something that the work he studies does not say, even if he claims to be saying the same thing' " (*BI*, 109), De Man, after agreeing with Todorov about the messiness of this situation, purposely compounds the problem: "not only does the critic say something that the work does not say, but he even says something that he himself does not mean to say" (*BI*, 109). Because interpretation is a function of the temporal structure of understanding, it possesses no "epistemological certainty." (*BI*, 109) The result of this structure of interpretation, of course, is that unlike the form of scientific description, the "ob-

ject" under investigation, the literary text, does not function, and
cannot be made to function, as a privileged center for critical discourse. It cannot be pinned down, confined, and contained; it
cannot be reified. Furthermore, the critic cannot count on his
own privileged position to provide stability. Since his discourse
cannot originate from an extrinsic system or model, his language
itself must be, from the beginning, part of the "game." [12] It cannot, or certainly should not, attempt to violate the essentially
linguistic structure it possesses by reducing it to a stable and
reified object. The critic must willingly enter into a relationship
which is marked by flux. As de Man points out, in such criticism
the text and the interpretation threaten to destroy each other. In
fact, Todorov recognizes the potential risk to verbal and critical
stability in this interpretive process. It is for him, however, only
another reason to try to escape its uncertainty:

> The work can be used repeatedly to show where and how the
> critic diverged from it, but in the process of showing this our
> understanding of the work is modified and the faulty vision
> shown to be productive. . . . Both texts can even enter into
> conflict with each other. And one could say that the further the
> critical text penetrates in its understanding, the more violent
> the conflict becomes, to the point of mutual destruction: To-
> dorov significantly has to have recourse to an imagery of death
> and violence in order to describe the encounter between text
> and commentary. One could even go further still and see the
> murder become suicide as the critic, in his blindness, turns the
> weapon of his language upon himself, in his mistaken belief
> that it is aimed at another. (BI, 109–10)

De Man's deconstruction of Todorov's extrinsic, scientific, structuralist criticism not only points out a difference [13] in every act of
interpretation between the text and the criticism, but also the ir-
remediable breach between all centered forms of discourse and
the language of literature and criticism. Those who attempt to
produce such logocentric criticism as the structuralists strive for
proceed from and remain in error. It is an attempt to escape the
risk of interpretation in which the critic engages the text with a

[35]

full awareness of the implications of reading and writing: "The necessary immanence of the reading in relation to the text is a burden from which there can be no escape. It is bound to stand out as the irreducible philosophical problem raised by all forms of literary criticism, however pragmatic they may seem or want to be. We encounter it here in the form of a constitutive discrepancy, in critical discourse, between the blindness of the statement and the insight of the meaning" (*BI,* 110).

Thus, there is a radical discontinuity (or differance), between the literary text and any reading of it, naive or critical. No extrinsic system can be imported into the gap to close it. There is no privileged point of origin to be found in the encounter between self and text. Reading is at best ambivalent because of the nature of the act. Criticism, in trying to render the immediate or immanental experience, is caught in the paradox of the mediate nature of language. It is de Man's object to make critics aware of the duplicity of their language and of the ambivalence of their act. This also offers one way of approaching de Man's attack on the idea of genetic continuity. The path from the divergence of reading and text to the discontinuity of literary interrelations, and therefore, to the impossibility of all continuous, i.e., genetic, literary history is clearly marked.

As we have seen in Bloom and Bate, genetic models of literary history, whether they are centered on organicism or causality, result in the idea of a continuous tradition. In Bloom's case, this continuity is assured by his theory of imitation. Essentially, the genetic structure is a nonlinguistic rhetoric based on the literal structure of life, but which can be applied to literature only metaphorically (GGN, 44). It has many variants within itself, however, and perhaps the most familiar one to literary historians is that of the neatly contained "narrative unit" (GGN, 44). In all such traditional literary histories, according to de Man, "history and interpretation coincide, the common principle that mediates them being the genetic concept of totalization" (GGN, 45).

Totalization occurs in this structure whether it takes the form of a line or the dialectic. In the former, " 'all things below' are said to be part of a chain of being heading toward its teleological end. The hierarchical world of Ideas and Images becomes a world of means moving toward an end and ordered in the prospective temporality of a genetic movement" (GGN, 44). This linear form becomes, in the Romantic period, at least according to the general understanding (GGN, 44), the dialectical process of evolving Spirit which climaxes in Hegel's *Logic* and *Phenomenology*. As de Man points out:

> "Das Resultat," says Hegel, "ist nur darum dasselbe, was der Anfang, weil der *Anfang Zweck* ist" (sic) (*Phenomenology of the Mind, Introduction*). The English translation of the words italicized by Hegel illustrates the interdependence and potential identity of end and beginning that characterizes a genetic concept of time: "The outcome is the same as the beginning only because the beginning is an end." (GGN, 44)

The dialectic then does not escape the genetic model. Although a study of Romanticism might show that the dialectic replaces the linear form of time, it would also show "that a dialectical conception of time and history can very well be genetic and that the abandonment of an organic analogism by no means implies the abandonment of a genetic pattern" (GGN, 45). Although the dialectic, "deconstructing" the linear or organic metaphor, does create "discontinuities" to the extent that no event or group of events can acquire full historical meaning, each event "can still be said to share in the experience of this movement [to totalization]" (GGN, 45). In the dialectic, the closed circular form of the system or of the argument's structure becomes the model of the genetic, teleological pattern. Linearity is disposed with and replaced by the "ultimate conformity of the end to the origin" (GGN, 45). Thus, there is no radical break or rupture in the genetic pattern, even in its dialectical manifestations. In the dialectic, the antitheses are resolved in synthesis, and all parts progress toward a totalization formed by a circle in which the end returns to the beginning thereby only changing the shape of the continuity. Furthermore, only deconstruction can reveal that the

[37]

Poetic Destruction

dialectic is blindly founded on the same ideals as the scientific, linear model:

> From a historiographical point of view, it is instructive to see a genetic narrative [*The Birth of Tragedy*] function as a step leading to insights that destroy the claims upon which the genetic continuity was founded, but that could not have been formulated if the fallacy had not been allowed to unfold. (GGN, 53)

When the deconstructive process is applied to traditional genetic assumptions of literary history, the centers of the various discourses are displaced from their privileged positions. Nietzsche, according to de Man, breaks open the tradition and allows what is obscured by it to appear.

In the last two essays of *Blindness and Insight,* de Man continues his reconsideration of the standard forms of literary history by exposing radical discontinuities between texts and within individual works. In both essays, the previously assured center of historical discourse is displaced by an equiprimordial and simulaneous binary opposition. I intend to discuss the first of these essays to show how de Man moves through the conflict between traditional literary history and what deconstruction reveals about literary language to call for a more satisfactory literary history which, as de Man puts it, is the same as literary interpretation, but not identical to it.

"Literary History and Literary Modernity" begins by throwing the ordinary understanding of "modern" into doubt and by suggesting that the "beginning" of this very essay is potentially absurd. The entire opening paragraph must be quoted for de Man's detailed rhetoric to function clearly:

> To write reflectively about modernity leads to problems that put the usefullness of the term into question, especially as it applies, or fails to apply, to literature. There may well be an inherent contradiction between modernity, which is a way of acting and behaving, and such terms as "reflection" or "ideas" that play an important part in literature and history. The spontaneity of being modern conflicts with the claim to think and

[38]

Poetic Destruction

write about modernity; it is not at all certain that literature and
modernity are in any way compatible concepts. Yet we all
speak readily about Modern literature and even use this term as
a device for historical periodization, with the same apparent
unawareness that history and modernity may well be even
more incompatible than literature and modernity. The in-
nocuous-sounding title of this essay may therefore contain no
less than two logical absurdities—a most inauspicious beginning. (*BI*, 143)

De Man concludes from all this that the modern and the historical are two synchronic, necessary functions at the "center" of the
act of literature. Within a given text there is a movement or
structure which attempts to detach that work from any vestigial
relationship with the past, but which simultaneously, using the
language of that past, records that act and desire. Furthermore,
the relation of "present" works to the tradition is not at all continuous. The initial impulse of being "modern" is, as Nietzsche
understood, "the ability to *forget* whatever precedes a present situation" (*BI*, 146); Nietzschean man must forget everything in
order to be able to do something (*BI*, 147): "Modernity exists in
the form of a desire to wipe out whatever came earlier, in the
hope of reaching at last a point that could be called a true present,
a point of origin that marks a new departure. . . . Thus defined,
modernity and history are diametrically opposed to each other"
(*BI*, 148). De Man's deconstruction has not yet brought the dia-
metric opposition of modernity and history to the point where
they are to be seen as two irreconcilable but absolutely necessary
and simultaneous "foci" of a structure.[14] But de Man's examination of Nietzsche's shrill and extravagant rhetoric shows that it
indirectly reveals the structure of differance in which history and
modernity are not only opposed but synchronic. From the start
of every act of creation, even in attacks upon the historical mind
itself, they are co-original and equivalued:

> From the start [of "Vom Nutzen und Nachteil der Historie für
> das Leben"], the intoxication with the history-transcending
> life-process is counterbalanced by a deeply pessimistic wisdom

Poetic Destruction

that remains rooted in the sense of historical causality, although it reverses the movement of history from one of development to one of regression. . . . This description of life as a constant regression . . . is a temporal experience of human mutability, historical in the deepest sense of the term in that it implies the necessary experience of any present as a *passing* experience that makes the past irrevocable and unforgettable. (*BI,* 148)

The irreducible opposition which de Man allows to emerge in Nietzsche's text between history and modernity becomes even more unescapable when the problem is transferred to the act of literature. De Man says that "the modernity of literature confronts us at all times with an unsolvable paradox" (*BI,* 151). Literature begins as a spontaneous, free act which has no past and is discontinuous from all which precedes it (*BI,* 151–52). "But the writer's language is to some degree the product of his own action; he is both the historian and agent of his own language" (*BI,* 152). Literature is, then, inherently based on a difference: the act and the "interpretation" of that act which remains always only mediate.

Although chroniclers of literary history assert the possibility of modernity as forgetful originality, de Man claims that their rhetoric often entraps them into saying the opposite of what they mean and, therefore, into putting the possibility of such modernity into question. Yet, the impulse to modernity is never overcome or synthesized; it is never *aufgehoben:* "Modernity turns out to be indeed one of the concepts by which the distinctive nature of literature can be revealed in all its intricacy" (*BI,* 161). It cannot, however, be given any priority in the definition of literature. "Modern" brings with it "history"; neither can exist alone: "The more radical the rejection of anything that came before, the greater the dependence on the past" (*BI,* 161). This is the unending and absurd paradox which defines all literature and which cannot be avoided by literary interpretations or literary history.

De Man's basic concern throughout this essay is the possibility of writing a history of literature which is marked by an awareness of such *differance* at the "heart" of literature. Positivistic and ahistorical modes of literary history are of no value since they misinterpret the nature of literary language and are absolutely inimical to it. Organic and dialectical histories assert the possibility of privilege and are different from the nature of literature. Since the structure of modernity-history is not genetic, "It follows that it would be a mistake to think of literary history as a diachronic narrative of the fluctuating motion we have tried to describe. Such a narrative can only be metaphorical, and history is not fiction" (*BI*, 163). The opposition between literature and history is absolute as long as historical language assumes any privileged rhetoric. The only history appropriate to literature must itself be marked by discontinuity. As a result, de Man calls for a displacement of the center of the rhetorics of all history. However, in perhaps his most valuable insight, he concludes that the task is not as monumental as it first seems because "what we call literary interpretation . . . is in fact literary history" (*BI*, 165).

This rather enigmatic but, I think, comprehensible remark can be amplified by examining the exchange between de Man, Louis Roberts, and Walter Kaufmann following de Man's paper, "Nietzsche's Theory of Rhetoric." In response, at first to Roberts, de Man emphasizes the importance of reading:

> I am very glad that you bring us back to the question of how Nietzsche is to be read. Perhaps we have not yet begun to read him properly. In the case of major authors this is never a simple task. There are likely to be long periods of continual misinterpretation. . . . Certain authors are privileged in provoking more and better misreadings than others, Plato, Rousseau, and Nietzsche being three striking cases in point. Every interpretation can be said in Nietzsche's terms to be both truth and lie, and this double aspect can best be understood with regard to the complex relationship between literal and figural meaning within the linguistic sign. Nietzsche uses at least two terms for "misreading": one is "Will to power" and the other is simply "interpretation." Both combine in the forceful reading that

presents itself as absolutely true but can then, in its turn, be undermined. (NTR, 49–50)

Interpretations are, then, misreadings. They do not and cannot "progress" linearly or dialectically toward enlightenment because of the synchronous binary opposition which structures all literary language. The further these critical interpretations penetrate into the "truth" of a text, the more they must recognize their own and the texts' "errors." Walter Kaufmann presses de Man on just this point of misreading:

> KAUFMANN: In connection with his own reading of *Hamlet* Freud says that this is merely one interpretation. Freud doesn't say it is a *misreading*. He says it is merely one reading, but there can be others, which is more nearly a way of saying that there can be many plausible, interesting, rich readings. But you are saying they are all misreadings. (NTR, 50)

De Man responds to this objection by claiming that all readings make some pretense to "totalization" and to "being right" and that as a result of this claim of privilege, such readers believe in the possibility of one reading, perhaps of a cumulative one. Beginning from a "pluralistic perspective," however, a unique and total reading is not possible. It is from this process of misreading, and not from the "progressive" movement toward enlightenment, that a new literary history can emerge:

> DE MAN: You can develop the reading only if you are to some extent committed to it. And this is not just a question of historical perspective. The ongoing process of understanding and misunderstanding takes place among historical events as well as among texts. By a good misreading, I mean a text that produces another text which can itself be shown to be an interesting misreading, a text which engenders additional texts. If you have a poor text, you cannot make up a very rewarding construction. But, with Nietzsche, the possibilities are endless. (NTR, 51)

Literary history, then, is this "ongoing process of understanding and misunderstanding" which is defined as interpretation or misreading. It is not an attempt to impose an order of development or dialectic upon a series of poems, but it is the process of allowing the truth to emerge from the error of interpretation, from the temporal process of encountering a text in understanding (*Verstehen*).[15] It has no "end" just as it has no "origin." It is not a history of texts, nor is it a history of interpretation; rather it is both and neither since the very identity without sameness between text and the interpretation of it comprises the difference which makes literary understanding and historical understanding possible. This means that "literary history" has no center, but rather two foci, the text and the ongoing misunderstanding of it. Such a history of the understanding and misunderstanding of texts would provide the kind of literary history de Man asks for:

> Could we conceive of a literary history that would not truncate literature by putting us misleadingly *into* or *outside* it, that would be able to maintain the literary aporia throughout, account at the same time for the truth and falsehood of the knowledge literature conveys about itself, distinguish rigorously between metaphorical and historical language, and account for literary modernity as well as for its historicity? (*BI*, 164)

Although such a history of interpretation provides the new literary history de Man is looking for, it does avoid one complication which requires a modification of de Man's text and a somewhat fuller analysis of the nature of interpretation. I intend to provide the beginnings of the latter in my next chapter on Heidegger's *Being and Time*. I can suggest, however, the simplification upon which de Man's already sophisticated theory rests.

In their interpreations of Rousseau, De Man's difference with Derrida centers upon the problem of whether or not Rousseau is mystified by the language he uses or whether he uses it indirectly,[16] that is, revealing its essential rhetoricity by employing it with full rhetorical flourish. De Man concludes, perhaps unlike Derrida—although the latter's strategy in the second volume of

Poetic Destruction

*De la grammatologie* remains naturally ambivalent—that "On the question of rhetoric, on the nature of figural language, Rousseau was not deluded and said what he meant to say" (*BI*, 135). In fact, it is de Man's theory that no poet needs to be demythologized: "when modern critics think they are demystifying literature, they are in fact being demystified by it" (*BI*, 18). De Man is not willing to grant that any "fiction writer" can be blind or trapped within the logocentric or metaphysical tradition. For de Man, all literature exists on the far side of this tradition and emerges from an awareness of the unprivileged nature of literary language. He expresses this universal idea in "Crisis and Criticism": "All literatures, including the literature of Greece, have always designated themselves as existing in the mode of fiction" (*BI*, 17). This remains de Man's unexamined presupposition about literary language and texts throughout *Blindness and Insight.* This unqualified "truth" of literature is always confused with logocentric presence by the misinterpretation of readers: "It is always against the explicit assertion of the writer that readers degrade fiction by confusing it with a reality from which it has forever taken leave" (*BI*, 17). This total separation of literature and "reality" is partially undercut in the last essay, "Lyric and Modernity." De Man establishes that the two foci of the lyric are allegory and representationalism, in which allegory "undermines and obscures the specific literal meaning of a representation," while the representation or reference to the world necessarily exists to make possible understanding of the poem (*BI*, 185). Allegory and representationalism are unreducible and unsynthesizable "origins," a fact which undercuts de Man's earlier claim for fiction's total separation from the world.

The pessimism and nihilism in de Man's work result from Rousseau's idea that poetic language merely names the void of "le néant des choses humaines," of the "presence of nothingness": "Poetic language names this void with ever-renewed understanding and, like Rousseau's longing, it never tires of naming it again. This persistent naming is what we call literature" (*BI*, 18). The poet cannot confuse the "name" with a "real" pres-

[44]

ence, according to de Man, because "the human self has experienced the void within itself and the invented fiction, far from filling the void, asserts itself as pure nothingness, *our* nothingness,
stated and restated by a subject that is the agent of its own instability" (*BI,* 19). Although this privileged position of poetic
knowledge is never once put explicitly into question by de Man,
there are some indications, "much more tentative utterances,"
(*BI,* 106) which suggest that, in fact, poets are not always privileged and are sometimes in need of deconstruction.

The problem is that the persistent naming of the void can in
itself be misinterpreted as a naming of a "center." The repetitive
offering of the same or similar name by a variety of writers
creates the illusion that language is not creating a fiction, but is
offering an "insight" which is not qualified in its privilege by
"blindness." Such constantly repeated names form a habit, what
Heidegger and Derrida would call tradition—as Bloom and Bate
would readily concede—which functions more or less unconsciously within individuals. When this tradition or habit is firmly
established (like the genetic pattern itself which is an element of
the metaphysical or ontotheological, logocentric tradition), it obscures what is fresh, imaginative, and individual in the particular
act of naming. This particularity of "original" naming is what de
Man, following Nietzsche, calls "modernity." De Man himself
admits that "modernity" not only is inseparable from history as
one of the foci of literature, but that it is capable of being reduced
by repetition to fashion or mode:

> Fashion (mode) can sometimes be only what remains of mo-
> dernity after the impulse has subsided, as soon—and this can be
> almost at once—as it has changed from being an incandescent
> point in time to a reproducible cliché, all that remains of an in-
> vention that has lost the desire that produced it. (*BI,* 147)

Literature, itself, is capable of such fashion to varying degrees.
The writer like Rousseau, for whom it can be claimed, as de Man
does, that he understood everything and is in no need of deconstruction, is rare. Derrida, in his study of Rousseau himself,

[45]

remains ambiguous about his knowledge of what Rousseau's language revealed (*BI,* 116–18). In other words, Derrida accuses Rousseau of some blindness. Derrida's role as interpreter in this situation then is to deconstruct the logocentric assumptions in Rousseau by examining the language of differance within which they are contained. Rousseau could be used to narrow the distance in understanding between de Man and Derrida on this problem; here, however, I can only suggest that both de Man and Derrida are right and wrong in their tales of Rousseau. De Man reveals Derrida's perhaps necessary blindness, that is, to the possibility that literature itself can approach total demystification at times, but as an observer, he is himself partially deconstructed by his exchange with Derrida. In the chapter on Rousseau, de Man's commitment to the absolute self-aware fictionality of all literature is revealed as an unexamined presupposition.

In "The Rhetoric of Blindness" itself, it is possible to find some evidence of Derrida's deconstruction of de Man, one of those "tentative utterances" which reveal the blindness of all critical discourse. In a discussion of the problem of misreading and literary interpretation—which, of course, leads to the topic of literary history—de Man hints at a possible blindness within a poetic or literary tradition which might require deconstruction:

> I spoke above of the blindness of critics with regard to their own insights, of the discrepancy, hidden to them, between their stated method and their perceptions. In the history as well as in the historiography of literature, this blindness can take the form of a recurrently aberrant pattern of interpretation with regard to a particular writer. The pattern extends from highly specialized commentators to the vague *idées reçues* by means of which this writer is identified and classified in general histories of literature. *It can even include other writers who have been influenced by him.* (BI, 111; italics mine)

This admission by de Man is the basis for the construction of a "tradition" which is blind to the insight of "modernity" provided by the "original" author. Later interpreters who come closer to an understanding of the writer must first, as Derrida does for Rousseau, destroy the sedimented interpretation which lies in between. Of crucial importance, however, in this admission by de Man, is the possibility that certain poets, influenced by predecessors who of course themselves understood fiction and the void, misinterpret their predecessors and are thus mystified and in need of deconstruction. In such situations, the interpreters' job is to demystify these later writers in the tradition to reveal what their acquiescence to the hardened tradition obscures, namely, the insight of their great predecessors.

Furthermore, this deconstruction or interpretation can be done by other poets upon their "traditional" forebears. The reading of previous texts is, of course, the necessary ground for the possibility of such deconstruction. While de Man does not anywhere admit this possibility explicitly—it would further complicate the business of literary history to have the texts themselves involved in the act of interpretation which he has reserved for critical works—he does implicitly suggest that this is precisely what happens.

In the "Preface" to *Blindness and Insight,* de Man explains that he chooses to deal with critical texts because the problems of reading, which are the key to understanding the nature of literary language, are clearest in them:

> The reason [for dealing with critical texts] is that prior to theorizing about literary language, one has to become aware of the complexities of reading. And since critics are a particularly self-conscious and specialized kind of reader, these complexities are displayed with particular clarity in their work. They do not occur with the same clarity to a spontaneous, non-critical reader. . . . Neither are the complexities of reading [i.e., of reading *other* texts] easily apparent in a poem or a novel, where they are so deeply embedded in the language that it takes extensive interpretation to bring them to light. (*BI,* viii)

Poems and novels then are implicitly misreadings, interpretations, of other poems, novels, and interpretations. In fact, one

[47]

might extrapolate from this that poems are interpretations of other poems and subject, therefore, to the same structure of blindness and insight, of differance, which "afflicts" critical discourse. Poetry exists in a condition of truth and error. A fuller justification of this notion requires a theory of language itself as interpretation which, I believe, can be found in *Being and Time*.

Literary history must be extended to include not only the series of critical misreading of a given text, but also the interrelationships among poems as they are interpretations, deconstructions, of each other. It must also be said, although justification for it must be reserved until the next chapter, that this process of interpretation is reciprocal: the later text does not merely open up the earlier and make it say what it did not mean to say, but the earlier text in turn opens up the later so that interpretation and literary history become integral, but not identical parts of the process of literary understanding.

De Man's own blindness is to this interpretive interrelationship among poems and forms. Because he misses this idea, which at times he himself approximates, his theory of literary history remains partially mystified. It is based upon the "privilege" that poets enjoy of not falling into the traps of language. As a result of this assumption, there is no need for a criticism of poetry which deconstructs and no need for a poetry of destruction. Interpretation and literary history are reduced by de Man to the process of unending "correction" of critical misreadings of major texts which leaves the actual relationship among poems in doubt. Once, however, the possibility of a destructive, hermeneutical poetry is allowed to emerge from de Man's own speculations on the nature of literary language, a closer approximation to the problem of critical interpretation becomes possible. Thus, interpretation, the way poems are read, is returned to the sphere of time and history in such a way that de Man's cautions about linear and dialectical genetic fallacies are no longer valid objections to this "new literary history."

[48]

Chapter Two

# Heidegger's Phenomenological Destruction: A Theory of Poetic Interpretation

I

American critical theory and literary history has been dominated for the past thirty-five years by the New Critics. Contemporary theoreticians like Bate, Bloom, de Man, and some few others in the United States have attempted to suggest alternative critical conceptions which escape the deadening influences of the New Critics' unrestricted formalism. Although Northrop Frye's *Anatomy of Criticism* and archetypal theory seemed for a while to offer a way out of the dead end of Brooks and Ransom and Tate and all the others, it became apparent that Frye's own "revolt" against mere close reading and his sweeping systematization of literature is only the completion of the New Critical impulse to stabilize literary conventions to produce meaning. For Frye, literature as an institution is hermetic and nonrelational. Furthermore, the New Critics' impulse to circularity, to deny time through closed or circular form—which I discuss more fully in my next chapter—climaxes in Frye's theory of circular literary history in which the ironic mode gradually returns to the beginning in the high mimetic, mythic mode.

Although the dissatisfaction with the New Critical vocabulary and method has not been too widespread in American universities—Brooks' and Warren's *Understanding Literature* has just been revised and reissued—individual critics have hoped, almost in isolation, to find more humane and vital approaches to literature. There has been a renewed interest in literary history and in the connection between literary interpretation and the possibilities of history. But even the best of these attempts falter upon inadequate theories of language and interpretation. De Man comes closest, I think, to being aware of the full range of complexities involved, but even he does not completely think through the implications of modern phenomenological theories of understanding, language, and time for literary texts and history.

The complexity of Modern and Postmodern literature requires an equally complex literary criticism. Unlike the New Critics, contemporary critics cannot afford the luxury of philosophical inexactness in justifying their enterprise. They cannot let their language remain uninformed by the insights of those like Nietzsche, Husserl, Heidegger, Gadamer, Derrida, and de Man. Nor can they hope to practice their craft authentically if their comprehension of the nature of language, understanding, and interpretation is not worked out upon as sound a basis as they can achieve. As de Man says, there is a crisis of criticism; there is a challenge to its first principles which must be responded to with all of the tools at hand. Modern and Postmodern literature offers a challenge not only to positivistic criticism—biographical and "influence" or "source" studies—but to the various "objectifying" modes of critical thought which developed to fill the vacuum when the scientific method was thrown into question by this literature itself. In response to this challenge by literature, criticism, if it is to remain adequate to its task, must restructure its grounds so that it can confront this literature—and undoubtedly that of the past—in a new way, that is, by revealing both what New Criticism obscures in it as well as what it remains blind to within itself.

Bloom and Bate, as we have seen, avoid the problem of language as rhetoric in constructing their own myths of influence. As a result, they actually establish exactly what they hoped to disprove. Both writers dismiss the possibility that language itself, as the store-house of tropes, ideas, and interpretations could be the burden or anxiety of the past. Both critics insist upon the priority of their atemporal models because they can postulate in them a constant pattern, an unchanging system which rests upon a continuous and, therefore, nonhistorical "tradition" and an equally unchanging psychology of self. Bate realizes that the eighteenth century's claim that the past inheres in language, that language can be and is used up by the past and hardens into tradition, is very dangerous to traditional modes of criticism which themselves rest on precisely this hardened, unchanging, accumulated tradition of language. However, Bate displaces the burden of the past from this radical conception of language and its relation to time to the simpler model of one self, for the sake of greatness, confronting the tradition and using it.

Bloom, of course, admits that he is trying to avoid all the decentering he sees in deconstructive criticism, in critical interpretation which realizes that language is rhetorical, that is, that it contains within itself sedimented patterns of expression which are inherited from the past and which block the poet's ability to create new works and to examine the world around him. Bloom admits that his enterprise is to reinstate and to rest upon that very tradition which he so desperately guards from the deconstructions of linguistically oriented critics.

The great lengths to which Bate and Bloom go to shift literary criticism and history away from literary language and form and toward nonintrinsic models for interpretation reveal their dread of the self-destructive potential in a criticism which is willing not only to reexamine the various critical interpretations of the past, but to challenge them in their most fundamental premises. Tradition must at all costs remain constant and sacrosanct for these critics. If it is not, then we are either deluded, as Bate would have it, or degenerate sadomasochists like Pynchon, as Bloom would have it.

In fact, both of these critics are reactionaries. They are trying to continue the solidification of the tradition which has dominated Western criticism for hundreds of years and which has also effected western poetry. De Man's work suggests some of the reasons for their defensiveness. Once the critic is stripped of the presuppositions upon which he bases his enterprise, the text and the reader are deprived of stability, and criticism emerges as radical flux, in which the text and the interpretation of it are constantly modifying, adjusting, and perhaps even destroying each other. In other words, literary criticism, and the tradition from which it cannot be separated, becomes susceptible to the same uncertainty and indefiniteness which threw science and mathematics into turmoil much earlier in the century. Ironically, it finally becomes "Modern," that is, it comes to share the potential dispersion of its central tropes (the "objectivity" of the text and the privileged position of the reader), just as painting during the cubist movement, for example, had its central tenets (representationalism, the unified plane, and color theory) disintegrated by theories of relativity and uncertainty. The privilege that criticism in some way "makes sense" of literature, especially of a Modern or Postmodern literature which quite precisely refuses to "make sense," can be displaced by destroying the extrinsic models of Bate, Bloom, Todorov, Frye, Culler, and the New Critics.[1]

Bate and Bloom, then, are aware of the potential threat to criticism's existence as a special, nonmodern event in the Modern world and they want to preserve its privileged status. It is not incidental that they are both primarily scholars of the late 18th and early 19th century. Nor is it mere accident that they both see Modernism and Postmodernism as the ultimate decline of the Romantic movement, the high point of a decline begun in the Renaissance. They sense in Modern and Postmodern literature a threat to the habitual interpretations of the entire myth of Tradition—promulgated by Eliot, Brooks, and the New Criticism and debunked by Frank Kermode[2]—as the decline of the west "beginning" with the death of the metaphysical imagination, the last vestige of the medieval metaphor of correspondence and the hierarchical Image of the Great Chain of Being.

As I pointed out in my first chapter, Bate and Bloom begin

with the assumption that the New Criticism does not provide an adequate theory of poetic history. But as I also indicated, Bate and Bloom's models are insufficient as well; they are essentially atemporal. For the New Critics, the nonreferentiality of closed poetic structure leaves no opportunity for a poetic history based upon the interrelationships of texts. For both Bate and Bloom, the tradition in some way becomes the *logos,* an incarnate order which the imagination uses as a bulwark against the chaos of nature and fragmentation. Paradoxically, while searching for a literary history, they coerce literature into a spatialized model of literary texts which appear to be stabilized and visualized because they are described as objects "out there." This "objective," scientific model enables criticism to clarify the ambiguities and uncertainties of literature itself. Once a text is "defined," it operates as the matrix of meaning; the model closes off possibilities for human action and creation. Indeed, it is only by virtue of this restriction upon possibilities that criticism can hope to offer, not misreadings as de Man rightly prefers, but what Kaufmann defends, a series of readings which are believed to be "right."

I hope that my "reading" of de Man's and Nietzsche's destruction of the traditional forms which this literary history often takes has suggested its inadequacy. It would be possible to extend this privative study of traditional forms of literary criticism and history from the perspective of Martin Heidegger, and the phenomenological critics generally, but I prefer instead to draw out of *Being and Time* an authentic mode of interpretation which results in a form of history that can justify the theory of poetic destruction which I hinted at in the last chapter. This justification needs to be outlined before I move directly to Heidegger.


II


There are essentially two facts to be drawn out of Heidegger which are necessary to justify the theory of poetic destruction: first, that all authentic uses of language are interpretations, specifically destructions; second, that interpretation as the completion of the moment of understanding (*Verständnis*) which discloses and un-covers (*aletheia*) is a process which leads necessarily to a more vital, and temporal, sense of literary history than those which I have already discussed and will discuss in the next chapter. My discussion of Heidegger begins by examining his methodology, i.e., phenomenological destruction (*Destruktion*), and his notion of truth. Circularly, his method is justified by the way in which it reveals truth as he defines it, while his idea of truth is validated only insofar as the method allows it to be seen as such. In his language, one might say that these two ideas are existentially-ontologically equiprimordial in *Being and Time*.[3] Therefore, in recounting my understanding of them there is no absolute priority in beginning with the idea of truth as *aletheia*, which dominates not only *Being and Time*, but remains a critical element of all phases of his thought.

The complete inseparability of Heidegger's "method" and his idea of "truth" can be seen in his derivation of the concept of "uncoveredness" from the traditional theories of truth as correspondence, judgment, and assertion (*BT*, 257). Heidegger destroys these traditional ideas in order to show that they are derived from the primordial character of truth which they obscure. When they are destroyed, they reveal that their sole basis is "Being-uncovered": "To say that an assertion '*is true*' signifies that it uncovers the entity as it is in itself. Such an assertion asserts, points out, 'lets' the entity 'be seen' (ἀπόφανσις) in its uncoveredness. The *Being-true* (*truth*) of the assertion must be understood as *Being-uncovering*" (*BT*, 261). Heidegger uncovers this primordial sense of truth from its concealment within the tradition. It is, as the intersection of destructive methodology and the discovery of *aletheia*, a *virtual* center in *Being and Time* and an appropriate starting point for the story of poetic destruction and literary history.

Heidegger himself points out in section 44b, *"The Primordial Phenomenon of Truth and the Derivative Character of the Traditional Conception of Truth,"* that the authenticity of this theory of truth

Martin Heidegger

validates his methodology. And, of course, the success of his methodology in finding justification for this idea of truth in the tradition shows *aletheia* to be "only the *necessary* Interpretation of what was primordially surmised in the *oldest* tradition of ancient philosophy and even understood in a pre-phenomenological manner" (*BT*, 262). This is one of the most important of Heidegger's "retrieves" from the tradition of a dis-closure which had been forgotten in the reified tradition of truth as judgment. He recalls Heraclitus's definition of truth as *aletheia,* and destroys Aristotle's concept of *aletheia* to show that it too "signifies what shows itself—*entities in the 'how' of their uncoveredness"* (BT, 262). Moreover, in a destruction which will have more import a bit further on when I deal explicitly with the "phenomenological destruction," Heidegger finds not only in Heraclitus but in Aristotle as well the idea that *logos* means "unhiddenness." This meaning is lost by translating it as "truth" and needs to be reclaimed (*BT*, 262).

Rhetorically, this section of *Being and Time* insists that the only means to truth is through a rethinking of the tradition. Destruction is not a purely privative process, although this is clearly a possible misconception which concerns Heidegger throughout *Being and Time:* "Must we not pay for this dubious gain [into the essence of truth as *aletheia*] by plunging the 'good' old tradition into nullity?" (*BT*, 262). After performing a brief destruction of Aristotle, Heidegger answers his own question: "In proposing our 'definition' of 'truth' we have not *shaken off* the tradition, but we have *appropriated* it primordially . . ." (*BT*, 262). The *rhetorical* juxtaposition of the definition of truth and the defense of the destructive orientation toward the past makes quite clear that, as W.B. Macomber argues in *The Anatomy of Disillusion,* "there is no *other* approach to truth except through constant and resolute reflection on tradition."[4] The reasons for this are varied and complex, but since I am not attempting a complete exposition of Heidegger here, only one is of immediate interest, the truth of Dasein as uncovering.

Following the definition of the essence of truth as *aletheia,*

Martin Heidegger

Heidegger moves to an exposition of the ontological disclosedness of Dasein as primordial truth, that is, "uncovering." "Being-uncovered," that is, "uncoveredness," is a second sense of truth and applies to those entities which are disclosed by Dasein (*BT*, 263). Although the largest significance of this interpretation for Heidegger is its justification of his own enterprise— "the disclosedness of [Dasein's] ownmost Being belongs to its existential constitution" (*BT*, 263)—it is thematically important to my story because it involves a crucial paradox: *"Dasein is 'in the truth.'"* And *"Because Dasein is essentially falling, its state of Being is such that it is in 'untruth'"* (*BT*, 263, 264). In other words, by arguing that there is no truth independently of Dasein, since Dasein alone discloses, the essence of truth is "adulterated" by the facticity and fallenness, the finitude, of Dasein's Being-in-the-World. Error and truth are equally existential possibilities of Dasein as special instances of the inauthentic and authentic modes of Being. Thus, Dasein must wrest from the hiddenness of untruth the possibility of disclosedness which it also contains:

> Proximally and for the most part Dasein is lost in its "world." Its understanding, as a projection upon possibilities of Being, has diverted itself thither. Its absorption in the "they" signifies that it is dominated by the way things are publicly interpreted. That which has been uncovered and disclosed stands in a mode in which it has been disguised and closed off by idle talk, curiosity, and ambiguity. Being towards entities has not been extinguished, it has been uprooted. Entities have not been completely hidden; they are precisely the sort of thing that has been [sic] uncovered, but at the same time they have been disguised. They show themselves, but in the mode of semblance. Likewise what has formerly been uncovered sinks back again hidden and disguised. (*BT*, 264)

Because of Dasein's propensity to fall into idle talk, destruction, or the authentic use of language, in an attempt to regain what has fallen back, must be violent. Furthermore, truth can only emerge when Dasein stands in a destructive relationship to the past, to

Martin Heidegger

what has been previously discovered, but which is now covered-over and remains as only a semblance of its "originality."

Heidegger explicitly charges Dasein with the role of confronting this constant falling back into hiddenness:

> It is therefore essential that Dasein should explicitly appropriate what has already been uncovered, defend it *against* semblance and disguise, and assure itself of its uncoveredness again and again. The uncovering of anything new is never done on the basis of having something completely hidden, but takes its departure rather from uncoveredness in the mode of semblance. Entities look as if . . . That is, they have, in a certain way, been uncovered already, and yet they are still disguised. (*BT*, 265)

This general need to reclaim what the past, the tradition has discovered, and covered over, "again and again," is the ground for the theory of literary history I am suggesting. Interpretation (I purposely leave this word vague at this point) of all kinds attempts to achieve this ongoing recovery. In fact, the retrieve of the past, in the present, for the sake of our possibilities, that is, of our future, is also the only way literary history can get beyond the traps which contemporary literature and interpretation pose for traditional histories.

Because of Dasein's facticity and fallenness, something which is uncovered can itself become obscure, but furthermore, it can, as discovered, block further unhiddenness. Thus, "truth" can in and of itself not only emerge from "untruth"—all disclosure must result from semblance or illusion—but become, once assimilated to assertion about the present-at-hand (*BT*, 266–67), part of the idle talk, the inauthentic illusion of the "they" world, of the obfuscating, inherited, unthought-of tradition. Macomber phrases the truth-untruth complex in a way which leaves no doubt as to its existential necessity in Heidegger's thought as well as to its ontological priority:

> The discovery of being can occur only on the basis of what has already been revealed, though partially and inadequately. Yet

[57]

> the partial revelation draws away from what is yet to be revealed—from its own limitations and imperfections—and thereby becomes an obstacle to further revelation, an illusion which has to be overcome. (*AD,* 126)

For this reason, interpretation, destruction, the violence necessary to wring truth from closure must be ongoing. Furthermore, it must be prepared to destroy previous destructive interpretations in order to bring to light, to let be manifest in themselves, the various facets and aspects of a being or idea which any *one* interpretation, or as de Man would have it, any one misreading, necessarily obscures. Destruction must be performed "again and again." As Macomber says, "illusion must provide the material of knowledge as well as its impetus and direction. . . . knowledge can never fully divest itself of its illusory origins if it is to make sense" (*AD,* 129).

"Di-vest," "dis-close," "un-cover," these are all privative terms. In fact, as Heidegger defines it, the process of getting to "truth" is a negative function. *"A-leitheia"* is a privative expression. Therefore, obtaining access to truth through semblance must be a violent process:

> Truth (uncoveredness) is something that must always first be *wrested* from entities. Entities get *snatched* out of their unhiddenness. The factical uncoveredness of anything is always, as it were, a kind of *robbery*. Is it accidental that when the Greeks express themselves as to the essence of truth they use a *privative* expression—ἀ-λήθεια? (*BT,* 265. Italics mine.)

The need for this violence signifies that *Dasein* is always and for the most part in untruth, in the inauthentic mode. It is difficult but necessary that he wrench himself out of this mode in order to let things be, to emerge out of their cover under the force of his active destruction of the obscuring tradition and semblance. But once again, this untruth or error is not something which is "destroyed" once and for all. Like the tradition itself, it can never be reduced to "nullity": "untruth is . . . to be found . . . at the center of [Dasein's] being as radically finite, as existence, project, or care. Truth and untruth belong together to the being of man, and not merely to the being of man but to the totality of being as such" (AD, 130).

According to Heidegger, what is disclosed falls into semblance by the agencies of idle talk, curiosity, and ambiguity. Of course, in the context of literature, the idea of idle talk is of most interest. In the immediate context of his discussion of the primordial and derivative senses of truth, Heidegger points out how the authentic use of language to bring about disclosure becomes, through its repetition in an assertion, an inauthentic expression of something present-at-hand in which Dasein's disclosedness is covered-up.

According to Heidegger, what is disclosed falls into semblance by the agencies of idle talk, curiosity, and ambiguity. Of course, in the context of literature, the idea of idle talk is of most interest. In the immediate context of his discussion of the primordial and derivative senses of truth, Heidegger points out how the authentic use of language to bring about disclosure becomes, through its repetition in an assertion, an inauthentic expression of something present-at-hand in which Dasein's disclosedness is covered-up. Assertion of something which is disclosed to understanding rests upon that understanding and its interpretive structure. Assertion is meant to maintain the existence of what has been disclosed: "The assertion . . . contains the uncoveredness of these entities. The uncoveredness is preserved in what is expressed" (BT, 266). Thus, language is authentic not only when it acts violently to bring about disclosure and to articulate it, but when it preserves what has been discovered in the act of understanding. Assertion makes possible the repetition of the truth disclosed primordially by an other. This in itself, however, is not inauthentic: "Dasein need not bring itself face to face with entities themselves in an 'original' experience; but it nevertheless remains in a Being-towards these entities" (BT, 266). However, the inauthentic, illusory use of language—the idle talk of the "they"—is made possible by the very nature of assertion: "What is expressed becomes, as it were, something ready-to-hand within-the-world which can be taken up and spoken again" (*BT*, 266).

Authenticity is lost when the assertion persists and becomes habitual, the unthinking common sense of the "they." What had been disclosed in language and preserved in assertion is covered-over. The "disclosed" becomes merely present-at-hand (*vorhanden*), i.e., an object absorbed by Dasein's abstract and theoretical judgment as Dasein stands off from the world. Dasein's *involvement* with the "disclosed" is eliminated; the "circumspective concern" (*BT*, 57–59) in which he discovered the interrelationship among things as implements in his environment as well as their actual usefulness as "ready-to-hand" (*zuhanden*) is conceptualized and objectified by repeated assertions: "In a large measure uncoveredness gets appropriated not by one's own uncovering, but rather by hearsay of something that has been said. Absorption in something that has been said belongs to the kind of Being which the 'they' possesses" (*BT*, 266–67). The language of the "they" is, of course, inauthentic precisely because it solidifies and covers-up; it preempts the possibility of individual discovery.

"Idle talk" not only covers-up something disclosed, but it also reifies language itself. In the process of transforming the insight or discovery made by language into the mime of hearsay, of what is overheard without understanding, the "they" world reduces language itself to an instrument which is present-at-hand. Language becomes a "thing" to be studied objectively, shaped, and abstracted. "Truth" in the world of the "they" becomes the degree to which the solidifed "statement" "about" some solidified "object" corresponds to the observable "facts of the case." The reification of the discovered by the idle talk of the "they" parallels the traditional metaphysical insistence that truth is a matter of judging the degree of correspondence between proposition and object.

Since Dasein primarily and for the most part belongs to the "they" world, language is usually inauthentic. Macomber suggests that inauthentic existence of the everyday world of the "they" is "untrue," which implies quite clearly that inauthentic language is also quite "untrue" (*AD*, 90). Indeed, such language, the "idle talk" of the "they" and the propositional-judgmental form of traditional notions of truth, makes possible the continuity of the tradition and the bourgeois world by holding off at a distance the potential revelations of Being and nothingness which threaten to upset it.

The inauthenticity, the "untruth," of language in the tradition needs to be destroyed to reveal what it obscures as well as to bring out of it—as Heidegger has done with Kant—whatever "truth" the tradition *intended to say* but could not because it remained to some extent trapped within its own historical inauthenticity. For the literary critic or historian, the predominance of untruth in language demands a destructive stance in the face of previous interpretations of texts—interpretations which are themselves articulated for the most part in the language of the tradition—as well as an awareness that insofar as a primary text is authentic—intending to bring the truth out from its cover—it too stands in a destructive relationship to earlier texts, tropes, forms, and structures of the language of the tradition.

The central role of language in the theory of truth is carried a step further in this section when Heidegger, destroying Aristotle once more, argues that "the λόγος is that way of Being in which Dasein can *either* uncover *or* cover up. This *double possibility* is what is distinctive in the Being-true of the λόγος: the λόγος is that way of comporting one-self which can *also cover things up*" (*BT*, 268). This dualistic definition of *logos* is of crucial importance because of Heidegger's earlier definition of *logos* as *Rede*, i.e., as speech (*BT*, 55–58). Ontologically, these two uses of language are equiprimordial and they are both basic to truth. But as a potential for disclosure and to avoid the "cover-up" also inherent in speech, *logos* must not be merely "speech" but destruction, that is, to fulfill the potential of *logos* to disclose, speech must violently draw out of the sedimented tradition of idle talk those "original" or "primordial" experiences of Dasein's disclosing. Heidegger's own "speech," that is, his own authentic use of language, is undertaken in the hope of reclaiming the lost

Martin Heidegger

idea of Being from the idle talk, the illusion, the inauthenticity of the tradition.

The phenomenological destruction of the metaphysical tradition which *Being and Time* performs is authentic speech, the *logos*. In its retrieve of the Being question from the tradition and in its disclosure of temporality as the horizon of Dasein and of Being, *Being and Time* establishes destruction as *the* hermeneutic stance of the authentic *logos*.[5] The "methodological" passages of the second "Introduction" point out that destruction, phenomenology, and interpretation (hermeneutics) are stages of the same process of "dis-closing" what the tradition has reduced to habit and the "natural attitude" as well as of exposing what it has chosen to ignore. As *Being and Time* develops, Heidegger establishes that *all* linguistic efforts to move away not only from the tradition but from the "idle talk" of the "they," possess the same destructive, interpretive, phenomenological structure as his own assault on the metaphysical tradition's cover-up of Being, nothingness, and temporality. For the authentic literary critic a recognition of this necessary destructive function in art which is authentic—that is, which brings out the nothingness and Being which the tradition covers-up—compels literary criticism and history to abandon the New Critical, Bloomian, genetic, and structuralist models. Verbal art can no longer be experienced as simply nonreferential, autotelic, and atemporal as these critical theories assume it can; rather, literature must be met as the temporal event of a human's understanding disclosure.

Sections six and seven of *Being and Time* conjoin destruction, phenomenology, and interpretation in the methodological center of the second "Introduction." The task of interrogating Being and the Being of Dasein necessitates an inquiry into the history of that interrogation (*BT*, 42). The fullest possibilities of the inquiry require that the past's interrogation of Being be made "positively" our own. Furthermore, the essential historicality of Dasein, which itself may be hidden, can be revealed in and by tradition. The very existence of a tradition as a context for Dasein and as an "object" of study makes clear the necessary existence of a human being in a situation defined by the "past" which lies "before" him, i.e., as the complex of expectations and goals which he gains, or loses, by his "place" within the tradition: "Dasein can discover tradition, preserve it, and study it explicitly. The discovery of tradition and the disclosure of what it 'transmits' and how this is transmitted, can be taken hold of as a task in its own right. In this way Dasein brings itself into the kind of Being which consists in historiological inquiry and research" (BT, 41). However, the condition for the possibility of seizing the tradition as an "event" to be studied is Dasein's "historicality" (Geschichtlichkeit). In other words, although Dasein can discover his historicality by learning he has and is in a tradition, Dasein can have a tradition and can study it only because he is always already radically temporal, i.e., historical. In a passage which is crucial in suggesting the importance of the destruction of the past for the possibilities of the future, Heidegger summarizes the relationship between Dasein's temporality and his potential for historiology:

> Dasein "is" its past in the way of *its* own Being, which, to put it roughly, "historizes" (*geschieht*) out of its future on each occasion. Whatever the way of being it may have at the time, and thus with whatever understanding of Being it may possess, Dasein has grown up both into and in a traditional way of interpreting itself: in terms of this it understands itself proximally and, within a certain range, constantly. By this understanding, the possibilities of its Being are disclosed and regulated. Its own past—and this always means the past of its "generation"—is not something which *follows along after* Dasein, but something which already goes ahead of it. (BT, 41)

Because Dasein is fallen, tradition (just like the *logos* itself) possesses, or is defined by, the potentiality for authentic and inauthentic existence. In both cases, the authentic is distinguished by disclosure, while the inauthentic, the untrue, is marked by covered-up-ness.

Just as the assertion might preserve a disclosure made by others and might, when part of authentic discourse, reveal what

[63]

Martin Heidegger

has been hidden to the other in the dialogue, so tradition may preserve whatever authentic insight into Being has been achieved. Tradition is inauthentic, however, when it degenerates into habit, into the dominant and "natural" view-point of the "they." When it remains unquestioned and assumed, it solidifies and conceals, it transmits untruth; it is no longer what Bloom calls *mishnah,* but a kind of "tradition" which betrays what it should pass on:

> Dasein is inclined to fall back upon its world (the world in which it is) and to interpret itself in terms of that world by reflected light, but also Dasein . . . simultaneously falls prey to the tradition of which it has more or less explicitly taken hold. . . . When tradition thus becomes master, it does so in such a way that what it "transmits" is made so inaccessible . . . that it rather becomes concealed. Tradition takes what has come down to us and delivers it over to self-evidence. (*BT,* 42–43)

Just as what is disclosed in *aletheia* falls back into semblance, into appearance, mere appearance, or metaphor, so the primordial access to Being which lies preserved in the tradition loses its urgency and meaning and becomes the accepted, present-at-hand, utilitarian, "natural" system of the "truth" of the crowd.

When the instrumentality of this hardened tradition fails, when it "breaks-down" (as the work of Hegel and Nietzsche in philosophy, of Heisenberg and Einstein in physics, and of innumerable poets shows the atemporal, Cartesian, anthropomorphic, and ego-centric Renaissance tradition to have done), then a sense, an intuition, of the meaning and importance which it has long obscured is recognized. Specifically, the culminating failure of western metaphysics in Hegel and Nietzsche—as Heidegger sees it—reawakens explicitly the Being-question as *the* forgotten issue of western tradition. This idea is clear in Heidegger's own large-scale reexaminations of Kant, Hegel, and Nietzsche as well as in his destructions of Thomistic, Cartesian, and Aristotelian theories in *Being and Time.* Heidegger's famous discussion of the hammer indicates that only when a tool fails to work does its ontological significance as an instrument within a larger context in-the-world become apparent. Similarly, the breakdown of the tradition reveals truth that could not be seen as long as, crisis-free, the tradition "worked." [6]

"Destruction" is the methodology by which the intuition granted by the failure of the tradition is articulated. In fact, destruction cannot proceed without an initial incomplete awareness of what is concealed; insofar as destruction emerges from the structure of interpretation, "it is . . . the working-out of possibilities projected in understanding" (*BT*, 189). Just as disclosure cannot result from complete hiddenness, but must emerge from semblance, or the appearance of something *as* something else, so destruction can only proceed from what Heidegger in his discussion of understanding calls a forestructure. This predisposition in the face of the tradition is the basis of the hermeneutic circle, which I shall discuss again further on; however, it is enough to say here that, since understanding can only emerge as a result of this failure of tradition, destructive interpretation is always circular and shares in the basic structure of the existential-ontological understanding of Dasein.

In his "definition" of destruction, Heidegger points out how his particular destruction of the metaphysical tradition begins from an intuition, a clue given by the failed tradition itself:

> If the question of Being is to have its own history made transparent, then this hardened tradition must be loosened up, and the concealments which it has brought about must be dissolved. We understand this task as one in which by taking *the question of Being as our clue,* we are to *destroy* the traditional content of ancient ontology until we arrive at those primordial experiences in which we achieved our first ways of determining the nature of Being—ways which have guided us ever since. (*BT*, 44)

But this destruction of the tradition, just like the cutting away of the concealing semblance or assertion to disclose the truth which is covered-over, does not reduce the "cover" to nullity. Rather,

[65]

Martin Heidegger

it opens it up to reveal what of value is concealed within the habitual ways of looking at the tradition:

> But this destruction is just as far from having the *negative* sense of shaking off the ontological tradition. We must, on the contrary, stake out the positive possibilities of that tradition, and this always means keeping it within its limits; these in turn are given factically in the way the question is formulated at the time, and the way the possible field for investigation is thus bounded off. (*BT*, 44)

These statements on method can be explicated to reveal broader implications for the possibilities of interpretation resting on a destruction. I intend to delay this explication, however, until other essential terms of the project and their interrelationships are developed.

Heidegger begins section 6 by postulating that "Dasein's Being finds its meaning in temporality" (*BT*, 41). It is the aim of his entire project to work out this proposition to establish the relationship—perhaps the identity—of Being and Time. His interpretation of the relationship of Dasein and tradition as well as his deconstructions of Kant and Descartes discloses temporality both as the ground of Dasein's Being—which thus makes possible the examination of the tradition—and as the validation of the destructive method of interpretation:

> In other words, in our process of destruction we find ourselves faced with the task of Interpreting the basis of ancient ontology in the light of the problematic of Temporality. When this is done, it will be manifest that the ancient way of interpreting the Being of entities is oriented towards the "world" or "Nature" in the widest sense, and that it is indeed in terms of "time" that its understanding of Being is obtained. (*BT*, 47)

Temporality as the ground of destructive methodology, and, more universally, of all understanding and interpretation, must be emphasized as an alternative to the timeless modes of literary interpretation and models of literary history which Modern and contemporary critics postulate. Most specifically, as we have

[66]

seen with Bate and Bloom, and as I will show in the next chapter for Brooks and many other New Critics, finitude, the ground fact of human existence and, therefore, of interpretation, prevents the very possibility of timeless models because each of them is based upon the possibility of an infinite, i.e., spontaneous, instantaneous, divine, mode of perception and interpretation.

Following his discussion of destruction in Section 6, Heidegger turns specifically to the deconstructed idea of *logos* as *legein*, as speech, which suggests the authentic orientation toward those entities which we encounter within the world. Just prior to his famous methodological discussion of phenomenology as hermeneutics, Heidegger intimates that phenomenology, insofar as it stands in the face of the world, must share implicitly in the "structure" of destruction. Hermeneutical phenomenology proceeds from a clue or intuition gained in the moment when the habitual or instrumental orientation toward an entity—which may be a text in the tradition—fails, and then progresses to make explicit and exhibit what is hidden by the semblance which must be stripped away.

Heidegger begins section 7, *"The Phenomenological Method of Investigation,"* by asserting twice that phenomenology is a methodological concept (*BT,* 49, 50). By the end of his discussion, though, phenomenology takes on thematic importance when it is identified with ontology itself (*BT,* 60). He divides "phenomenology" into its two constitutive linguistic elements, "phenomenon" and "logos." His opening etymological—perhaps even destructive—definition of the former parallels his definition of truth:

> Thus φαινόμενον means that which shows itself, the manifest. Φαίνεσθαι itself is a *middle-voiced* form which comes from φαινω—to bring to the light of day, to put in the light. Φαινω comes from the stem φα—like φως, the light, that which is bright—in other words, that wherein something can become manifest, visible in itself. Thus we must *keep in mind* that the expression *"phenomenon"* signifies *that which shows itself in itself,*

the manifest. Accordingly, the φαινόμενα or "phenomena" are the totality of what lies in the light of day or can be brought to the light. (*BT*, 51)

In fact, since "phenomena" may need to be brought to light, phenomenology possesses, like *aletheia* and destruction, a privative function. Because these phenomena can fall back into hiddenness, they must often be forcibly disclosed. However, this uncovering only occurs because the phenomena which do not manifest themselves in themselves, but are concealed in semblance, appearance, and "mere" appearance, always include in themselves "the primordial signification," namely, "the phenomena as the manifest" (*BT*, 51). Phenomena possess the same dual possibility for disclosure and cover-up as the *logos* and tradition, the authentic self and the "they" self. In fact, this dual potential rests upon the structure of the *logos* which Heidegger's "destruction" of the traditional interpretation of the *logos* reveals.

Heidegger lays bare the idea of *logos* by explicitly identifying destruction with phenomenology: "In Plato and Aristotle the concept of the *logos* has many competing significations, with no basic signification positively taking the lead. In fact, however, this is only a *semblance,* which will maintain itself as long as our Interpretation is unable to grasp the basic signification properly in its primary content" (*BT*, 55). This "primary content" of the *logos* is *legein* or discourse; as such, it shares in the same revelatory or disclosing structure as phenomena, *aletheia,* and destruction (*BT*, 56). Heidegger explicitly identifies these various elements of his methodology as a prelude to establishing that *logos* as discourse is "just not the kind of thing that can be considered as the primary 'locus' of truth":

> Furthermore, because the λόγος is a letting-something-be-seen, it can *therefore* be true, or false. . . . The "Being-true" of the λόγος as αληθεύειν means that in λέγειν as αποφαίνεσθαι the entities of which one is talking must be taken out of their hiddenness; one must let them be seen as something unhidden (ἀληθές); that is, they must be *discovered.* Similarly, "Being

Martin Heidegger

false" (ψεύδεσθαι) amounts to deceiving in the sense of *covering up:* putting something in front of something (in such a way as to let it be seen) and thereby passing it off *as* something which it is *not.* (*BT,* 56–57)

Only the *noein* can be primordially true, i.e., free of the possibility of covering-up. "Discourse," *logos* as *legein,* is a way to truth, is a mode of "dis-covery" only when "it is genuine," when it does not reveal something in appearance, mere appearance, or metaphor. Although "discourse" becomes "fully concrete" when it takes on the character of "vocal proclamation in words," the mere presence of oral speech is not enough to assure the process of "un-covering." This point must be made against those[7] who would argue for the priority of oral language to writing on the grounds that the former, as nonliterary, i.e., "authentic," is the primary way to reveal what the tradition obscures. Heidegger does not grant speech such complete privilege. "Discourse" as orality possesses the dual possibilities of authenticity and inauthenticity. Only when it violently breaks open the tradition can it be authentic. "Writing," as Derrida suggests throughout his work,[8] can be equally "primordial" in the task of "de-constructing" the tradition. The far-from-oral poetry of Wallace Stevens, for example, offers perhaps the fullest Modern paradigm of writing in the service of disclosing nothingness. It is primarily in linear writing of logocentric metaphysics that the West has reified its past and its vital re-sources—as Heidegger's written destruction of written texts makes clear—and, therefore, it must be to a confrontation with the essentially literate structure of that tradition that hermeneutic destruction must turn. Certainly Charles Olson senses the necessity for confronting this written tradition in order to make it "speak" again when he attacks "discourse" in his *Special View of History*[9] and praises the opportunities afforded the contemporary poet by the typewriter to break open the lines and hard forms of the tradition in order to show what it conceals.[10]

Heidegger's analysis of the structure of phenomenology has

## Martin Heidegger

proceeded by his dis-assembling the constituent parts of the term
to uncover what they contain or conceal. In order to clarify the
formal nature of phenomenology as term and method, he "re-as-
sembles" these parts—phenomenon and *logos:* "to let that which
shows itself be seen from itself in the very way in which it shows
itself from itself" (*BT*, 58). And as we have seen in all the other
terms of this structure of "dis-closure" which I have been drawing out of *Being and Time,* Heidegger points out that Being,
which is allowed to show itself in this way, "can be covered up
so extensively that it becomes forgotten and no question arises
about it or about its meaning" (*BT*, 59). In order to prevent this
obscuring of what is disclosed, Dasein actively destroys or
interprets whatever semblance threatens to cover-up the phenomenon.

Michael Gelven, in his *Commentary on Being and Time,*
suggests that in his formal definition of a phenomenology which
requires interpretation to reveal the "thing itself," Heidegger
threatens himself with a contradiction:

> The difficulty is that many phenomenologists argue that Hei-
> degger's "hermeneutic phenomenology" is a contradiction in
> terms. They maintain . . . that in the tradition of Edmund
> Husserl—the father of modern phenomenology—the whole
> purpose of this method is to achieve a vision of consciousness
> untainted by "systems" or interpretations: to let the facts speak
> for themselves, as it were. . . . If Heidegger's methodolgy is
> *interpretive,* and if phenomenology means to let the facts speak
> for themselves, in whatever sense that can be taken without
> being ridiculous, then surely a hermeneutic phenomenology is
> impossible. (*C*, 34)

Gelven decides that this is really not a contradiction but a dilemma which Heidegger avoids because of the specific nature of
his task: the analysis of existential experience. However, the necessary connection between "interpretation" or "hermeneutics"
and *aletheia* and destruction which I have been suggesting all
along can provide a more satisfactory explanation than the one
Gelven offers.

[70]

Martin Heidegger

Heidegger not only labels his variety of phenomenology "hermeneutic," but he also identifies it with destruction: "The phenomenology of Dasein is a *hermeneutic* in the primordial signification of the word, where it designates this business of interpreting" (*BT,* 62). In historical terms, it is "a phenomenological destruction of the history of ontology" (*BT,* 63). Since discourse, *logos, aletheia,* phenomenon, and phenomenology itself all possess the potential for hiddenness, of allowing what they reveal to fall back, to be *"buried over"* (*BT,* 60), they must be structurally completed by hermeneutics or interpretation to assure their authenticity: "the meaning of phenomenological description as a method lies in *interpretation"* (*BT,* 61). In other words, when a truth or a phenomenon is covered-over and presents itself only as a semblance, it can only be regained and re-dis-covered when "our *passage* through whatever is prevalently covering it up" is "secured by the proper method." (*BT,* 61). Phenomenology itself is violent (*BT,* 61), because, in the face of the cover-up, of the semblance, it must "exhibit" and "explicate" the truth or phenomenon. "The λόγος of the phenomenology of Dasein has the character of a ἑρμηνεύειν, through which the authentic meaning of Being, and also those basic structures of Being which Dasein itself possesses, are *made known* to Dasein's understanding." (*BT,* 62). The key phrase in defining Heidegger's violent destructive phenomenology is "making known to Dasein's understanding."

Yet, circularly, this process begins from the phenomenon or truth itself which is present as error or semblance and "explicit to our awareness by further analysis or discrimination of the given, rather than by any inference from it" (*BT,* 106–7, n. 1). The understanding, then, performs this preliminary disclosure in the very nature of its structure as constituent of the "world." Thus, Dasein's act of uncovering the world in understanding is analogous to phenomenology and in a similar way requires interpretation or hermeneutics to render what is "intuited" or incompletely understood "explicit."

But, like phenomenology itself, and the other disclosing

[71]

Martin Heidegger

structures which emerge from Heidegger's Dasein analytic, understanding also is capable of inauthenticity, i.e., of covering-up. "Understanding is either authentic, arising out of one's own Self as such, or inauthentic." And its inauthenticity "arises" when Dasein does, "Proximally and for the most part, understand itself in terms of its world" (*BT*, 186). In other words, when Dasein abandons or forgets its own nature as "potentiality-for-Being," when it falls into the hardened world of the "they" self and accepts what is, "naturally," ignoring its potential for possibility, for change, for becoming something other than what-it-is, then it covers-over primordially. In effect, at this point, having forgotten the nature of its own Being, it even loses the possibility of disclosure and abandons itself and the world to hiddenness, habit, and opacity. Of course, such an extreme cover-up can never be total. Just as truth emerges from error and phenomenon from semblance, Dasein's "Being-possible is transparent to itself in different possible ways and degrees" (*BT*, 183).

In the Being of its possibilities, Dasein is essentially temporal. This idea of temporality as the ground of Being and Dasein has been worked out by Heidegger commentators since the appearance of the text. Recently, an attempt has been made to ground a temporal literary hermeneutics upon *Being and Time*. In his forthcoming *Icon and Time*, William V. Spanos argues for a return to the primordial sources of literature and reading by a process of understanding based upon the temporal disclosure of discourse. These studies alleviate the necessity for outlining Heidegger's demonstration of the primordiality of temporality. In this context, it is only necessary to suggest how the structure of understanding as the potentiality-for-Being of Dasein is fundamentally temporal. Although Heidegger establishes this in the repetition of the "existential-temporal analysis of Dasein" of Division 2, chapter 4, section 67a, it is already contained in the discussion of "Being-there as understanding," section 31.

As possibility, Dasein is not "a free-floating potentiality-for-Being. . . . In every case Dasein, as essentially having a state-of-mind, has already got itself into definite possibilities" (*BT*, 183).

[72]

Martin Heidegger

Dasein's "past," his "having-been," results from his thrownness (*Geworfenheit*). Dasein is already always in a world, a situation, to use Sartre's term, which is constituted partly by his own possibilities. At the same time as understanding "has" a past or "having-been," as "projection," it "has" a "future," "Why does the understanding," Heidegger asks, "always press forward into possibilities? It is because the understanding has in itself the existential structure which we call *'projection'* " (*BT*, 184–85). This does not mean Dasein conducts itself according to a fixed plan; projection is a stable element of Dasein's structure: "As long as it is, Dasein always has understood itself and always will understand itself in terms of possibilities" (*BT*, 185). Commenting on this passage, Michael Gelven explains: "This means that to throw before ourselves our own possible ways of existing is an essential characteristic of what we are" (*C*, 87). Dasein's Being as understanding, that is, as potentiality-for-Being, is defined by its temporal structure: thrownness and futurity.

Dasein's third ecstasy, the Present, is discussed in this section as "sight," "a universal term for characterizing any access to entities or to Being, as access in general" (*BT*, 187). In other words, "sight" is the element in understanding's structure which disposes Dasein toward disclosure. In "sight," "Dasein *'sees'* possibilities, in terms of which it is" (*BT*, 188). But it is not until the repetition of the analysis of Dasein in light of temporality that the idea of "sight" becomes clear as constituting the "Present" ecstasy of Dasein's understanding: "as an authentic Present of waiting-towards, the moment of vision permits us *to encounter for the first time* what can be 'in a time' as ready-to-hand or present-at-hand" (*BT*, 388).

Thus, understanding is a structure of disclosure. In fact, it is primordial disclosure since it reveals the world, the context of Dasein's existence, and constitutes his possibilities. Whenever Dasein interprets, therefore, whenever it brings what is understood into light, it does so from a position already within the context and limitations of that which it interprets. This is the heart of the hermeneutic circle. The nature of Dasein's under-

[73]

Martin Heidegger

standing as the basic disclosure of the world necessitates that all interpretation which exhibits whatever is understood and explicates whatever is disclosed, must be circular, caught within the realm of what is being interpreted. In other words, it is impossible to escape from the context of world defined by understanding to a standpoint of interpretation which goes beyond being in and of the material or events being interpreted. A Hegelian claim to see all of history from the end of its working out, and therefore to understand it "objectively" and "abstractly," founders upon Heidegger's demonstration that the Being of understanding itself prevents such atemporal, infinite knowledge.

Heidegger defines interpretation as "the development of the understanding" (*BT*, 188). In the process of interpretation, the possibilities of what is only preliminarily understood in *Verständnis* are worked out. Hermeneutics is the way to pass through the veil of hiddenness to the phenomenon, to Being, only because structurally, in intepretation, "the 'world' which has already been understood comes . . . explicitly into the sight which understands" (*BT*, 189). Dasein is capable of phenomenological destruction only because of the disclosing structure of understanding. But just as phenomenology must be hermeneutical because of Dasein's potential for inauthenticity, understanding, which is the ground of all acts of disclosure, must find its meaning, its explicitness, in interpretation. In "circumspective concern," Dasein not only understands, but discloses *"something as something"* (*BT*, 189). In other words, the hermeneutical-interpretive process of destructive phenomenology reveals and names something by disclosing this something's relationship to or involvement with Dasein because understanding is ontologically completed in its structure by the primordial interpretation of what a thing that is ready-to-hand "is for" (*"es ist zum"*) (*BT*, 189). Heidegger labels this function of understanding the "apophantical *as*": "we are not simply designating something; but that which is designated is understood *as* that *as* which we are to take the thing in question" (*BT*, 201). Our relationship to and involvement with the thing is defined or disclosed in this structure.

[74]

Martin Heidegger

It is a completion of a potentiality contained in understanding: "That which is disclosed in understanding—that which is understood—is already accessible in such a way that its 'as which' can be made to stand out explicitly. The 'as' makes up the structure of the explicitness of something that is understood. It constitutes the interpretation" (*BT*, 189). Interpretation, then, is a fundamental structure of Dasein's understanding; thus, all specific acts of interpretation possess a hermeneutical or phenomenological function. The ontological-existential structure of understanding, of Dasein's primordial Being as potentiality-for-Being is completed by a structure of what I call primordial interpretation which exhibits, explicates, and reveals the involvement of Dasein with whatever is intuited in understanding. In fact, the primordiality of the interpretive structure in the process of disclosure causes Heidegger seemingly to contradict the major thrust of his argument for the equiprimordiality of understanding and discourse. He suggests at one point that understanding and interpretation are ontologically prior to discourse: "That which is understood gets Articulated when the entity to be understood is brought close interpretatively by taking as our clue the 'something as something'; and this Articulation lies *before* our making any thematic assertion about it" (*BT*, 190). The importance to Heidegger's argument of the priority of discourse to interpretation—which I will discuss shortly—is temporarily upset in this statement. Heidegger is clearly preoccupied with the essential nature of interpretation as a primordial element in the larger structure of understanding.

The burden of this explication of Heidegger has been to suggest why all interpretive or hermeneutical acts share in the essentially destructive process of the ontological structure of primordial interpretation. The latter, in all cases, as we have seen, completes understanding by drawing out what is incompletely understood and exhibiting it as a possibility of Dasein. In the face of the understanding's potential for hiddenness, for inauthenticity, primordial interpretation explicitly presents understanding with its own possibilities for disclosing. Proceeding from the

[75]

constitution of the "world" by the understanding, interpretation clarifies Dasein's fundamental involvement with what is disclosed as in-the-world (*BT*, 190–91). Just as the hermeneutical method provides the proper way through whatever specifically covers up a phenomenon or truth, primordial interpretation is the passage through the potential for inauthenticity which threatens to cover-over Dasein as disclosedness itself. In effect, primordial interpretation is the necessary process by which Dasein becomes open to the world, authentic, and capable of disclosure, rather than remaining fallen, inauthentic, and in error. Further, all acts of secondary interpretation, of hermeneutics, which are made possible by primary interpretation, necessarily share in the disclosing of a structure charged with preserving the disclosive potential of Dasein itself. Disinterested, distanced, analytic knowledge of an object of interpretation is impossible. Interpretation can only present the working out, the "explicating," not of a text, but of the understanding of a text as a possibility of Dasein. Heidegger explains the nature of this "explication" in his analysis of the "fore-structure" of understanding.

Heidegger characterizes this "fore-structure" as a "fore-having" (*Vorhabe*), "fore-sight" (*Vorsicht*), and "fore-conception" (*Vorgriff*) (*BT*, 191). The "fore-structure" is essentially temporal in nature. The "fore-having" directs an interpreter out of Dasein's past and present while "fore-sight" and "fore-conception," although conditioned by the past, are primarily futural. The "fore-structure" establishes that prior to any act of interpretation, Dasein is in-the-world. Also, because of Dasein's situation, all interpretation emerges out of and toward Dasein's interest in or involvement with those things in-the-world which he intends to interpret. Dasein is necessarily predisposed toward the "object" of his interpretation, thereby making "objective" interpretation impossible.

In the "fore-having," Dasein's involvement with things in an entire complex of relationships which compose his environment or world directs interpretation toward those things which Dasein "already" understands: "As the appropriation of understanding, the interpretation operates in Being towards a totality of involvements which is already understood—a Being which understands" (*BT*, 191). An interpretation can only be the working out of what is understood but not yet appropriated, that is, not yet "unveiled" (*BT*, 191). This appropriative interpretation unveils "under the guidance of a point of view. . . .[a *Vorsicht* which] 'takes the first cut' out of what has been taken into our fore-having, and does so with a view to a definite way in which this can be interpreted" (*BT*, 191). As a result of this fore-sight which directs understanding's movement into the future of interpretation, an object of understanding becomes conceptualizable, authentically (by disclosing something hidden) or inauthentically (by continuing to perpetrate the cover-up): "In either case, the interpretation has already decided for a definite way of conceiving it, either with finality or with reservations: it is grounded in *something we grasp in advance*—in a *fore-conception*" (*BT*, 191). Authentic interpretation *cannot* escape this fore-structure. Even the process of dis-closure, of dis-covering, must emerge out of the world and a disposition toward the world. Interpretation as a process of stripping away, of performing the phenomenological reduction—that is, of bracketing all the presuppositions of the tradition—itself emerges not from a completely passive, *tabula rasa* consciousness, but from an active interest, an involved predisposition to unveil totally something which is given only incompletely in understanding.

The circular structure of Heidegger's own project which I outlined above results from this "fore-structure." Since truth cannot emerge from complete hiddeness, but only from error or semblance, interpretation or hermeneutics can only exhibit what is "intelligible" (*verständlich*) and not something which is completely foreign and distanced from our possible involvement. "An interpretation," according to Heidegger's structure of understanding, "is never a presuppositionless apprehending of something presented to us." Furthermore, in a passage which certainly greatly influences Paul de Man, Heidegger adds: "If, when one is engaged in a particular concrete kind of interpreta-

## Martin Heidegger

tion, in the sense of exact textual Interpretation, one likes to appeal to what 'stands there,' then one finds that what 'stands there' in the first instance is nothing other than the obvious undiscussed assumption of the person who does the interpreting" (*BT*, 191–92). Therefore, all interpretations are not only destructive, i.e., involved in appropriating through the veil what is understood, but they are circular and themselves based on presuppositions. It is this latter fact which requires the ongoing process of interpretation which needs to be performed "again and again" in the examination of the primordial material contained within the tradition and in the attempt to bring about *"a-letheia."* Clearly, this fact lies behind de Man's idea of a literary history which would be composed of a series of "mis-readings." They would be "misreadings," of course, because they must each necessarily rest upon an unexamined interpretive presupposition and because they would be, as interpretations, merely "working-out" those presuppositions.

Heidegger insists that this structure is not the vicious circle of logic and it would be a mistake to try to somehow escape from the circle. For interpretations to be authentic, these basic conditions must be acknowledged beforehand as essential: "What is decisive is not to get out of the circle but to come into it in the right way" (*BT*, 125). This circle contains a possibility for attaining "primordial" knowing. Proper attention to the nature of the "fore-structure," rather than futile, inauthentic attempts to evade it—and consequently the finitude of Dasein's understanding—assures the unique "historiological knowledge" which the hermeneutic circle offers:

> To be sure, we genuinely take hold of this possibility [for primordial knowledge] only when, in our interpretation, we have understood that our first, last, and constant task is never to allow our fore-having, fore-sight, and fore-conception to be presented to us by fancies and popular conceptions, but rather to make the scientific theme secure by working out these fore-structures in terms of the things themselves. Because understanding, in accordance with its existential meaning, is Dasein's

## Martin Heidegger

own potentiality-for-Being, the ontological presuppositions of historiological knowledge transcend in principle the idea of rigour held in the most exact sciences. (*BT*, 195)

Although I have already treated some of the historical and historiological implications for Dasein of Heidegger's methods of destruction and interpretation in the context of my discussion of "phenomenology," this fuller account of historical as opposed to the scientific knowledge which structuralists such as Tordorov and Culler as well as the New Critics desire, is crucial to my understanding of literary history. Yet, before I can move to a discussion of this central idea, it is necessary to examine Heidegger's notion of discourse explicitly to show not only that all interpretation is destructive or explicatory, but also that all authentic speech is itself hermeneutical, i.e., disclosing and destructive interpretation, as well.

As I have noted above, Heidegger's momentary claim for the priority of understanding and interpretation over that of discourse appears to contradict the major impulse in *Being and Time* to see *logos* as *legein* (*Rede*) as equiprimordial with understanding when viewed existentially. Heidegger's discussion of discourse indicates a distinction between language and speech. The former "has its roots in the existential constitution of Dasein's disclosedness" (*BT*, 203). In other words, language as a phenomenon is made possible by the potentiality-for-Being which is Dasein's understanding. However, discourse, the *logos* as *Rede*, is *not* language, but rather "the existential-ontological foundation of language." (*BT*, 203). We have already seen Heidegger, in his discussion of *logos*, suggest the possibility of identifying *legein*, discourse, with *noein*, " 'to be aware of,' 'to know' " (*BT*, 47). It is by virtue of this identification that *logos* as the authentic use of language can be distinguished from the inauthentic use of language in idle talk.

Discourse is "an existential state in which Dasein is disclosed." It reveals the basic structure of disclosedness of Dasein. Furthermore, discourse articulates or expresses Dasein's state of

[79]

Martin Heidegger

Being-in-the-world and, as a result, reveals itself to have a *"worldly"* character itself (*BT,* 204). Consequently, discourse as speech, as talk, is always "talk about something" (*BT,* 204). Not merely assertive language is always "about" something, but all discourse, as disclosure of Dasein's relationship to and involvement with the world, is referential: "What the discourse is about is a structural item that it [i.e., discourse] necessarily possesses; for discourse helps to constitute the disclosedness of Being-in-the-world, and in its own structure it is modelled upon this basic state of Dasein" (*BT,* 205). Dasein, however, does not find itself in a world, nor does it create its own world, by "talking about" and "naming" things which it finds "out-there." Rather, discourse as *"ex-pression,"* has the form of articulating Dasein's "Being-outside" (*BT,* 205). *Rede,* that is, expresses the non-dualistic, non-Cartesian nature of Dasein's Being-in-the-world. Speech does not bring man into relation with the world. It does not "overcome" the split between the mental and the natural—a split which, of course, totally motivates Harold Bloom's misreadings. "In talking, Dasein *ex*presses itself [spricht sich . . . *aus*] not because it has, in the first instance, been encapsulated as something 'internal' over against something outside, but because as Being-in-the-world it is already 'outside' when it understands" (*BT,* 205). Thus, all language, as discourse, speaks already within the world, within a context of involvements which in fact it discloses. The opposition between language and nature which Bloom sees as the motivating cause of poetic anxiety is reduced to a fiction by Heidegger's analysis of discourse. In fact, as I have tried to suggest in my rhetorical analysis of his works, the "anxiety of influence" stems from the conflict between a poet's desire to use language authentically, i.e., discursively, to reveal the structure of Dasein's involvements with his world, while being restricted in the process by the sedimentation of language which has occurred in the reification of "idle talk" into tradition.

The import of Heidegger's theory of discourse lies in the essentially authentic use of language to disclose by destroying or

Martin Heidegger

overcoming "idle talk." Yet, discourse need not be speech in order to be authentic. Ultimately, discourse need not even involve language as any "totality of words" (*BT*, 204). Discourse comes to be seen as an element in Dasein's structure of disclosure *upon which* all language is based, but which is not necessarily itself linguistic. Perhaps, put most extremely, it could be said that "discourse" *is* authentic language, cutting away the veils screening the involvement of Dasein with the World as well as the language of the tradition which has for so long obscured the priority of the Being-question and other "phenomena" which are "true."

Heidegger explicitly recognizes that one of the possible achievements of his theory of understanding and discourse is "the necessity of reestablishing the science of language on foundations which are ontologically more primordial" (*BT*, 209). He is criticizing both the solidification of language into meaning and the solidification of its rules into grammar as this is brought about by the misinterpretation of *logos* as " 'logic' " (*BT*, 209). This criticism is of utmost importance to my argument. Heidegger's retrieve of the *logos* as *Rede* from the tradition of *ratio* is partially intended to *re-found,* to *re-discover* the potentialities of a language which would rest upon a *"positive* understanding of the basic *a priori* structure of discourse" (*BT*, 209). Such renewal is necessary because it would free language from its "error" of assertion (*Aussage*). The latter, of course, is a derivative mode of language which congeals the discovery of discourse into the utilitarian form of the proposition, which, in its turn, in its Being-present-at-hand, is an instrument of the technological mind. Heidegger sees the entire tradition of language theory and language usage as defined by the Greeks' notion of *logos* as assertion. Of course, this misinterpretation of language brings about the forgetfulness of Being, the hiddenness of truth, and the cover-up of the primordial temporality of Dasein.

Therefore, when Heidegger begins his project, he is confronted by a language which itself contains not only the history of all past disclosures, but which itself is the instrument of their cover-up. His problem is to get through the veil which the very

[81]

usage of language drawn from the tradition will superimpose upon the disclosures he is attempting by his "re-membrance" of Being. As a result, of course, he breaks radically with traditional philosophical language. Yet, his etymological analyses and his verbal pyrotechnics revivify some of the petrified issues which lie concealed behind long-unexamined and habitually misused terms. *"Logos"* is the classic example of Heidegger's verbal destruction in *Being and Time.*

At the end of his second "Introduction," Heidegger in fact announces to his readers that the "awkwardness" of his prose is purposeful and meaningful: "it is one thing to give a report in which we tell about *entities,* but another to grasp entities in their *Being.* For the latter task we lack not only most of the words but, above all, the 'grammar' " (*BT,* 63). In historical attempts at ontology, the Greeks were compelled to impose "formulations" of an "altogether unprecedented character" upon the language (*BT,* 63). In other words, there is historical justification for his own attempt to retrieve language from the grammar of logic which has elevated the petrifying assertion to the pinnacle of philosophical meaning. By laying bare the ontological structure of truth and understanding, Heidegger undercuts the priority of the *logos* as *ratio,* i.e., what the tradition thinks of as the condition for the possibility of disclosure, "reason" itself, and, by his discussion of discourse as constituent of Dasein's disclosedness, Heidegger also shows "assertion" to be itself a derivative form of language.

But in his own project, Heidegger works *through* the language of the tradition to break it down and to reveal what it has concealed about itself and Being. In the process, he discloses the possibility for the condition of an authentic, nontraditional language, the structure of Dasein's disclosedness. Thus, his attempt to uncover the question of Being through a nontraditional language has actually disclosed the reasons why his attempt is valid. Through discourse and understanding, a positive grammar of language as uncovering, as destruction, as interpretation, becomes a necessity. The language of assertion, which rests upon the possibility of "objective" understanding, is completely overthrown by the hermeneutical structure of understanding. Dasein cannot stand off at a distance, detached from whatever he does, thinks about, lives with, or studies. His basic constitution as Being-in-the-world, disclosed by understanding, involves him immediately in a complex relationship with whatever he studies and lives with. Once reminded of the roots of language, one can proceed to uncover, to disclose, to maintain, and to communicate without necessarily falling into the trap of formalization and logic.

For the literary critic, such as Paul de Man, certain writers perform the function of disclosure which discourse as an ontological structure of Dasein makes possible. Discourse must be seen as the condition for the possibility of all authentic language. What Heidegger reveals is that language contains the possibility for uncovering at all times, just as it can be idle talk for the most part. Language can proceed from *logos* as discourse or *aletheia* to reveal what tradition, habit, and inauthenticity cover-up for the most part. Furthermore, as Heidegger's own retrieves indicate, many writers and thinkers participate in the structure of disclosure to greater and lesser extents. Kant, for example, "discloses" the temporal ground of Dasein, although proximally and for the most part, he is unaware of the position his language—as the potential for truth—reveals. His understanding and primordial interpretation as structures of disclosure constitute the insight he, as fallen, cannot articulate fully. Although Heidegger's destruction, i.e., his interpretation, is necessary to allow Kant's discovery to emerge explicitly, the revelation is essentially that of Kant's language.

The insights gained by this examination of Heidegger's theory of *logos* can now be summarized. The structure of Dasein's disclosedness as potentiality-for-Being grounds the entire complex of disclosure which is composed of *aletheia,* destruction, phenomenology, and interpretation. Yet, the potentiality to un-

[83]

cover is always and for the most part itself covered over by Dasein's inauthenticity. But tradition and habits cannot completely obscure truth since understanding, as constituent of the world, always, to some degree, is aware of the Being of entities and of Dasein. Two crucial ideas for literary interpretation and literary history emerge from this discussion to support my original proposition that literary texts are themselves interpretations. All language is capable of authenticity and inauthenticity, i.e., it both discloses and covers up, often in the same movement. Therefore, for language to maintain what has been disclosed in a state of openness, it must itself be kept from solidifying into idle talk or "tradition" by the process of destruction. All authentic language reflects this destructive process. Criticism of literary language, insofar as it is authentic, must be aware of this interpretive process within the language being studied. Authentic, destructive language opens up those forms, ideas, and tropes which lie within the earlier texts of the tradition. Moreover, literary history itself, as I have suggested in my discussion of de Man in chapter one, if it intends to be authentic, must be cognizant that there is ongoing hermeneutical interaction within and among literary texts to maintain what has been disclosed, and they must recognize that "history" and historiological knowledge are the record of this necessary, unending interpretation.

Dasein's potential for this type of interpretation lies in the temporal structure of his understanding, his "relatedness backward and forward." It makes possible a look at the tradition which tries to redeem the issues, the problems, from their hibernation in the idle talk of habit. In fact, to this point, my analysis has been directed toward showing that Heidegger's theory of understanding realizes that all authentic language potentially reveals truth by destroying what obscures it. Now, however, it is necessary to deal with his ideas of repetition, retrieve, and history to defend the model of literary history which I am suggesting is more vital and valuable than the genealogical and positivistic models of so much Modern criticism.

Martin Heidegger

## III

There is a fairly extensive literature dealing with the relationship of Heidegger's theory of history and his own model of historical interpretation in *Being and Time* and other works.[11] I intend to extend the conclusions of some of these theories to the area of literary history. The problem for the literary critic is this: how does an individual work stand in relation to the "tradition"? There is a strong sense that this problem needs to be dealt with, and I have tried to suggest some of the reasons why a few of the more important recent attempts are only partially successful. As Paul de Man's essay on "Literary History and Literary Modernity" suggests, the claim by contemporary writers to be doing something "new" and "different" is a universal claim of all literature and is always counterbalanced by the necessary relationship to the past in which every text stands by definition of being linguistic. Slavish imitation of the "tradition," of course, leads to conscious and unconscious parody (Bloom offers Pynchon as an example of the former and Mailer of the latter), and as Bloom suggests, sterility, loss of value, and the death of literature. Because Dasein, and especially the artist, stands already within a world and within a tradition, he cannot act independently of it. Certainly, Modern and Postmodern writers, though, have been trying to get completely beyond what they see as the deadening habits of thought, perception, and writing which define the "western" mind since the Renaissance. Some critics, like de Man and Derrida, are aware of the difficulty of this effort and some major writers, such as Whitman, Stevens, and Olson, are prepared to admit that the tradition must somehow be re-begun and made to "work" once again in a kind of Kierkegaardian repetition, since it cannot, in fact, be evaded. How, though, can this be done? How can the horrors Bloom so rightly fears be avoided? Even more importantly, how can literature regain the vitality and meaning which it always possesses as a possibility by virtue of its linguistic existence?

The inability to escape from the tradition which Heidegger

and Nietzsche both sense is paradoxically the key to answering these various questions. This "entrapment" is what Heidegger calls the hermeneutic situation. Calvin O. Schrag defines this situation in historical terms:

> In seeking to understand the history of metaphysics we are involved in interpretation. But in every work of interpretation the interpreter, with his questions and intentions, is already positioned within his data. He operates within a hermeneutical situation, and his understanding is conditioned by this situation. This situationality of always already operating within a context of given, although provisional, meanings is what keeps the interpreter within the history of that which he interprets. The interpreter is himself historical. He is denied the unconditioned freedom to stand outside of history so as to make a judgement on it. This leads us to a rejection of the Hegelian claim that one can place oneself at the end of history and speak from the standpoint of a disembodied logos.[12]

Thus the writer in using language is already and always within the world and the tradition constituted by that very language. This explains why the modern impulse to be antitraditional is always defined by its position within the tradition. In "Tradition and the Individual Talent," T.S. Eliot insists that poetry cannot be trapped within mere "novelty," (which de Man calls fashion), or mere imitation. "Tradition," Eliot says, "is a matter of much wider significance." Although Eliot's insistence that every new work of art is not only informed by the tradition, but actually modifies "the *whole* existing order," is a step toward understanding the relationship of each new work to the tradition from which it emerges, his claim that tradition might be seen as an ideal and timeless order is not justifiable.[13] Indeed, that all authentic texts exist in a state of flux and of unstable, destructive, intertextual relationships disrupts both any linearly successive and organically integral images of order.

Heidegger's theory insists upon the historicity of the tradition and its interpreter. Neither one is a privileged unchanging center or firm point of reference for the interpretive act. All

Martin Heidegger

linguistic texts share to some degree in the interpretive, disclosing structure of the *logos,* in the potentiality for truth and error, and thus in a mixed relationship to other disclosures and cover-ups which precede and follow them. Once again, this suggests the change and risk which a fully temporal and hermeneutic theory of literary interpretation and history brings to the study of literature. Yet, it does not require the gloom and despair which brings Bloom to deny the future potential of literature. Indeed, this situation, fraught with possibilities, opening up language and literature to potential change, and perhaps even disorder, becomes the basis of poetry's future: "Our hermeneutical situationality is not a matter of fatalistic determination. It is layered with possibility, temporalized in such a manner that it projects the openness of the future as it recollects the destiny of the past." [14]

"The openness of the future" is the central *human* fact of this sort of literary history. Within the hermeneutical situation the poet can destroy the history of literary interpretations, of literary texts as such, as well as the habitual-critical interpretations of those texts. This means he can reclaim for human possibility those potential problems and issues which are lost in the systematization of Dasein's disclosures in past language. In *Kant and the Problem of Metaphysics,* Heidegger explains the orientation toward the ontotheological-metaphysical tradition which his own interpretations, his own writings, assume:

> It is true that in order to wrest from the actual words that which these words "intend to say," every interpretation must necessarily resort to violence. This violence, however, should not be confused with an action that is wholly arbitrary. The interpretation must be animated and guided by the power of an illuminative idea. Only through the power of this idea can an interpretation risk that which is always audacious, namely, entrusting itself to the secret élan of a work, in order by this élan to get through to the unsaid and to attempt to find an expression for it. The directive idea itself is confirmed by its own power of illumination. [15]

[87]

Martin Heidegger

Heidegger goes on to describe this method of close destruction of a previous text in order to express what its language *"intended to say,"* a repetition (*KPM*, 208). Of course, as William V. Spanos suggests, Heidegger's idea of repetition as destruction emerges from Kierkegaard's earlier treatment of the same idea.[16] For the Danish philosopher, it is a movement based soundly on the incarnational paradox, while for Heidegger, it stands forth from the secular analysis of Dasein's understanding. In this context of ongoing interpretation, Heidegger's definition is of more immediate importance:

> By a repetition of a fundamental problem we understand the disclosure of the primordial possibilities concealed in it. The development of these possibilities [in an interpretation] has the effect of transforming the problem and thus preserving it in its import as a problem. To preserve a problem means to free and to safeguard its intrinsic powers, which are the source of its essence and which make it possible as a problem. (*KPM*, 211).

This general program of repeating the traditional "problems" in such a way as to regain their authentic Being as issues is known as the "retrieve." Programmatically, the "retrieve" must regain all the fundamental experiences which motivate the problems of the tradition and exhibit them as such in order to find a new beginning. The retrieve does not nostalgically hope to return to some lost beginning, some mythic *illo tempore,* but to displace that beginning and to establish another:

> This means nothing less than to *re-trieve* the beginning of our historical-spiritual Dasein in order to transmute it into another beginning. This is possible. It is indeed the crucial form of history because it takes its start in the ground occurrence. But a beginning is not retrieved by reducing it to something past and now known and merely to be imitated. The beginning must be begun again, more originally, with all the strangeness, darkness, and insecurity that a true beginning brings with it. Retrieve as we understand it is anything but a better way of continuing the past by the methods of the past.[17]

[88]

Martin Heidegger

In fact, Modern and Postmodern writing, in its antipathy for traditional ways and ideas, tries repeatedly to start over. Yet, these attempts are generally defined by their relation to the past. Particular writers—like those dealt with in this study—Whitman, Stevens, and Olson—in fact adopt the specific method of retrieve which Heidegger suggests here. They break open the traditional poetic models which obscure the vital sources of their art, a possibility for poetry which de Man is reluctant to admit. Wallace Stevens, for example, employs the form of romantic quest against itself, not merely to destroy it by describing its "inadequacy" to the Modern world, but to reveal what it obscures, what, as a form, it "intends to say" and could not. In Whitman and Olson, the fracturing of the line of English verse is another example of destroying the literary tradition for the purposes of beginning again—as Heidegger hopes—by allowing the potential, the possibility, of language to exhibit itself as such writers actively explore its "sites," its "occasions."

The possibility and potential value of this type of retrieve lies within the temporal structure of Dasein. Dasein's understanding is essentially temporal and Heidegger derives the three "ecstasies" which constitute this temporality from Dasein's disclosedness, that is, his "relatedness backward and forward," his simultaneous structure of "having been," of the now, and of futurity. Dasein is not an entity with a "life span" completed between the poles of beginning and end (*BT,* 426). As Thomas Langan puts it when commenting on the unique temporal structure of Dasein:

> In the full "now" of authentic existence, all projections are made in view of my radical thrownness, with death before me as the ultimate conditioning possibility, so that existence becomes a self-extension from birth to death lived in the dense moment of caring projection. Because the Dasein knows the course it is taking and resolutely wills it, the historical motion is not a passive undergoing, such as the material living thing experiences, but an active "letting itself happen," the free shouldering of a destiny. For this reason Heidegger terms the

[89]

motion of Dasein's self-extension a *Geschehen*—a "happening," from which of course he would derive the word *Geschichte* (historical destiny). (*MH*, 57)

It is precisely this temporal structure which differentiates the model and value of the literary history I am proposing from the traditional positivistic, structuralist, New Critical, and Bloomian theories. Dasein is *both* forward and backward, looking at all times, in all nows; in fact, both orientations are determined by Dasein's projection into possibility, into change, into time itself. Bate reduces the past to ideal orders which can never be radically changed. Along with Bloom, his "past" is defined by continuity and stability. Yet Dasein's own structure, his own Being is potentiality, possibility, which, although it emerges out of a situation, or rather, because it is grounded in existence, looks authentically back to its past to find new possibilities for a new beginning, which have either been forgotten or never exhibited in interpretation.

The look backward, though, is always simultaneously a look forward, toward the actualization of these possibilities in a more authentic—and that means more open and less forgetful—tradition. Once again, Langan's comments on the theory of repetition are important: "Repetition, the act of making present the possibilities of the past in view of [Dasein's] resolute projections, is the basis of 'handing on a tradition,' which is what occurs when I actualize historical possibility on the basis of what has been done, and thus make possible new advances for the future" (*MH*, 59). The need to preserve what is disclosed is an ongoing process and its renewal requires viewing the past in terms of the future. This does not mean coercing the past or imposing "modern" theories upon it; rather, it implies allowing the past to define itself, allowing the interpreter to see in the light of what Heidegger calls a text's "élan," so that the intention of past language—its potential—can be constantly renewed. Insofar as language is used authentically in literature—and it can never be completely authentic since, as we have seen, *logos* is both discourse and idle talk—literary history is a series of interpretations of what has preceded in the light of what are freely seized as future possibilities. In the tradition, the solidification of the language which made the "original" disclosures obscures the sources for the most part, and language's habitual forms need to be overcome. The severity of Postmodern and Modern destruction does not, however, obscure the potential for disclosure which exists in all language and specifically in antitraditional writers like Swift and Sterne.

This theory presents us with a model of interpretation which is more explicit than the one suggested by de Man in *Blindness and Insight*. It recognizes the temporal orientations of many writers as destructive stances. It requires a practical criticism which involves the critic in dealing with texts which are themselves often in need of interpretation, of destruction, and which are, to the degree that they are authentic, interpretations of their own tradition as well. Authentic criticism, then, is no longer merely the analysis of one text as a closed system, or of one poet in terms of his "formative biographical influences," nor even of his psychological attempts to be his own father, a Gnostic out of time, but an interpretation of an interpretation of an interpretation, and so on "again and again." Finally, such a process leads the authentic critic back in his own history of interpretations— which, of course, are themselves destructive interpretations as all authentic histories probably must be—to a Nothing. Clearly de Man senses this in his own work as well as in his reading of Heidegger. "To put it simply," as Theodore Kisiel says in his introduction to Werner Marx's *Heidegger and the Tradition,* "the backtrack that attempts to get to the bottom of things ultimately reaches a point where the bottom falls out, and all that can be said is *es gibt:* 'there is a giving.' " [18] When Derrida "defines" *la différance* as the ground of all conceptualization, as the possibility of thought and discovery, he certainly alludes to Heidegger's demonstration that at the origin, the fundamental center, there is only Nothing, the withdrawal of Being which marks the ontological difference between Being and beings.

[91]

Martin Heidegger

Ultimately, then, there emerges a theory of literature which sees all language as based on nothing and manifesting itself as fiction emerging out of and reflecting nothing. Insofar as it pretends to special freedom from error, it is inauthentic. De Man "erred" precisely by claiming absolute demystification for literary texts. All language has a dual potential because it emerges from the Nothing and Being of the source of all interpretations. The *"es gibt"* makes possible conceptualization and idle talk; it enables both tradition as *mishnah* and tradition which no longer "works." Authentic critical interpretation confronts this constant destructive shifting among truths and errors with no hope at all of making sense of it all. It cannot be straightened out or closed off. As Heidegger says of the hermeneutic circle, it cannot be avoided, only gotten into in the right way. Fundamentally, this means recognizing the existence of the permanent hermeneutical situation and allowing it to inform the practical acts of interpretation which a critic performs. If literary interpretation is to be realized as an authentic possibility and not merely an abstraction, destruction must be employed in practice, in the process of disclosing the very interpretive impulses of poets of undoubted authenticity. Following my destruction of the inauthentic method of the New Criticism, the chapters on Whitman, Stevens, and Olson will attempt to do just that.

Chapter Three

## Cleanth Brooks
## and Modern Irony:
## A Kierkegaardian Critique

I

In an attempt to deal with the problems of temporality and the tradition which contemporary literature raises with such violence and insistence, critics who are authentically responsive to this material have attempted theories of literature and criticism with the assumption that the New Criticism has come to an end. Yet, New Critics of the second and third generation still influence the study of literature in the universities of the United States. Often these teachers and scholars were trained by other devoted New Critics, fresh from the battles to establish the primacy of the literary text over the life of the poet and general cultural history in the study of literature. As a result of the success of these defenders, the New Criticism has become pervasive. It has become an unreflective set of critical habits rather than principles, which coerces the reading processes of those who have been trained in colleges and universities. Even though the New Criticism has been declared dead and buried many times in the last ten or fifteen years, it effects education and research in literature even at advanced levels with such a tenacity and stubbornness that many of its practitioners are no longer aware that they are, in fact, employing a method, and certainly they do not suspect what the implications of that method might be.

The New Criticism also has provided a terrain suitable for the introduction of French structuralism and poststructuralism into the United States. The proliferation of major journals and of important books in these fields in the last five years suggests that the much more technical and precise language of the structuralists and poststructuralists is not at all inimical to the New Criticism. A destruction of the New Criticism might, by opening up the metaphysical assumptions underlying it, suggest some of the reasons why the structuralists and poststructuralists have been welcomed in the American academy. Also, there might appear in the process some idea of how a destruction of structuralism itself—which is perhaps only the newest version of the New Criticism—could proceed.

Bate and Bloom begin with the assumption that the New Criticism is dead, but they do not bother to analyze what it obscures or what it assumes because the theories which they propose are not meaningful departures from the larger tradition of metaphysical aestheticism which subsumes the New Criticism. Indeed, like Brooks, Ransom, and Tate, they use literature as a bulwark against nothingness in an attempt to recover a lost paradise in the "fall" into historical existence. De Man is aware of the refusal of Modern criticism to recognize the essential nothingness at the "center" of all literature and he certainly reveals the weakness of any criticism which does not attempt to take the basic "fact" of nothingness into account as a permanent feature of all critical writing. Yet, de Man does not perform the radical destruction of the New Criticism which is necessary. His discussion of American formalism fails to bring out both its atemporal assumptions and its basically metaphysical nature. He does not expose how the New Criticism as cover-up of time, the absurd, and finitude, of nothingness, Being, and the world is a continuation of the inauthentic tradition which Heidegger recognizes as the primary blocking agent to thinking about truth. A destruction of the New Criticism along these lines would also suggest why it resists so much contemporary literature which insists precisely upon finitude, absurdity, nothingness, and the world.

Furthermore, since the American "tradition" in poetry is defined essentially by a destructive relationship to the forms of the past European tradition, the New Criticism emerges as in-authentic especially in the context of those poets treated in the second half of this study. Indeed, the New Criticism, in its various manifestations—the rigorous verbal analysis of Brooks and Warren, the more catholic but equally reactionary insight of Tate, or the Adamic, neo-Kantian theories of R.W.B. Lewis and other theoreticians of American mythology—is exactly the cover-up which the metaphysical tradition perpetrates to obscure the poetry of destruction itself. The New Criticism, in its extreme denial of stature to Whitman and Olson (as well as many others like Lawrence and Williams), and in its reduction of Stevens to an accountant of the imagination, hides the poetry which threatens its metaphysical self-interest, i.e., its desire to use literature and the academy as a way out of historical time into a world of eternity and timeless truths.

These poets can be used to destroy the New Critical interpretations which have grown up around them and reduced them to habits of our culture. In other words, it is possible to reveal what the New Criticism conceals in individual poems by turning those texts against the "standard readings" of them. But a more radical examination of the New Criticism's *a prioris* is needed to disclose the dehumanized New Critical stance toward poetry as a *metaphysical* stance which inauthentically covers-up.


II


Irony is, of course, the most pervasive category of Cleanth Brook's criticism, and it shares along with Burke's "paradox" and Empson's "ambiguity" a position so dominant in modern literary study that to question it is to question the best practical criticism and much of the best critical theorizing of this century. Nonetheless, the time for reevaluating Modernism's ironic stance is overdue.

During the 1960s, critics such as Nathan A. Scott, Jr., J. Hillis Miller, Frank Kermode, and later in the decade, William

V. Spanos, called for a critical discourse which would be open to the thematic nightmare of Eliot, Yeats, Kafka, and Beckett in a way which the highly disinterested language of "ambiguity," "paradox," and "irony" is not.[1] Most importantly, these critics searched for a concept of form to replace the "verbal icon," just as the nontraditional, open nature of what is called "destructive" or "deconstructive" anti-art had replaced the classical closed forms—the concrete universals—of such modern poems as "In a Station of the Metro," "Musée des beaux arts," "Lord Weary's Castle," and Empson's "Arachne."

At the same time that this critical dissatisfaction was beginning to emerge, the unsympathetic response of New Critically dominated universities and journals to the works of poets like Charles Olson, Robert Duncan, Sylvia Plath, and others revealed that the New Critics were unable to understand this postmodern poetry because it is modelled upon nonironic poets like Whitman, Lawrence, and W. C. Williams, whom Eliot and Brooks had designated as anathema to the "tradition" and, therefore, to academic study.[2] These new poets returned to sources of poetic vitality forgotten by the "tradition," and they let the possibilities of a nonsymbolist, immanental poetry—that is, one which shows that man and nature are inextricably united and that man is an object in nature—emerge from within the hardened, sedimented New Critical interpretation of Modernism, thereby not only destroying the "tradition" but also letting these poets be heard.

I intend to restrict myself in this essay to a study of Brooks, not only because to include Empson, Burke, Tate, Ransom, and all the others consciously or unconsciously associated with the New Critical attitude would require a much longer essay to satisfactorily discriminate among their various theories, but also because Brooks is both paradigmatic of much of what is now called "Modernism" and is perhaps its ablest critical representative.

Because irony is the "center" of the New Criticism, any destruction of its discourse or of its interpretation of Modernism must begin by rethinking the "center" in an attempt to displace it. Also, because irony has become habitual—part of what Hus-

Cleanth Brooks·

serl would call the "natural attitude"—among practical and evaluative critics both as a kind of structure necessary to all poems
and as a criterion for judging "good" poetry, it is crucial to
reduce irony, to lay bare its unexamined assumptions, and to
make clear to those who employ it and defend it as necessary to
literary discourse exactly what is at stake in the "game" they
have chosen to play.

It is necessary to begin by placing Brooks in his historical
context for two reasons: first, to show how his version of the
New Criticism exemplifies the modern temperament as a turning
to the aesthetic as a means to what I shall call "absolute freedom"[3] and as a movement away from time, finitude, and the
world; second, to make clear the nature of his own view of his
historical situation. The latter is of primary importance in understanding irony. Since, as Heidegger argues, all interpretation and
discourse is radically temporal and is made possible by the historicity of Dasein, an interpretation of irony must emerge from
its "source" in the "times" of both Brook's texts and of my critique of them. My historical awareness of recent public events in
literature and criticism is the condition for the possibility of my
destroying Brooks's "irony"; analogously, Brooks's own awareness of and relationship to his dominant actuality—scienticism,
historicism, and positivism—alone makes possible what I shall
call his pervasively ironic stance.

According to Brooks's interpretation of his historical situation, the modern age is defined by naturalistic science, by positivism, and by causal history. This world view imbues not only
science, but also education, economics, and even poetry. It demythologizes superstition and Christianity and it destroys the
idea of analogy and correspondence, upon which the unified sensibility rests. It replaces faith in God with faith in the machine
and in progress—unending repetitive change. Its factories reduce
the complex phenomenon, man, to a being functioning in only
one direction, to one end, suppressing all that seems irrelevant,
to the particular purpose for which he acts.

Thus, positivistic science and historical naturalism simplify

[97]

Cleanth Brooks

human experience, render it deterministic by virtue of the law of
causality, and dissociate the human sensibility. T. E. Hulme,
who is a major influence upon the New Critics and Brooks
through Pound and Eliot, writes in his commentary on Bergson
that positivistic historians reduce history to an "extensive manifold," that is, to a sequence of abstract counters, related causally,
which proceed from a definite beginning to a predictable conclusion.[4] Allan Tate echoes Hulme, and is quoted by Brooks, when
he describes the naturalistic view of history as a "logical series"
which is " 'quantitative, the abstraction of space.' " This "natural" conception of time as an external phenomenon consisting of
discrete units causally and logically related is, of course, exactly
what Bergson in *Time and Free Will* calls the "spatialization of
time."[5] As Tate goes on to say, in such a theory of time, " 'The
past becomes a causal series, and timeless,' " reducing history
to an agent of utility. Thus, the natural view of time "suggests
'an omnipotent human rationality' " capable of fixing the past
in an irreducible, unchanging, logical order.[6] This causal abstract progression results in historical determinism and in the
ultimate achievement of absolute control over man and nature
through scientific predictability and technological progress.
Man is "caught"[7] within the limitations of a historical period,
in an irreversible history which painfully limits human freedom and restricts human aspirations toward any Ideal or Absolute.

Science achieves this coercion of man and nature by first
coercing thought and language. It imposes the linear form of
pure logic on the mind and it drives language into propositional form. As a result, experience is "perceived" on the basis
of and as having the shape of the propositional form of the
declarative sentence, which is itself structured by the "logical"
form of subject and predicate. In expository prose, proposi-
tions are related logically, and the mind following the argument moves inexorably from one "position" or "counter" to
the next until the conclusion is reached. This mode of discourse mirrors the "extensive manifold's" causal progression

[98]

Cleanth Brooks

of objects in an abstract series and thus reflects the mind
which orders the positivistic, mechanistic world picture. Since
no single proposition can amend or qualify its own statement
or contain its own negation, propositional form is seen by
modern critics as a simplification of experience, as an abstraction which does not reflect the complex and often contradictory world. That is, the Moderns see the proposition as a
linear, nonhieroglyphic, unironic distortion of language's
ability to reflect complex experiences.

Under the impact of the "new science," according to
Brooks's historical interpretation, poets and critics, beginning
with Hobbes, admit the priority of the propositional form of
language and see metaphor and other nonlogical verbal forms
as only the embellishment of statement. This admission results
in a separation of form and content, of essence and phenomenon; it is a fall from the "unified sensibility" of Dante and
Donne, both of whom see the unitary nature of metaphor and
its value in conveying the poet's attitude toward his subject.

In ironic or contextualist poetry and criticism, meaning is
not a result of statement, but of a metaphoric complex of verbal relationships and qualifications, existing on the page.
These linguistic patterns alone create and convey meaning appropriate to the complexity and order of the ironist's vision.
In traditional theories on the metaphor, Brooks argues,
"There is no need for an ironical function—for imagery which
will do other than ennoble" (MP, 28–29). Such theories support
the dissociation of sensibility. The new science compart-
mentalizes the mind, "separating into neat categories the emotional and frivolous, the dignified and the mean, the 'poetic' and
the 'non-poetic'. . . . The tendency of the [Restoration and
Neo-Classical] period toward order . . . tended to remove the
conflict of opposites which is the very life of metaphysical poetry" (MP, 31). While the "Hobbesian poet tended to substitute
the rational act of sorting out the discordant and removing it
from the context," metaphysical and modern poets—that is,
ironic poets of context—fuse what in "ordinary experience is

inharmonious" (*MP*, 34).[8] For the positivist, according to Brooks, the universe is ordered on a progressive model and the primary human faculty is reason; for the authentic poet, the world is ordered by analogy and the primary human faculty is imagination: "Insisting upon imaginative unity, he refuses to depend upon non-imaginative classifications, those of science or logic" (*MP*, 43). Modern poetry and the New Criticism attempt to replace this logic of concepts with a "logic of imagination," to use Eliot's phrase.[9]

In "Irony and 'Ironic' Poetry," Brooks defines irony as the "obvious warping or modification of a statement by the context" (IIP, 232). Furthermore, he asserts: "The relation between the parts of a poem—even of a simple lyric—is often intricate, and it is always important. Each part—image, statement, metaphor—helps build the meaning and is itself qualified by the whole context" (IIP, 237). This definition assigns a unique cognitive and human value to poetry. By creating a complexity which results from the ironic qualifications of context, the ironic poem not only supersedes the limitations of a logical order of perception but also goes beyond a vision of actuality defined solely by causal science. Only poetry which is contextual, that is, ironic, is able to deal completely with and "represent" the manifold complexity of human experience. In place of the simplifying scientific worldview, the poet puts the complex, analogic vision of a pervasive ironist.

It is, of course, well known that the "great originals" for Brook's theory of synthesis and complexity are Donne and the Coleridge of the fourteenth chapter of the *Biographia*.[10] Brooks finds in "The Cannonization" the kind of poetry which demands of the critics a recognition of the imagination's autonomy and of its superiority to reason. In the poem, the seeming opposition between love and religion is really nonexistent. Although these two concepts are contradictory to the strict rationalist, Donne builds the poem on the paradox. As Brooks says, modern man, "habituated as he is to an easy yes or no," is uncomfortable with a situation which does not fit his predetermined categories of positivistic experience. As a result,

> He refuses to accept the paradox as a serious rhetorical device; and since he is able to accept it only as a cheap trick, he is forced into this dilemma. Either: Donne does not take love seriously; here he is merely sharpening his wit as a sort of mechanical enterprise. Or: Donne does not take religion seriously; here he is merely indulging in a cynical and bawdy parody. (*Urn,* 11)

Brooks hypothesizes that biographical and historical critics are forced by the principle of noncontradiction to exclude the seemingly contradictory; his own explication of "The Cannonization" shows, however, that poems are not organized upon a logical basis. Donne's poem is built upon a structure which transcends the limits of logic by accepting contradictions, and Brooks's analysis of it demonstrates the complexity of a poetic mode of apprehension and organization which is not hampered by the *a priori* categories of a simplifying system external to the experience. Thus, Brooks not only offers an alternative to progressive, linear structure, causality, and chronology, but he also destroys them by annihilating their linguistic equivalents and verbal structures, the proposition and paragraph.

Analogously, Brooks's reading of Coleridge's theory of the synthetic imagination which yokes incongruities into a harmonious whole provides a description of a method of ordering experience which is an alternative to the extensive manifold. Since the unified sensibility is built on correspondence and not on logic, metaphor, which joins opposites on the basis of analogy, can help create a unified picture of the world which is more complex than that offered by science (*Urn,* 248). Ironic metaphor—paradox and ambiguity—can incorporate complexities and contradictions into an analogic order beyond the limits of systematic thought. When made complex enough, as in Yeats's *A Vision* or Eliot's *The Waste Land,* it can include and reconcile the total complexity of history and can do it without the abstract fragmentation of linear sequence, without the succession of parts in time.

For Brooks, poetry is an alternative to science only by virtue of irony. By allowing relationships between parts which are not causal, it permits no unqualified statement. In the verbal mosaic of the poem, irony qualifies each part, every statement, image, and metaphor. Thus, Brooks denies the modern positivistic-naturalistic stance of his age for a more spiritual Absolute which is an Image of life, which is as complex as life, and which is perfectly harmonized by the ironic context of language:

> It is not enough for the poet to analyse his experience as the scientist does, breaking it up into parts. . . . His task is finally to unify experience as man knows it in his own experience. The poem, if it be a true poem, is a simulacrum of reality. (*URN,* 212–13)

The ironic poem reestablishes the unity of experience lost in the seventeenth century's "dissociation of sensibility." When the poet returns to the "tradition" of Donne, he acknowledges the complexity of experience: "The poet attempts to fuse the conflicting elements in a harmonious whole" (*MP,* 37; see 43).

Not only does this theory of poetry and complexity overcome, for Brooks, the "dissociation of sensibility" and the fraudulent, coercive simplifications of science, but it achieves for the ironist, poet or reader, aesthetic and psychological freedom from causality and, hence, from determinism. In a poem structured on qualifying irony, no part has chronological priority, except in the most crude sense of visual encounter with the signs. There is no hierarchy of value among parts. There is no "beginning," no "origin," from which all else must follow.[11] Irony dictates that each part is a beginning simultaneously with every other part. The poem must be read reflexively so that the patterns of all the contextual interrelationships can be seen synchronically. The absence of *arché* and of progression thus lifts the ironist above the traps of the extensive manifold. Experiencing the ironic mode of

organization frees the poet or reader from the causal ordering of
the world, "from the constraint imposed upon him by the continuity of life." [12] In fact, in his M.A. thesis, *The Concept of Irony*,
Søren Kierkegaard recognizes this liberation as the foremost aesthetic and psychological aspect of the ironic vision:

> But the outstanding feature of irony . . . is the subjective free-
> dom which has at every moment the possibility of a beginning
> and is not generated from previous conditions. There is some-
> thing seductive about every beginning because the subject is
> still free, and this is the satisfaction the ironist longs for. At
> such moments, actuality loses its validity for him; he is free and
> above it. (*CI,* 270)

The text of *The Waste Land* which emerges from Brooks's interpretation of the poem is a paradigm both of the ironic method
and of the ironic consciousness. His text of *The Waste Land* frees
the ironist—the poet, the critic, and the readers of both the poem
and its interpretation—from time by recreating, restoring, and
discovering the complex unity of experience. I am not implying
here that the structure of *The Waste Land* "is" or "is not"
"ironic." Since no text has meaning apart from the interpretations of it, no statement can be made about what a poem "is,"
but only about what certain interpretations let it "mean."
Brooks's interpretation allows (or perhaps, coerces) the text to
"mean" irony and complexity:

> The basic method used in *The Waste Land* may be described as
> the application of the principle of complexity. The poem works
> in terms of surface parallelisms which in reality make ironical
> contrasts and in terms of surface contrasts which in reality con-
> stitute parallelisms. . . . The two aspects taken together give
> the effect of chaotic experience ordered into a new whole,
> though the realistic surface of experience is retained. The com-
> plexity of the experience is not violated by the apparent forcing
> upon it of a predetermined scheme. (*MP,* 167)

The apparent chaos of reality is realistically maintained by the
ambiguous surface of the poem; but explication reveals the ex-

quisite ordering of detail behind this surface chaos. The revelation of the poem's structure gives "the effect" of the construction of a new whole by resolving apparently discordant elements in a poem, but it does not give a truly new order because the contradictions which it resolves are only apparent antitheses. Brooks's precise wording becomes important at this point. He goes on to describe the method of *The Waste Land* in this way: "The statement of *surface* similarities . . . are ironically revealed to be dissimilarities, and the association of *apparent* dissimilarities . . . culminates in later realization that the dissimilarities are only *superficial*—that the chains of likenesses are in reality *fundamental*" (*MP*, 172; my italics). By negating the positivistic-naturalistic actuality of the world, irony clears the way for poetry to reveal the fundamental, the ground, the original analogies constituting reality; it allows the poet "to reconcile the irrelevant or *apparently* warring elements of experience" (*MP*, 33; my italics).

> If the poet, then, must perforce dramatize the *oneness* of the experience, even though paying tribute to its diversity, then his use of paradox and ambiguity is seen as *necessary*. . . . He is rather giving us an insight which *preserves* the *unity of experience* and which at its higher and more serious levels, triumphs over the *apparently* contradictory and conflicting elements of experience by unifying them into a new *pattern*. (*Urn*, 213–214; my italics)

Despite his constant insistence that his critical theory is not influenced by any ideology or nonliterary consideration (see, for example, *Urn*, 253ff), there lies behind what R.S. Crane calls Brooks's "critical monism" [13] a Gnostic faith in a lost but recoverable world ordered not by logic but by analogy. The structure of Brooks's criticism rests upon a foundation which may be best described as a "spiritual monism" reinforced by an almost visionary belief in the existence of an Ideal Absolute order in a separated world or Spirit. The ironic poet "re-discovers" and "represents" this order and returns man to these lost "origins," where he may be refreshed by the creative source of unity and wholeness. The poet lifts the veil of chaos and suspends the deadening restrictions of the actual. He returns us to the source of the "tradition," where, before the Fall into scientific time, which progresses, defines, and determines, all men participated in the medieval world picture of correspondences and the beneficent stillness which it bestows. By virtue of a presumed macrocosm-microcosm relation between Word and World, irony creates poetic simulacra of a lost, unfallen reality which is Absolute.

Yet Brooks, as ironist, experiences the limitations of his aesthetic creed. The kind of freedom and order which he desires cannot be "actualized" in the world; only in the Word can he "re-create" and "re-discover" the nonactual completion and stillness which he desires. In fact, the ironic poem functions magically to "represent" the unified perception of the order. Its "intention" recreates the dream of the Idea; and its "structure" requires that this Image be grasped only by the unfallen apprehension which intuits unities—that is, perceives time instantaneously and spatially—and thereby annihilates, by the necessities of its internal organization, which is a simulacrum of the newly refound order, all simplifying, fallen, temporal modes of perception. Thus, although irony returns a completely ordered, although nonrational world to the present, it also necessitates that History itself be abandoned for a closed, complete, Ideal Image. As Kierkegaard points out in *The Concept of Irony,* irony is a valuable way to negate the inadequate; it is negatively useful when its rebellion against a given actuality is justified historically. Negatively, of course, Brooks's position is useful and justifiable. The positivists had seemingly appropriated historical reality and Time itself and made them tools for their own imperialistic, coercive, dehumanizing ends. As a result, irony infinitely negates time and history. However, the poetic image of the Ideal put forward as the Word, the autotelic ironic poem, is offered as an alternative not only to positivistic actuality but to

[105]

all historical and temporal actuality as well. In fact, it becomes a conscious modern strategy to detemporalize Time by turning it into space through the agency of irony and the ironic poem.

Like Brooks, other modern ironists consciously try to create infinitely "complex," totalizing Images with which to replace history. These are often, but not always, modelled on the mythic paradigm of the cyclic theory of eternal return. Allen Tate, for example, announces that he wants to replace naturalistic, utilitarian history with what Brooks calls "concrete history," in which, Tate says, " 'images are only to be contemplated, and perhaps the act of contemplation after long exercise initiates a habit of restraint, and the setting up of absolute standards which are less formulas for action than an interior discipline of the mind.' "[14] The "natural view" of history is displaced by irony's desire to create Images of history. The abstract, spatialized counters of the extensive manifold become Absolute and inviolable, like Brooks's ironic poem.

If the extensive manifold of the positivists spatializes in the Bergsonian sense, that is, dissects and externalizes the living and continuous *durée,* then Tate, Brooks, and the other ironists spatialize history in Joseph Frank's sense of the term. They replace temporal events with Images whose interior relations are solely predicated upon a nontemporal, spontaneous recognition of the ironic interrelationship of parts. Echoing Pound, Frank points out that "an image is defined not as a pictorial reproduction but as unification of disparate ideas and emotions into a complex presented spatially in an instant of time."[15] This "imagizing" of time has its roots in the ironist's desire to be negatively free of the limitations of historical circumstance and continuity.

In order not only to feel free of temporal continuity but to destroy linear time itself, the ironist consciously joins forces with myth to "actualize" his atemporal Absolute. As Kierkegaard explains, the ironist, feeling free by virtue of negation, mistakenly loses his individual ego and believes he shares in the eternal ego which is timeless: therefore, as Kierkegaard points out, the ironist must not admit his own past:

Cleanth Brooks

> Insofar as irony should be so conventional as to accept a past,
> this past must be of such a nature that irony can retain its
> freedom over it. . . . It was therefore the mythical aspect of
> history . . . which especially found grace in its eyes. Authentic
> history, on the other hand, wherein the true individual has his
> positive freedom, because in this he has his premises, must be
> dispensed with. (*CI, 294*)

As I have argued earlier, there is neither beginning nor logical
and causal progression in an ironic poem. Each and every part is
coequally a beginning. When irony is applied to history in this
way, we have myth. The ironist recognizes no beginning in history and no causal series which restricts him. There is always the
possibility of return since time is either analogic, as in Tate,
cyclic, as in the primitive concept of eternal return,[16] or both, as
in Yeats's *A Vision*. In any case, the ironist treats history as an
ironic poem, often by reducing it to myth.

Brooks's interpretation of *A Vision* is the "center" of *Modern
Poetry and the Tradition* because it is a paradigm of the New Critical conjunction of "irony" and "myth." Brooks's "text" of Yeats
attempts to totalize complexity and to externalize it as Absolute
in an Image based upon the theory of the eternal return, that is,
upon Yeats's theory of the phases of the moon and of the Great
Year. As Brooks notes, Yeats begins with a hostility to all-per-
vasive science which is both abstract and nonevaluative. What
Yeats wants, according to Brooks, is an account of experience
which would go beyond the limitations of any abstract system:
"a philosophy which was at once 'logical and boundless.' " Unlike science, it will not exclude any element of an infinitely complex experience; yet, it will be "logical" in order to prevent the
multiplicity of life in Time from disintegrating completely.
However, the spatial and visual metaphors of Brooks's discourse
impose the ideal of "boundary" upon the ideal of "logical" and
thereby translate Yeats's desire into the ironic vision. Irony becomes the necessary price for the unified sensibility:

> The system is . . . an instrument for, as well as symbol of, the
> poet's re-integration of his personality. . . . The system, to

put it concisely, allows Yeats to see the world as a great drama, predictable in its larger aspects . . . but in a pattern which allows for the complexity of experience. (*MP,* 175–76, 200; my italics)

In Brooks's "text" of *A Vision,* "logic" becomes "pattern" and "drama." Time and experience are formed into a harmonious, unchanging artwork whose organization is cyclic, like the temporal orientations of primitive cultures, and is analogical, like Tate's view of concrete history.

As Mircea Eliade shows,[17] prehistorical civilizations transform both linear time and random change into patterns of repeating cycles. In order to escape from both senseless flux and the historical limitations of his own temporal situation, primitive man constructs aesthetically and ontologically comforting mythodramatic patterns. By means of these mythic projections, he can predict all meaningful events, that is, those which regularly occur. This constant structure of return lets primitive man feel psychologically and ontologically free of the past; it is always possible for him to begin again. In this light, then, the primitive and cyclic show themselves to be special cases of the ironic urge to contain all possibilities while standing outside any temporal actuality.

In a similar way, Allen Tate's view of history as a group of Images reduces time to spatial patterns. He changes linear history and random flux into aesthetic structures modelled, as we have seen above, on plastic art forms. Concrete history unifies temporal events so that they may be "fixed" or "arrested" for contemplation.[18] Tate transfers the stasis of plastic art to history, and Brooks extends this transfer to literature. In his interpretation of *A Vision,* Brooks "a-temporizes" history by binding it within a pattern of recurring Images for contemplation.

Even though history becomes a "drama," in Brooks's interpretation of Yeats's system, it remains atemporal since drama is defined essentially by the ironic interrelationships of its patterns of Images and metaphors; drama is taken over into the realm of permanence and plastic form.[19] This seems to be part of

Cleanth Brooks

what Brooks sees in Yeats's comment on Dante and Villon:
" 'They and their sort alone earn contemplation, for it is only
when the intellect has *wrought* the whole of life to drama, to
crisis, that we may live for contemplation, and yet keep our in-
tensity' " (*MP,* 201; my italics). Brooks's "text," "Yeats: The
Poet as Myth-Maker," reduces history to a series of cycles structured by analogy and repetition; myth itself becomes an artwork,
an Image contemplated as Absolute; as Kierkegaard would put it,
it is time alienated from itself and externalized.

The spatial view of history is a necessary result of irony's
substitution of the image of history for time. In Brooks's case,
the mythic view of history and the structure of poetry exists in a
macrocosm-microcosm relation: "The essential structure of a
poem resembles that of architecture or painting: it is a pattern of
resolved stresses" (Urn, 203).[20] Both the poem and the myth of
history are "bounded" and self-referential and thereby create
something fixed and removed from change. They actualize the
Absolute in the spatial form of the Image, the Word, as it were.
Joseph Frank's discussion of spatial form in modern literature, although begun from different premises, reaches the same conclusion:

> Time is no longer felt as an objective causal progression with
> clearly marked-out differences between periods; nor has it be-
> come a continuum in which distinction between past and
> present are wiped out. And here we have a striking parallel
> with the plastic arts. Just as the dimension of depth has van-
> ished from the sphere of visual creation, so the dimension of
> historical depth has vanished from the content of the major
> works of modern literature. Past and present are apprehended
> spatially, locked in a timeless unity that while it may accentuate
> surface differences eliminates any feeling of sequence by the
> very act of juxtaposition. (*WG,* 59)

In *Anatomy of Criticism,* Northrop Frye argues that every
ironic mode sooner or later returns to myth as a way of perception. Just as in Brooks's reading of Yeats, this is generally ac-
companied by a return to cyclical theories of history and to the

[109]

oracular style of "The Second Coming." In the twentieth century, Frye notes, "The return of irony to myth . . . is contemporary with, and parallel to, abstraction, expressionism, cubism, and similar efforts in painting to emphasize the self-contained pictorial structure."[21] This mythic structure, in other words, is one mechanism available to the ironist for developing a nonreferential, harmonized, "bounded" image. Frye's conjunction of irony, myth, and space parallels Brooks's interpretation of Yeats, in which much the same triad releases the ironist from the burdens of the past and present. By annihilating actuality, by explicitly recognizing the freedom from time inherent in cyclic returns, and by totalizing history in a plastic image of circles which in its infinite potential for "complexity" "actualizes" in the Word what is impossible in the World, this central essay establishes the Ironic and New Critical primacy of Word over World and Eternity over Time.

One of the metaphysical implications of the culmination of irony in spatial form is the perpetuation of dualism: mind vs. body, subject vs. object, Word vs. World, poetry vs. reader, all of which Brooks sets out to overcome in his attack on the dissociated sensibility. In "The Heresy of Paraphrase" (*Urn,* 192ff), Brooks develops a theory of context which makes a poem "inviolable." As a result of his determination not to allow science to compromise poetry, he insists that form and content are one, or, in other words, that there is not or should not be a separable content in a poem. No poem is paraphrasable; each poem is, in fact, its own language. The "meanings" of words are so altered by context, by the ironic interrelationships in which each word exists with every other in the poem, that no word in a poem is translatable into "discourse." When Ivor Winters paraphrases "the night wore" as "the night passed," Brooks upbraids him: "But the word *wore* does not mean literally that 'the night passed,' it means literally that 'the night wore'—whatever *wore* may mean" (*Urn,* 201). Brooks is justified in criticizing the careless explicator, but his theory forces even an apologist such as Murray Krieger to claim that this theory of poetic context results in poetry so inviolable that it cannot be responded to in any manner except silent admiration.[22]

Silence is, of course, the goal of irony, but as Kierkegaard indicates, such silence returns to " 'haunt and jest' " the ironist (*CI, 275*). The nonreferential structure of the poem denies the "translation" into ordinary language, commonly understood, of the ironic context. The unique language of each poem isolates work from work and work from man, who thinks, apprehends, and communicates through a system of signs whose signification is normally at least partially understood by a group. By abrogating this community of language, Brooks denies most people, with the exception of the elite, access to poetry. By making it so special, so different, so "other-worldly," the ironist alienates those whom he announces he intends to save from the dehumanized actuality and, consequently, he achieves a diversity directly contrary to the unity he so desperately seeks.

Ever wary of the "affective fallacy," Brooks does not try to define the aesthetic response to the ironic poem. Such "interests" would move him beyond the "text," that is, the words on the page, into a larger "context" which, by its contact with the reader, would violate the "disinterest" of aesthetic distance. Eliseo Vivas, however, describes the effect of the ironic poem upon its reader as "an experience of rapt attention which involves the intransitive apprehension of the object's immanent meanings and values in their full presentational immediacy."[23] This "aesthetic response" turns the reader away from the World and toward the Word. In the ironic poem, as Brooks describes it, language is autotelic and self-purposive. As a result, in the aesthetic apprehension of such an object, the observer remains "caught," rapt in attention, as he contemplates the order within the image which irony recreates. He follows the pattern of the interrelations of the poem and does not leave them for the duration of the experience. Thus, when the object of contemplation pretends to incorporate and order history, as in Brooks's interpretation of Yeats's *A Vision,* the observer need never suspend his contemplation to return to the World. The complex pattern that is "history," although it should be grasped intuitively, in the moment, requires all of Time for its complete explication, just as history requires all of time to unfold itself. This is, of course, the ultimate goal of the ironic position. When man abandons actuality to contemplate the Absolute realized as an artifact, irony's victory is complete. Actuality is denied in favor of a synthetic and synchronic image. Paradoxically, however, irony, which for Brooks should overcome the dualism of thought and feeling, form and content, not only further separates man from poem, as we have seen, but it also furthers the isolation of each individual in his own windowless monad. During the aesthetic act, the subject is turned away from "actual" history, from others, and from those "natural" aspects of his own Being in time. The haunting and jesting stillness of irony brings Brooks to the position directly antithetical to that he professes to desire.

While there can be little disagreement that the ironic strategy of Brooks and many of the other New Critics is to a large extent responsible for saving the study of poetry, and even fiction, from the destructive impulses of the academic and journalistic classifiers who learn their methodology from modern technology, it must finally be recognized that this same strategy has itself had profoundly destructive effects, that, in fact, it has failed in two most important areas: it has not overcome dualism and united the sensibility and it has caused a loss of human significance, of content, in the study of literature. It is time to expand the account of the failure of Modernism's ironic strategy and to suggest an alternative view of irony, and thus of literature, which might better succeed.

Søren Kierkegaard's study *The Concept of Irony* offers another attitude toward irony which is remarkably similar to one of the defining impulses of Postmodernism. It is, of course, impossible to do more than outline Kierkegaard's study here and to suggest its immediate relevance for Brooks's failure. I only hope to show that Kierkegaard points to a strategy potentially more capable of dealing with the modern problems of art and life than Brooks's theory of contextual irony.

Cleanth Brooks

The failure of Brooks's theory of pervasive irony can be attributed to the necessary loss of Time and, consequently, of the World, which it entails. As William V. Spanos argues in "Modern Literary Criticism and the Spatialization of Time: An Existential Critique," we have begun to see "that behind the strategy of the New Criticism lies the impulse to disengage literature from the defiling contingencies of life in historical time."[24] Kierkegaard's analysis of irony makes it quite clear that the movement away from time which Spanos finds in the New Criticism and which he explains by the New Critics' inability to stand in the face of dread and the existential nothingness which it reveals, has its formal impulse in the urge to "ironize," to become negatively free of all restrictions, to stand or hover above actuality in order to attain to the infinite perception and knowledge of the gods. The separation of time and eternity upon which the ironic impulse is based is dualistic and dissociates the human sensibility. That is, it divides the temporal Being-in-the-World which Heidegger defines as the ground of Dasein from the spiritual aspirations of man to the Eternal and his intuitions of something beyond the material.

Following Hegel, Kierkegaard defines "pervasive" or "unmastered" irony as "infinite absolute negativity":

> It is negativity because it only negates; it is infinite because it negates not this or that phenomenon; it is absolute because it negates by virtue of a higher which it is not. Irony establishes nothing, for that which is to be established lies behind it. It is divine madness which rages like Tamburlaine and leaves not one stone sitting upon another in its wake. (*CI*, 278)

The destruction of the actual world is "divine" not only because it is madly inspired like Plato's poet but also because it is accomplished from the vantage point of a being who, hovering, becomes a bird or an angel who sees and is satisfied to see "what is passed, or passing, or to come." From this transcendent perspective, the ironist sees history as an image, an artifact which removes the pain of time and the frustration of actuality. The

[113]

Cleanth Brooks

ironist loses his substantiality, his continuity with the material world in the practice of his "art." For Kierkegaard, Socrates is the archironist, and he approvingly paraphrases, from *The Clouds,* Aristophanes' satiric description of Socrates' ironic position vis-à-vis Time and the World:

> He [Aristophanes] has therefore assigned Socrates a place in the Thoughtery in a suspended basket. . . . But whether he hangs from the rafters in a basket or stares omphalopsychically into himself, and in this way frees himself to some extent from earthly gravitation, he still hovers in either case. It is this hovering which is so extremely descriptive: it is the attempted ascension into heaven which fulfills itself in rising to a glimpse of the entire realm of the ideal, when this staring into oneself causes the self to expand to the universal self, pure thought with its content. (*CI,* 180)

The movement out of time which the ironist makes by hovering removes all substance, all content, from his existence and makes him *disinterested.* By destroying all actuality from the infinite and timeless perspective of irony he kicks himself free of the earth: "The actuality which shall give him content is not, hence he is free from the restraint in which the given actuality binds him, yet negatively free and as such hovering, because there is nothing which binds him" (*CI,* 279). This "hovering" is the key to "destroying" Allen Tate, who, as Paul de Man would say, is blind at the moment of his greatest insight.[25] Tate's interpretation of the Angelists—Poe, Mallarmé, and Valery, among others—condemns them for dismissing material forms "for the illusory pursuit of essence."[26] However, his commitment to irony does not allow him to see that Angelism, like cyclic history, is only a special case of the ironic vision; it is an example of the ironist's movement not only out of time but into a world of form without content, and ultimately, into "pure poetry" (see *CI,* 321). Since irony springs "from the metaphysical problem concerning the relation of the Idea to actuality" and because "metaphysical actuality is beyond time . . . it is impossible for the actuality desired by irony to be given in time" (*CI,* 295). Irony, therefore, like Angelism, maintains a dualism of existence and essence, and it insists upon the priority of an ordered but empty realm which is beyond this world, behind irony, and which exists as an image held in the eye of the ironist. As a result of this priority, even Solger, whom Kierkegaard guardedly approves as a theoretician and practitioner of irony, "is unable to grant the finite any validity, unable to render the infinite concrete" (*CI,* 327). While he may, like Brooks, transcend the limits of his actuality, he does so only by dividing man and denying his temporal and earth-bound interests.

Spanos' "Modern Literary Criticism and the Spatialization of Time" thoroughly establishes the motive for the New Criticism's withdrawl from existence in time as the pain resulting from the opposition between the unstructured messiness of Being-in-the-World and the hard, neat outline of plastic form which these critics impose upon verbal art. In so doing, Spanos, like Kermode, Hough, and many others, has established the primary importance of the Image to both modern literature and to the New Critics.[27] It is the most crucial element of their attempt to spatialize time. We have seen how Brooks's theory of contextual poetry results in the creation of closed poems which are gemlike artifacts to be apprehended instantaneously along the model of the perception of plastic art. We have also seen how this reductive transformation of a poem—a verbal event, a process—to a static image by means of explication and context is intimately related to Brooks's insistence upon irony as *the* structural device of poetry which allows even the totalization of history in a mythic image.

Kierkegaard, however, goes further than any of these modern critics to demonstrate that the projection of images to stop time and to overcome the limitations of a historical period is only another special instance of the ironic vision. From the perspective of the hovering ironist, each and every historical actuality is incomplete and partial; it is not complex or "complete" enough. Each and every actuality is only part of time; the uncertainty and instability of actuality results from its incompleteness, from its change, its constant movement from one partial state to another. This unsettling observation causes the ironist pain. Existentially, the vision of change reveals death, dread, and nothingness; metaphysically, and perhaps theologically, it demonstrates the supposed inadequacy of the real world to the vision of spirituality and infinity the ironist intuits. Most importantly, "incompleteness" denies the metaphysical freedom of choice among an infinitude of possibilities which all history and a universe of potentialities might offer an imaginative mind. As a result, the ironist hovers and imagizes in order to see all possibilities of time at a glance as empty forms "essentialized" in a mental world, in a mind expanded infinitely to contain all potentialities.

A series of questions presents itself at this point: Why is the ironist willing to abandon time, history, and the world for essences and emptiness? Beyond relief from the dread and pain of change, and the threat of death, does the ironist gain anything in his hovering? Are the rewards of the image and of totalization viable ones not only for literary criticism but for literature and life itself?

These questions can be answered tentatively by saying that the ironist achieves a vision of formal possibilities, empty of content, formed in an image, apprehended simultaneously, culminating in the infinite repose and stillness which only such intuitive contemplation allows. In other words, the reward of unmastered irony is Godhead. It is a continuation of the basic tradition of anthropomorphizing the earth, and its possibility is greatly facilitated by Nietzsche's announcement that God is dead. It is an act of complete and total freedom which allows the ironist as artist to impose order upon all possibility or any small world which he chooses to create by drawing on his vision of potentiality.

In *A Portrait of the Artist as a Young Man*, Stephen Dedalus, driven by the uncertainty and instability of his personal life—which reveals to him his own ontological precariousness in the world—proclaims to the rather lascivious Lynch that the modern

[116]

Cleanth Brooks

artist must, like the deistic god, become *disinterested* in his creation and, while off paring his fingernails, view it from afar.
Stephen's proclamation, along with Hulme's speculations on the
cold, hard, dry, static nature of modern art, has had a decisive
impact upon New Critical theory and practice. Kierkegaard's interpretation of irony opens up this relationship in a new way and
lets the ironic vision which lies hidden behind Stephen's thomistic language emerge as the center upon which the structure of his
aesthetic discourse is built.

There is no need to detail here how Stephen's triad of *clari-
tas, integritas,* and *quidditas* can result in a reified and autoletic object which suspends any conflict between the ironist's desire for
the perfection of aesthetic form and a world in which Lynch can
scribble obscenities on the bottom of the *Venus Praxiteles.*[28] It is
enough to point out that the neo-Kantian *disinterest* of both Stephen and the New Critics is only another of the particular
strategies of the ironic vision. In fact, it should be clear that
Stephen's "aesthetic" is both a metaphysical and an ontological
statement, which, like all such statements, must, as Kierkegaard
points out in *Repetition,* emerge from and therefore founder on
the *"interest"* of the thinker.[29]

I emphasized Brooks's treatment of Yeats in order to
suggest that the text of this interpretation is a paradigm of just
this aspiration to Godhead. It is the clearest example in modern
criticism of the ironist's desire to become other than human. The
freedom from time and pain, from history and determinism,
which Brooks gains, provides the ironist, as Kierkegaard says, "a
certain enthusiasm, for he becomes intoxicated as it were by the
infinity of possibles; and should he require consolation for all that
has passed away, then let him take refuge in the enormous re-
serves of the possible" (*CI,* 279).

But this is not a purely negative function designed merely to
escape from the discomfort of a dread-ful situation. The positive
value of the ironist's position is the ability to create freely, totally, and instantly upon will—to impose an order which mirrors
that of his own mind or imagination without suffering the rebuff

[117]

Cleanth Brooks

of actuality, which might, in its own Being, resist his coercive efforts. In a way which parallels Kierkegaard's insistence that authentic freedom is possible only within actuality, Wallace Stevens explains that the very existence of poetry requires the opposition of what he calls "imagination" and "reality": "It is not only that the imagination adheres to reality, also, that reality adheres to the imagination and that the interdependence is essential."[30] The ironist, unwilling to endure the restrictions necessarily resulting from this interaction, destroys the World to unencumber his imagination.

The ironist has at least two particular strategies open to him in this enterprise. He can contemplate the totality of the possible if he chooses or he can arrange from these possibilities any pattern which he finds congenial. Of course, all the patterns which he creates will be timeless and perfect forms, abstract transformations, and not moments in history. He is not open to or dependent upon the world for knowledge; rather, he creates his "worlds" instantly and holds them forever in new patterns which never exhaust or change the pattern, the Image of history—in other words, which never have historical or human significance.

In *Kant and the Problem of Metaphysics,* Martin Heidegger, in dialogue with Kant's *Critique of Pure Reason,* not only establishes that the ground of human being and human perception is time, but that it is to be differentiated from the infinite perception and knowledge of the Godhead, which is creative and instantaneous.[31] Since ontologically man is defined by temporality, he is finite and, in the ironist's sense, "incomplete." Dasein is dependent upon the outside world for knowledge and creativity. The ironist sees this condition as a limitation, while Heidegger sees in it the possibility of openness, of receptive waiting, of a chance for a more authentic rediscovery of Being:

> To begin with, we can say negatively that finite knowledge is noncreative intuition. What is presented immediately and in its particularity must be already on hand. Finite intuition looks to the intuitable as something on which it is dependent and which exists in its own right. That which is intuited proceeds (*herlei-*

[118]

Cleanth Brooks

> *ten*) from such an essent and for that reason is also termed *in-
> tuitus derivatus,* "derivative." Finite intuition of the object is not
> able by itself to give itself an object. It must let this object be
> given. But not every intuition as such is receptive—only the fi-
> nite is so. Hence the finitude of intuition lies in its receptivity.
> (*KPM,* 30–31)

Not only does this early statement of Heidegger help define his
later notion of *Gelassenheit,* but it points out that the ironist must
necessarily leave the World, the basis of man's finitude—and as
Heidegger would have it, the ground of man's Being—because
he cannot be receptive or open to "essents," to things, to objects.
The ironist must retreat into an empty but perfect stillness which
cannot possibly overcome the dualism inherited from the Cartesian tradition or create or explicate a literature which is meaningful in a world of content, of historical incompleteness, crisis,
messiness, and finitude. Irony does not "care" (*Sorge*) for the immediate, but for what-is-not, for what is absent and nonexistent.
Despite its "victory" over determinism, irony allows Dasein no
context in which to exercise his freedom concretely. It removes
him from the arena of action and choice, takes him to the only
"world" still available to the ironist, and thus reduces Dasein's
freedom to an abstraction or empty form. In order to be authentically free, as Kierkegaard puts it, man must feel himself "assimilated into a larger context" (*CI,* 296). Irony feels so "free" that it
dispenses with "Authentic history . . . wherein the true individual has his positive freedom" (*CI,* 294).

Modern literature does not, of course, in its highest moments, conform to the model which I have been drawing from
Brooks's poetics. Modernism is not by any means so unquali-
fiedly unearthly and dehumanized as the coercive New Critical
reading of it might suggest. The middle poetry of Yeats, for example, while dealing with the ironic strategy, never accepts it as
a fully satisfactory stance or solution. The seemingly closed and
ironic form of "Sailing to Byzantium," for example, is a major
instance of Yeats's treatment of irony and spatialization, but it is
by no means a solution with which the Yeats of *The Tower* can

[119]

Cleanth Brooks

rest. Significantly, "Sailing to Byzantium" is followed immediately by the title poem of the volume, which arrives at almost a diametrically opposite "conclusion." For Yeats, these opposites are not held in tension in imagistic form as alternatives among which he cannot or will not choose. They are not possibilities at which he glances aesthetically or which he holds in suspension out of time and action, resolved in images which give Yeats and his readers a temporary victory over time. They are humanly weighed alternatives, dealt with at different moments by the persona of the volume in his own dramatic, that is, human, time; in other words, they are a discrete and discontinuous series of stances toward the world, each of which is carefully articulated by the proper and appropriate voice.

Both the "rhetoric" and the "dramatics" of Yeats's major poetry contradicts any interpretation of him as an ironist in the Brooksian sense. In "Sailing to Byzantium," the "conclusion's" repetition of the opening stanza's tripartite rhetoric returns the reader from the timeless Byzantium and golden birds "such as Grecian goldsmiths make," to the sensual world of "Fish, flesh, and fowl." (I will come back to the problem of circular form a bit further on.) The poem does not "end" in an image apotheosizing the birds's instantaneous vision of history, but on the temporal metaphor of change: "Of what is passed, or passing, or to come."[32] Rhetorically, the poem does not come to rest in a timeless vision.

Too many of Yeats's critics ignore the fact that his poems are "dramas."[33] "Sailing to Byzantium" presents the actions and emotions of a pathetic old man who is facing death—the undeniable evidence of his finitude and ontological insecurity. The poem proceeds from this fundamental situation. The old man leaves "that country" not only to gain permanence and immortality but "to sing," that is, to create poems independently of his life in time by achieving an instantaneous vision of the infinite possibilities of history through his own transformation into artifact.

A point which other critics have made before must be made

Cleanth Brooks

again. Yeats is not his persona. The complex theory of the mask, which Ellman, among others, has developed at length,[34] prevents such simple identification. Yeats does not ask that his "heart" be "consumed away"; rather, he dramatizes a futile attempt to project the self beyond time. The attempt is futile because ultimately, as Sturge Moore first pointed out, the persona does take his form from a natural thing and because, even as a "golden bird," he can sing of only what he tried to flee, time itself.

Another point which perhaps has not been made enough is that the theory of the mask is not Yeats's version of the disinterested artist. Again, the complex psychology of the mask does not allow for the complete separation of poet and persona, for the neo-Kantian distance between artist and artifact. Throughout his work, especially in the *Autobiography*,[35] Yeats is thoroughly conscious of the close interdependence of reality and imagination, of his "true self" and his various masks. The tension between these elements is necessary to Yeats's creativity and reminds us of Stevens' insistence upon the essential interrelationship of world and mind in art—an interdependence the ironist abhors.

The closed or circular form of "Sailing to Byzantium" has been suggested as evidence that Yeats, as an ironist, tries to create a nonreferential, autotelic poem which is a hard, dry, image.[36] As I have pointed out, such theories require that the poem be seen as a static pattern of radically detemporalized verbal tensions which can absorb its reader in the peaceful intricacies of artifice. I believe, however, that the circular form of this poem works in a different way, which, unfortunately, I can only hint at here.[37]

The temporal process of reading this poem appears closed by the "conclusion's" triadic rhetoric, which interlocks with the structure of stanza one. For the process of reading to be reduced to the instantaneous vision of the poem as image, there must be a harmonious balance of tensions at the point of this intersection. The poem, then, could work reflexively and the "complex" meaning of the "beginning" could be "seen" in light of our own awareness of its "end."

Cleanth Brooks

In "Sailing to Byzantium," however, the "return" to the opening creates an ideational discordance which the rhetorical similarity cannot contain and cannot harmonize. The beginning is not "fulfilled" and "seen" in its complex relationship to the end; following the return to the opening, its meaning is radically changed by the reader's new interpretation, which comes from having learned in the process of reading the poem that the initial "dualism" of "that country" and Byzantium—as well as the numerous other binary ironic tensions in the poem—is only a strategic fiction which the persona adopts as a stance in the face of time and finitude. The persona has throughout the poem been "caught" in that temporal world which prompts the desired fiction of "Byzantium." The dualistic strategy around which the structure of the poem is built is itself a specific pose of the ironic consciousness. When this stance is "reduced" or "deconstructed," the metaphysical "interest" of the persona appears as the motive for his comforting projection of a lost, but recoverable, artificial paradise. In other words, what on first reading appears to be a movement out of the world and time into art and eternity, is shown by the circular form of the poem to be only an impossible myth, a fiction generated by a being in time who seeks the comfort of an Ideal dream and who hopes to find the Absolute freedom of infinite perception in an image of history.

These "changes" in the repeated readings of the poem's beginning result from the time expended and the awareness gained in the process of reading the poem. They are made possible by a kind of irony unlike Brooks's, but similar to Kierkegaard's notion of "mastered irony" and very much like the "form" of his *Fear and Trembling,* which I will discuss later.

Perhaps most importantly, unlike the kind of response which, as I have indicated, Vivas attributes to a "viewing" of an ironic text, the reader of this poem is not allowed to rest in the supernatural or supratemporal position, gratified by an instantaneous vision of history. A careful reader has his normal "ironic" expectations—centered in this poem on the dualistic oppositions—frustrated and finds it impossible to rest in a simple har-

[122]

Cleanth Brooks

mony of unresolved tensions. He cannot become disinterested like Yeats's golden bird because he is now aware that to do so is in fact to choose, on the basis of a metaphysical "interest," a stance toward the world which, although it tries to leave the world, is conditioned by human finitude and by death itself. He learns that, like the golden bird he must sing of time despite himself.

It is not enough, however, merely to suggest how certain modern masterpieces are successful in escaping the deadly effects of the urge to ironize and become Godhead. It is much more important to see that certain works exist in the ironic matrix, are in fact apparently as pervasively ironic as Brooks could wish, and yet, because they do not emerge from any metaphysical "interest" in overcoming the world, they are not finally committed to the ironic vision. Kierkegaard, as is the case in almost all areas where irony is concerned, is also helpful here. He provides a language to describe the movement out of irony which some modern pieces make and suggests a solution to the problems which originally give rise to Brooks's need for unmastered irony.

It is important, however, to note that the existential implications of this movement away from unmastered irony, which has its roots in Kierkegaard's own pseudonymous works and certain works by late modern authors like Yeats, are the pervasive themes of most literature which has come to be thought of as postmodern. Although contemporary writers continue to oppose their texts to the dehumanizing, positivistic, technological society we live in, they do not, like the ironist, do so to reject history and time itself. This new openness to a nonscientific, nonlinear time, which can be found, for example, in Ionesco's plays and Beckett's fiction, is central to an understanding of how postmodern writers are reacting against not only their society but also the ironic interpretation of the modern world perpetrated for the most part by the New Critics. Sartre, of course, is a major spokesman for the movements against both scientism and disinterested art. His critical method is the obverse of the New Critics'. He begins his criticism not from a distanced look at a

Cleanth Brooks

disinterested object, but by first establishing the metaphysical interest of a particular author. Writing of Faulkner's *The Sound and the Fury,* Sartre claims, "A fictional technique always relates back to the novelist's metaphysics. The critic's task is to define the latter before evaluating the former." If we proceed in the same way to evaluate Kierkegaard, we will find that, as Sartre says of Faulkner, Kierkegaard's metaphysics is a "metaphysics of time."[38] This is, of course, a crucial fact and poses an interesting question: If Kierkegaard, like Yeats, is an acknowledged ironist, how can this be reconciled with his temporal metaphysics, that is, with his engaged human interest in art, time, and history?

We can find a beginning to the answer to this paradox in the final section of *The Concept of Irony,* in which Kierkegaard provides an outline for a theory of irony which, in fact, emerges out of his temporal interest:

> When irony has first been mastered it undertakes a movement directly opposed to that wherein it proclaimed its life as unmastered. Irony now limits, renders finite, defines, and thereby yields truth, actuality, and content. . . . Irony as mastered moment exhibits itself in its truth precisely by the fact that it teaches us to actualize actuality, by the fact that it places due emphasis upon actuality. (*CI,* 338, 340)

In mastered irony, the poet hovers not above the actual, but above his own creation. He transcends the work's visible irony, just as Yeats in "Sailing to Byzantium" goes beyond the ironic fiction of his persona and refuses to be wholly infatuated by the external projection of the persona's "mind." Goethe is Kierkegaard's example of a poet who, by mastering irony, "succeeded in making his existence as a poet congrue with his actuality" (*CI,* 337).

Kierkegaard's "authorship," of course, as Stephen Crites has shown,[39] is one of the fullest examples of this type of irony. The "open form" of his pseudonymous works reveals some of the implications for aesthetic form of a temporal metaphysics. The

[124]

Cleanth Brooks

congruence of art and life in the temporality of mastered irony is the ground for positive freedom for the self and true poetic creativity and the authentically poetic life: "the poet only lives poetically when oriented and thus assimilated into the age in which he lives, when he is positively free within the actuality to which he belongs" (*CI*, 338). No matter whether or not this "positive" freedom takes the form of engaged ethical, political, artistic, or religious action, it is an existential movement and, as such, needs to deal with possibility not in the abstract but in the concrete. In mastered irony, "possibility is not so prudish as not to betake itself to actuality, but actuality is possibility" (*CI*, 338). This reversal of the ironist's position results in a movement into history:

> the content of life must become a true and meaningful moment in the higher actuality whose fullness the soul desires. Actuality in this way acquires its validity . . . as a history wherein consciousness successively outlives itself, though in such a way that happiness consists not in forgetting all this but becomes present in it. (*CI*, 341)

The self "becomes" in this scheme as the mind evolves toward those levels where the commitment to the temporal and to what is immediately present becomes more and more radical. In fact, as the "stages" change, each succeeding one contains its predecessors so that nothing is lost, discarded, or dissociated, but merely appropriated and transcended. What is absent does not, as it does for Brooks and other modern ironists, lure the self away from what-is.

For Kierkegaard, mastered irony can end dualism and overcome the divided sensibility because it is grounded on a view of man which locates value in temporality, in man's existence in and dealings with the world. The incarnational paradox, the mystery of Spirit and Eternity inhering in matter and time, suffuses Kierkegaard's "authorship." In *Sickness Unto Death*, for example, Anti-Climacus defines man as a synthesis, in fact, as a double synthesis: "Man is a synthesis of the infinite and finite, of

[125]

Cleanth Brooks

the temporal and eternal, of freedom and necessity."[40] Despite
the parody of Hegel in the passage from which these lines are
drawn, the fact of temporality as the medium in which man, the
conjunction of time and the eternal, forms a self for himself is
quite clear. Man's synthetic nature is both painful and the
grounds for his potential salvation. Irony corrects those who
plunge into the finite with no thought for the eternal, while mastered irony can correct those who suspend themselves above the
earth by returning them to time.

The paradox that life, the synthesis of time and the eternal, is
found in the actual by virtue of the Incarnation is what Johannes
Climacus in *Concluding Unscientific Postscript* defines as the absurd:
"The Absurd is—that the eternal truth has come into being in
time, that God has come into being."[41] Yet, even this fact depends upon the essential actuality of man: "the paradox . . . is
essentially conditioned by the fact that a man is in existence, so
that the explanation which takes away the paradox, fantastically
transforms at the same time the exister into a fantastic something
or another which belongs neither to time nor to eternity—but
such a something or another is not a man" (*CUP,* 162). The
location of man and truth in time leaves only what is present to
be encountered as the "abode" of the Absolute.

I know that I run a risk of being misunderstood here when I
insist upon paradox to *differentiate* between Kierkegaard and
Brooks. Brooks, many will remind me, can no more do without
paradox than Kierkegaard himself. Yet, "The Language of Paradox" provides ample material for precisely such differentiation.
While for Kierkegaard the paradox is the incomprehensible
*absurdity* of the Incarnation which insists upon the temporal *locus*
of both man and the sacred, for Brooks "paradox" is always no
more than a linguistic trope used to contain signs or counters in a
pattern or hierarchy of language and imagery. In fact, Brooks's
understanding and use of "paradox" is only another strategy of
the hovering and spatializing ironic mind. Its *interest* lies in *containing* the absurd and irrational in a nonlogical—indeed, an
alogical—spatial form:

[126]

Cleanth Brooks

> The poet must work by analogies, but the metaphors do not lie
> in the same plane or fit neatly edge to edge. There is a contin-
> ual tilting of the planes; necessary overlappings, discrepancies,
> contradictions . . . . even the apparently simple and straight-
> forward poet is forced into paradoxes by the nature of his in-
> strument. . . . The method is an extension of the normal lan-
> guage of poetry, not a perversion of it. (*Urn,* 9–10)

Furthermore, paradox is not merely a tool in the service of an
ironic project resolved upon reducing poetry to patterns of
stresses and connotations; it also—and this is central to the difference between Brooks and Kierkegaard—emerges from a view
of being which is, as I argued above, radically harmonized, ordered, and readily intelligible to the vision of the hovering ironist.

One of the problems of Kierkegaard's authorship is that his
pseudonyms usurp the aesthetic and literary and compel art and
literature to function ironically, to create private worlds of "recollection" and "theater" as locations for their self-created Absolute. In *Repetition,* for example, Constantine Constantius, in a
meditation on masks, acting, and the theater, develops the simile
of life as a "well-made" play or a farce consisting of a series of
perfect moments. Constantine extends the aesthetic distance of
these metaphors to his role in life as an observer and to his
demands in his domestic life for unchanging order.[42] Similarly,
in another example which could be multiplied throughout Kierkegaard's "authorship," Hilarius Bookbinder, the "editor" of
*Stages in Life's Way,* presents " 'In Vino Veritas,' a recollection
subsequently related by William Afham" which epitomizes the
desires of Kierkegaard's personae to impose aesthetic form upon
life or to withdraw into a world of art and memory.[43] Because
Kierkegaard's "authors" impress literature in the service of
irony, he must master the ironic movement (in a language cur-
rently more at-hand, he must destroy the ironic structure to
reveal and evaluate the hidden "origins" of the ironic movement)
in order to express his own anti-ironic, temporal vision of language and art in an appropriately temporal, verbal medium.

[127]

Cleanth Brooks

*Fear and Trembling* is representative of the fictional technique, and in its open-ended structure is itself a formal aesthetic
equivalent for mastered irony and Kierkegaard's fundamental Incarnational metaphysics. The visible irony of Johannes destroys
both the "actual" world of the Copenhagen merchants and the
"Ideal" world of the Hegelian synthesizers and systematizers.
The latter try to proceed along the acquisitive route of the "extensive manifold"; as Kierkegaard says in *Fear and Trembling,*
they try to go beyond faith and abstractly to absorb the spatialized wisdom of their fathers in order to rest secure in an
unearned system which contains, explains, and predicts everything.[44] But Kierkegaard, although sympathizing with his persona's destruction of his dominant bourgeois actuality, turns an
ironic glance back upon him and his artifact. Johannes creates
ironic and aesthetic forms to try to define and enclose Abraham,
particularly in the book's opening movement. Kierkegaard,
however, confronts Johannes's creation with the temporal, inde-
finable, absurd act of faith and reveals the inability of ironic or
"aesthetic" form to contain or "explain" a radically human and
temporal, that is, changing, event. Technically, Kierkegaard lets
Johannes strain the lyrical, dialectical, and ironic modes to the
limit trying to enclose something essentially alien to the ironic
and aesthetic, until these categories and the ironic strategy behind
them burst from the strain. Paradoxically, the movement into
time which Johannes cannot make himself (he cannot become a
Knight of Faith; he remains a Knight of Infinite Resignation who
has abandoned the world for heaven) is made by his work, which
in its own "inadequacies" points beyond itself to time and the
world as the proper medium for actualizing his topic. In its openness, its burst ironic forms, that is, in its temporality, *Fear and
Trembling* is a formal alternative to Brooks's use of irony.

Although I cannot perform here the full interpretation of
*Fear and Trembling* which would be necessary to show that it is,
in fact, a paradigm of mastered irony and of a temporal metaphysics, we can catch glimpses—in its open forms, in its "destructions"—of existential movements which cannot be worked

out in the closed form of an Image or artifact, movements such as that of Faith, whose only proper medium is human time. By examining the imagination in the light of the actual, i.e., in the light of the paradoxical synthesis of human being, Kierkegaard masters irony and hovers above the particular works which the ironic mind creates. Like Goethe, he properly evaluates each work as an important moment in the existence of the poet's and reader's consciousness according to his model of stages. Each work of Kierkegaard's pseudonymous authorship deals with a human possibility from a particular point of view, but each work transcends that point of view by showing the weaknesses of the imaginative object or process it projects. Ultimately, each work "concludes" by opening out to a new possibility "higher" and more involved in the actual than the perspective of the persona.[45] This pattern appears in works as diverse as *Either/Or, Repetition, Fear and Trembling, Concluding Unscientific Postscript,* and *Stages on Life's Way.* In all of these works, higher temporal possibilities, often suggested by the persona himself, break the aesthetic form into fragments, prevent the contemplation of an image or "explanation"—disrupt the "perfect" world created by the artist-god—and demonstrate that the highest stage of consciousness is paradoxical; that is, they reveal the infinite in the finite and not in the image of the Absolute.

Kierkegaard's works, therefore, are themselves part of the temporal process of raising levels of consciousness and returning readers to the paradox. The process of reading such works obviates the dangers of stillness and isolation described by Eliseo Vivas and cultivated by Brooks. In fact, criticism becomes more than the deadly process of explication, more than an attempt to drive time and the world out of life and literature. Language and form now "refer" and are allowed to be "affective." They make possible the discovery of value and spirit in the human unity of the here and now.

While it is true that for Kierkegaard time is based on the Christian Incarnation, other artists have adopted his technique to refer man to a world not necessarily sanctified by God. Beckett,

Cleanth Brooks

Ionesco, Sartre, the late Yeats, and many postmodern poets employ Kierkegaard's technique of mastered irony to destroy the potentially sterilizing pervasive irony of Modernism by revealing in their own work the false and atemporal assumptions behind the modern "Tradition." They open literature to the implications of absurd time.[46] Their negation of irony by irony is a dialectical turn to the World and a reevaluation of World over Word. They are committed to the paradox that in and through the profane, what is sacred, creative, and valid is to be found in the here and now. Like Kierkegaard himself, they absurdly reveal the interpenetration of the spiritual and the profane.

Ultimately, an understanding of Kierkegaard's notion of mastered irony is essential to comprehending much postmodern literature from Sartre and Thomas Pynchon to Wallace Stevens and W.C. Williams.[47] The openness of form and the repetition of reading based not on memory but on emergence explain how and why the literature of the absurd and poetry of immanence are not accepted by the New Critics or the French Structuralists. Kierkegaard prefaces *Stages on Life's Way* with a quotation from Lichtenberg: "Such works are mirrors: when a monkey peers into them, no apostle can be seen looking out."[48]

The great achievements and the great failures of much of Modernism are associated with its ironic stance. In its rebellion against abstraction and determinism, we applaud its tenacity. In its unwillingness and perhaps inability to appreciate the impossibility of withdrawing into the construction and contemplation of a static, complex unity, we see an ultimate urge to abandon life in this, our own historical period. Conrad shows us in both Jim and Axel Heyst that the desire to leave the world of action, moral choice, and time eventuates in death, and even Freudians see the urge for mystic contemplation as at least partially a death-wish. Unfortunately, the ironic Moderns' attacks on positivism were not completely successful; fortunately, perhaps, neither was their urge to stillness.

Chapter Four

# *Leaves of Grass*
# and the Center:
# Free Play
# or Transcendence

Whitman is quite rightly viewed by critics as having established the native American tradition of poetry. Contemporary
poets, reacting against early Modernism's condemnation of
Whitman, constantly return to his work as a source of definition
for the American poem. Ezra Pound's belated acknowledgement
of his indebtedness to Whitman in "A Pact" seems to have
triggered the reconsideration by poets like Williams, Roethke,
the Black Mountain School, and the "bard" of the fifties, Allen
Ginsberg. Criticism did not catch up with the renovation of
Whitman until the revisionist work of Roy Harvey Pearce,
which insists upon the nature of Whitman's poetry as act or process and not as form or structure, not as achieved artifict.[1] Indeed, although there have been a variety of "Whitmans" defined
by the critical biases of the misreader, the New Critical devalua-
tion of Whitman for his loose, unstructured forms has dominated
the Modern understanding of our poetic tradition. Cleanth
Brooks, for example, would purge him from the canon of poetry
because his form is not tight (*MP*, 71, 76). Some more sympathetic critics, like R.W.B. Lewis, have tried to "save" Whitman
by arguing that his "aesthetic" is, in fact, the one which lies
behind the New Criticism itself. In 1955, Lewis writes in *The*

*American Adam* that Whitman "adapted [the Kantian aesthetic] to artistic creativity with a vigour and enthusiasm unknown before James Joyce and his associates in the twentieth century."[2]

Pearce's "revisionary" reading of Whitman diverges from these typical Modern analyses by insisting that *Leaves of Grass* is a different kind of poetry than that written by the metaphysicals, symbolists, or New Critics themselves. Whitman's poetry is process and not product: "Like Pound after him, Whitman worked toward a new Paideuma: one entirely of process, of guiding, strengthening, energizing, and redefining the sensible self by putting it into direct contact with the world wherein it could be free, creative, and whole."[3] There is no need to debate the issue which Pearce defines. The standard interpretation of Whitman has now shifted to a position like Pearce's in the critical and poetic writing of W.C. Williams, Charles Olson, Robert Duncan, Stanley Burnshaw, John Vernon, and others.[4] These writers have deconstructed much of the mystification surrounding Whitman perpetrated by the New Critics and in the process of this deconstruction have opened up our definition of poetry itself. However, generally and for the most part, there is another myth surrounding *Leaves of Grass* which requires some destruction: the insistence upon Whitman as the American Adam, as the self alone, creating spontaneously, having sloughed off the skin of European systems in his driving attempts to be "new" and adequate to the American experience.[5]

Generally, Whitman's urge to "make it new," as Pound says, has been taken naively, as a program of simply dismissing the past in his own poetry and prose. In fact, however, Whitman's attitude toward the past is more "constructive," by which I mean, of course, more "destructive," than the mere reduction of the past to, in Heidegger's term, "nullity." Yet, Whitman's attitude toward the past and his sympathies toward the tradition are ambiguous. His idea of "indirection" suggests his program should be more completely destructive than it is. Nonetheless, by deconstructing Whitman's prefaces and other prose works, a project of retrieving the past, tradition, and Europe emerges

[132]

from the primarily rhetorical insistence upon making it new. Ultimately, of course, the retrieve of authentic problems and potentialities from the past vitalizes the "new" poetry and tradition he begins for America.

My treatment of Whitman, then, has two parts, each of which is also subdivided into two arguments. In the first section, I will examine Whitman's prose to exhibit the destructive retrieve which programmatically motivates even the 1855 edition of *Leaves of Grass;* but I will also show the extent to which Whitman's program remains mystified, partially in error, by accepting uncritically some of the language of the tradition he tries to avoid. The second section treats some of the poems to indicate how they are deconstructive yet, almost simultaneously, entrapped within a tradition marked precisely by the possibilities of transcendence and of centered discourse. Whitman can be said, particularly in his relationship to Emerson, which Harold Bloom sees as the defining aspect of the former's poems, to have initiated the American tradition of destroying the past, i.e., whatever has become a *fixed* part of the objectified tradition which obscures more than it reveals.

I

> He drags the dead out of their coffins and stands them again on their feet. . . .
>
> —"Preface," 1855

Whitman's "Preface" to the 1855 edition of *Leaves of Grass* remains the most important single document in American poetics. Precisely because it calls for a native strain of American poetry which would surpass the worn out limits of traditional, i.e., European poetry, American poets return to it again and again to find renewal for their own program for poetry. Roy Harvey Pearce's fine essay in *Historicism Once More,* "Whitman and Our Hope for Poetry," points out that Modernist American poets,

Eliot, Pound, and Stevens, found in Whitman a figure of the lonely poet struggling to define a place for himself in a world essentially hostile to poetry. They tried to separate the prophet and politician from the "shape-shifter" who irrevocably altered the patterns of English verse. Essentially, as Pearce argues, "Their Whitman was the lonely Adamic figure—in Emerson's phrase, the self against the world." [6] More recent American poets have another interpretation of Whitman which is largely a reaction against that of Eliot. Their concern is to find in Whitman as source a poet who revitalizes the idea of poetry's intimate relationship to the ecological and political structure of the nation and the world. Again as Pearce argues, Duncan and his contemporaries are attracted to Whitman because he asks the necessary poetic question: "What . . . were the conditions which would have to obtain if the land were to be restored to productive order?" [7] In effect, the importance of this question denies Whitman the Adamic autonomy which Modern and formalist analyses of his texts usually claim as his major achievement. His primary concern for the outside world, the direction of his poetry toward this fundamental, "*pre*-political" [8] recognition of the role of the poet in the world, throws into doubt the interpretation of Whitman as totally free and independent creator of absolute novelties. [9] It also throws into some doubt the centrality which Adamic interpretations normally impose upon the idea of "self" in Whitman's verse and suggests that a much more complex relationship between "self" and "other" is at the "heart" or "origin" of his poetry. [10]

R.W.B. Lewis's treatment of Whitman in *The American Adam* is probably the paradigm of all Modernist interpretations of Whitman. The fundamental "mystification" of Lewis's misreading lies in his assumption of the possibility of absolute novelty, of freedom from the past and tradition, of a human potential for absolute beginnings at any time. Lewis's misreading emerges from his disguised New Critical presupposition that language magically can free itself and its user from the immediate historical past either to return to some ahistorical scene which actually transcends time—Eliade's *illo tempore* [11]—or simply to begin again, free of historical consequences. In other words, the New Critical insistence upon the ability of the poet as ironist to choose at any time from an infinity of possibles unrestricted by historical actuality and the ecstatic temporal structure of Dasein is transferred in Lewis's study of Whitman to the myth of the American Adam who is free of Europe, its traditions, its language, its rhetoric, and its failures. To some degree similar assumptions underlie all interpretations of Whitman which see him in an exclusively American context. They habitually presuppose as *fact* not only Whitman's success in freeing himself absolutely from the past, but the very possibility of such an escape.

The basically New Critical assumptions behind the Adamic interpretation of Whitman can be made clear in a look at a few passages from Lewis. The strategy which Lewis assigns to Whitman is essentially a mythic attempt to overcome time by returning to the point when man exists out of history in an unfallen state:

> In the poetry of Walt Whitman, the hopes which until now had expressed themselves in terms of progress crystallized all at once in a complete recovery of the primal perfection. In the early poems Whitman accomplished the epochal return by huge and almost unconscious leaps. In later poems he worked his way more painstakingly up the river of history to its source. (*AA*, 42)

> . . . his ambition [is] to reach behind tradition to find and assert nature untroubled by art, to re-establish the natural unfallen man in the living hour. Unfallen man is, properly enough, unclothed as well; the convention of cover came in with the Fall. (*AA*, 43) [12]

The return to mythic origins behind tradition allows the poet to feel free of time and all its psychological effects and artistic demands; it obliterates memory as a result of doing away with time:

> Whitman's hope was unspoiled by memory. . . . While European romanticism continued to resent the effect of time, Whitman was announcing that time had only just begun. . . . It

Walt Whitman

> was this that Whitman had the opportunity to dramatize; and it
> was this that gave *Leaves of Grass* its special quality of a Yankee
> Genesis; a new account of the creation of the world—the cre-
> ation, that is, of a new world; an account this time with a
> happy ending for Adam. (*AA*, 45)

Poetically, this creation of a new world free of the past allows
Whitman to create absolutely new poems, with a new language,
about new experiences:

> How can absolute novelty be communicated? (*AA*, 42)

> Nor is there, in *Leaves of Grass*, any complaint about the
> weight or intrusion of the past; in Whitman's view the past had
> been so effectively burned away that it had, for every practical
> purpose, been forgotten altogether. In his own recurring fig-
> ure, the past was already a corpse; it was on its way out the
> door to the cemetery; Whitman watched it absent-mindedly,
> and turned at once to the living reality. (*AA*, 44)

> The exalted mind carried . . . with it a conviction of absolute
> novelty. (*AA*, 46)

The basic similarities of the presuppositions behind Lewis' analysis of Whitman and those of the New Critics and other ironists
indicate the degree to which even Whitman's defenders have
misread him under the influence of the antihistorical, antiexisten-
tial impulse of Modern American criticism. A closer look at
Whitman's "Preface" exhibits Whitman's constant concern with
the "presence" of the past, his awareness of the basically historical nature of man, who cannot escape his past and tradition—
especially if he hopes to have a future—and his expressed desire
not be bury the dead, but to stand "them again on their feet"
(*LG*, P, 718).

Lewis can analyze Whitman in these terms because to some
extent the poet is amenable to a logocentric language which attempts to find a firm, nonhistorical base for poetry and human
affairs. In fact, Harold Bloom makes explicit and extends the
critical analysis of such logocentric language which is only im-

[136]

plicit in Lewis. Bloom sees Whitman as *the* Emersonian poet, which implies, according to Bloom, a "peculiarly American re-centering" of the *logos* as incarnate word, in opposition to the "deconstruction" or "destruction" of the *logos* as transcendent center (*MM,* 176). As I have shown in my first chapter, Bloom argues that the presence of the voice *"over* the scene of writing" "remains stubbornly logocentric" (*MM,* 176). As Kabbalist, Bloom insists on the priority of the self-presence of voice as privileged *logos* over the absence of writing as destructive discourse. In effect, Bloom agrees with Derrida's basic analysis that voice is logocentric while writing is essentially deconstructive. For this reason, the obviously "oral" Whitman, the singer of songs who discourses liberally and apparently spontaneously, must for Bloom represent the antidestructive forces of the onto-theological tradition of metaphysics. Paradoxically, both Lewis and Bloom conclude that Whitman is in a way free of time, out of history, but from different, in fact, antithetical positions. For Lewis, Whitman's absolute departure from the tradition, his Adamic independence, frees him totally from the past and history; for Bloom, Whitman's imitations of the logocentric tradition, particularly his imitation of Emerson, his commitment to the priority of imagination over world, establishes both his priority over nature and over the precedence of other poets and texts in history.[13] But from either perspective on Whitman, it is the logocentric, i.e., timeless, centered discourses of his critics which somehow manage to remove him from any direct involvement in history and from any direct, creative confrontation with his past, his tradition.

Because Bloom sees all poems "as instances of *the will to utter*" (*WS,* 393), he cannot recognize how Whitman's poetry is essentially a generous, projective dis-closure of past forms. Bloom's trope of speech is power and will whereas Whitman's trope, like Heidegger's, is care. Rather than Heideggerean "discovery," Bloom suggests that "surprise" is the defining trope of American poetry. Once again, by looking at this figure of "surprise" in the context of my previous discussion of Bloom and the

New Critics, we can see that Bloom's troping on American poetry is conditioned by his critical, subjective need to lie against time and reestablish the possibility of "new beginnings":

> "Surprise," as Emerson uses it, does not seem to mean to en-counter suddenly or unexpectedly, or to take or to be taken unaware. It means for him the *pathos* of Power, the sudden manifestation of the vital will. It means Victory and ecstasy, a seizure, as in the etymology of the word. Is it not the most American of tropes for poetic power? . . . For *surprise* is the American poetic stance, in the peculiar sense of surprise as the poet's Will-to-Power over anteriority and over the interpreta-tion of his own poem. (*WS*, 5–6)

I do not intend to deny the utility of these metaphors for reading Whitman, but I would like to suggest that, like the now familiar rhetoric of the Adamic critics, they are willfully and consciously blind to the important temporal structure of Whitman's poems. I also want to suggest that it is not the sublime seduction offered by the illusion of absolute beginnings, of "successive re-begettings" (*PR*, 243), projected by a subjective will to power that marks Whitman's major achievement.

On the contrary, it is Whitman's destruction of the Gnostic priority of "self" that gives his best poetry its most generous attitudes toward the past, toward the future, and toward others. In other words, I am refusing the Bloomian argument that says one forgets the self only to augment the self, to be powerfully victorious over time and nature. Bloom characterizes the "American Sublime" this way:

> The Emersonian repressiveness attains to a discontinuity with everything that is anterior, and in doing so it accomplishes or prepares for a reversal in which the self is forgotten . . . and yet through seeing introjects the fathering force of anteriority. By seeing the transparency, the poet of the American Sublime *contains* the father-god, and so augments the poetic self even as he remembers to forget that self. (*PR*, 247–48)

This figure is analogous in its interpretive power to the Freudian device of counterformation since it empowers the reversal of all other figures. One cannot disprove this figure nor argue its decidability; one can only suggest the subjective, methodological interests at stake in its invocation. Having already done this in my discussion of Bloom in chapter one, I offer here a reading of Whitman which, by refusing to yield to this figure, attends to the temporality of his poetry.

Whitman's 1855 "Preface" lends support to both of these critical theories. But as Paul de Man points out for all critical language, this "Preface" possesses a structure of blindness and insight, or in Heidegger's terms, of an error needed to reveal truth simultaneously, i.e., destructively.

The 1855 "Preface" begins with a statement of the relationship of the American poet to the past. Lewis sees Whitman's description of the tradition as "corpse" as proof of the poet's view that he can and must cut himself off completely from the past. Yet, Whitman's initial statement indicates exactly the opposite and calls into question the possibility of reading the "corpse" metaphor literally as Lewis does:

> America does not repel the past or what it has produced under its forms or amid other politics or the idea of castes or the old religions . . . . accepts the lesson with calmness . . . is not so impatient as has been supposed that the slough still sticks to opinions and manners and literature while the life which served its requirements has passed into the new life of the new forms . . . perceives that the corpse is slowly borne from the eating and sleeping rooms of the house . . . perceives that it waits a little while in the door . . . that it was fittest for its days . . . that its action has descended to the stalwart and well-shaped heir who approaches . . . and that he shall be fittest for his days. (*LG*, P, 711)

*Leaves of Grass* actually begins not only by asserting the "death" of the past poetical forms of defunct political and religious customs, but also by quietly indicating the American poet's relationship to that past. In effect, the American poet is the "heir" of the tradition, not a rebellious child. He is most importantly the place where the new life of mankind will find expression in new forms. A transference of poetic energy has occurred; the forms of

Walt Whitman

the tradition have lost their meaning and power and are no longer equal to the new world which throbs with the unstructured, unhabitual lives and problems the old world has effectively forgotten. Whitman's metaphor insists, furthermore, upon the European loss of a vitality, of a life itself which has been transferred to the West.

Although from the beginning, the "Preface" establishes a more complex relationship to the past than the simple Adamic model which Lewis suggests, it gives no evidence of any creative use of the past as a program for the American poet until further into the essay. Indeed, some argument could be made along the lines of the Adamic model for Whitman's denial of the past. For example:

> No reminiscences may suffice either. A live nation can always cut a deep mark and can have the best authority the cheapest . . . namely from its own soul. [. . .] —As if it were necessary to trot back generation after generation to the eastern records! As if the beauty and sacredness of the demonstrable must fall behind that of the mythical! (*LG*, P, 712)

But this particular disclaimer of the priority of the past—which Harold Bloom would undoubtedly see as Whitman's attempt to disown his father—is specifically a rejection of a simple return to the past, of an attempt to move literature out of the here and now of the poet's language to re-cover the mythical, i.e., literary records which have no relationship to the vitality of the present. In other words, this is a rejection of all naive attempts to move out of the historical moment back in time to the "mythical." It is a rejection of all attempts to "re-collect" the past not from the perspective of the present with an eye to the future, but merely from the perspective of the past, of what is not only habitual, but dead. It is, in effect, a denial of the efficacy of the imitative orientation which lies behind both Walter Bate's and Harold Bloom's theories of poetic creation and poetic history. Such imitation is a "re-cover-ing," an adding of another layer of the habitual to what already obscures the vitality and processes of discovery

[140]

which define life in the States, which, in fact, are the "essence" of America: "As if men do not make their mark out of any times! As if the *opening* of the western continent by *discovery* and what has transpired since in North and South America were less than the small *theatre* of the antique or the aimless sleep-walking of the middle ages!" (*LG,* P, 712. My italics.) America is the product and process of dis-cover-y. The rhetorical opposition of openness and discovery not only with antiquity but theatricality indicates that the cover-up is, to some extent, defined by the "dramatics," the "literariness" of the past, which obscures the antithetical notion of ongoing, human processes in the world of actuality—a world, that is, defined by the sense of place and "now" which the entire *Leaves of Grass* insists upon.

This early paragraph from the "Preface" not only further questions the Adamic or New Critical reading of Whitman, but it also throws some doubt on the correlate idea that insofar as Whitman is concerned with the past he attempts to return to some primordial "origins" which precede the fall into history. He fully rejects the movement back to the mythical as another form of ahistorical, or inauthentic, recovery. His insistence that "reminiscences" will not "suffice" certainly not only attacks the nostalgic "Euro-philes" in the States, but also the Platonic-Hegelian notion of "recollection." The American poet cannot adequately testify to the defining quality of his nation—discovery and openness—while partaking in the luxury of "recollection" which, as Kierkegaard's analysis of Hegel and parody of the aesthetes shows, removes the poet from his actuality and "returns" him to an aesthetic "scene" constituted by the imaginative, selective purgation of memory of all unpleasant and disturbing details.[14] In other words, a reflective art which absorbs the poet and his audience in the transformation of the past into pleasing objects of contemplation is totally inadequate to the vitality of American poetry. This assault on the idea of "reminiscence" is, paradoxically, perhaps the ultimate attack on the Adamic myth. Insofar as the very possibility of the idea of returning to the past as a paradise—either an actual return to a mythic time before the

Walt Whitman

Fall or an aesthetic return to a pleasing scene of the personal or cultural past—is denied, then the total inadequacy of the Adamic-Edenic myth/metaphor to the analysis of Whitman becomes obvious. In fact, the broader and more basic myth of the Fall itself, and its Miltonic-American version, the Fortunate Fall, is also completely destroyed as a possible basis upon which to criticize Whitman. De Man suggests that most criticism is deconstructed by the literature it attempts to analyze, and quite clearly, an important, innovative, i.e., discovering author like Whitman can be seen to destroy the normal varieties of literary interpretation which habitually build up around him. The "normal" attitude toward such writers which assumes some privileged position in further critical discussion of them must be violently destroyed if further insight into these authors is to result, and not merely inadequate reminiscences of the prior "true" interpretations.

Whitman insists that the future forms of the new American art will be different from those of the past. In fact, his periphrastic description of this new poetry can be reclaimed by employing Paul de Man's heuristic term "indirect" in an analysis of Whitman's claims for a native poetry:

> the expression of the American poet is to be transcendent and new. It is to be indirect and not direct or descriptive or epic. Its quality goes through these to much more. Let the age and wars of other nations be chanted and their eras and characters be illustrated and that finish the verse. Not so the great psalm of the republic. Here the theme is creative and has vista. Here comes one among the wellbeloved stonecutters and plans with decision and science and sees the solid and beautiful forms of the future where there are now no solid forms. (LG, P, 714)

De Man's analysis of Rousseau indicates that Rousseau is fully aware of the potential for being misunderstood which lies within all literary language. In order to make this clear and in order to avoid the inescapable mystification of poetic language, Rousseau employs an "indirect" method. Commenting on Derrida's read-

[142]

ing of Rousseau, de Man explains this procedure: "What happens in Rousseau is exactly what happens in Derrida: a vocabulary of substance and of presence is no longer used declaratively but rhetorically, for the very reasons that are being (metaphorically) stated" (*BI*, 138–39). As I have suggested in my own destruction of Lewis' New Critical Adamic reading of Whitman, Lewis has misconceived the language of the "Preface" as literal truth and not as the rhetorical statement of a self-conscious writer whose prose works in a destructive way. In other words, the clear comments which Whitman makes concerning the "abandonment" of the past and the need for an authentically American poetry are all undercut by the "more tentative utterances" (*BI*, 102) which reveal the important connections to the past and tradition Whitman insists upon. Considered historically, Whitman's "Preface" faces a unique situation: he cannot directly call for a more creative understanding of the past since the habitual mode of then current American poetry, in fact, stands in an imitative, derivative relationship to old British forms. As a result of the paradoxical situation in which Whitman finds himself, a direct request for an authentic look at or interpretation of the past would be misinterpreted, misconceived as further support for the already entrenched conservatism of American letters which Whitman propagandistically attacks elsewhere.

Whitman can only bring his readers to understand what he wants to say by moving his language a little off center. By calling for the blatant and absolute novelty which Lewis, among others, interprets as a literal program for poetry, Whitman assumes the risk of constant misinterpretation. Like Rousseau, like all major innovative writers, he is aware that he is necessarily doomed to constant misreadings. In fact, as Heidegger's theory of truth points out, such indirect use of language is a necessary strategy in the face of inevitable misreading. To disclose something new, it must emerge from something old. Truth comes from error, *aletheia* from semblance, and so on. The "truth" of this more complicated, indirect method of dealing with the past is purposely covered over with a lie, a call for the undesired and impossible, so that the "truth" may in fact begin to emerge when the text is read indirectly, i.e., rhetorically and destructively.

This analysis of the key term "indirection" can be extended by an examination of another key in Whitman's poetics, "destruction": "The power to destroy or remould is freely used by [the poet] but never the power of attack. What is past is past. If he does not expose superior models and prove himself by every step he takes he is not what is wanted" (*LG, P, 715*). The rhetorical identification of "destroy" and "remould" as well as its differentiation from any idea of "attack," overcomes the notion that this destruction is, in Whitman, a reduction to "nullity." Once again, a naive or direct reading would suggest the Adamic myth, a return to the garden by an elimination of the past, by making a new "beginning." Yet, Whitman does say that the "past is past." But this too can be interpreted in the light of the larger rhetorical structure and intent of this passage. If in fact the past is gone forever, then the poet's power to destroy is redundant and unnecessary. Also, precisely insofar as the "re-" of "re-mould" is purposeful and Whitman has not misspoken himself, then the pastness of the past, to paraphrase T.S. Eliot, does not deny its "presence." That is, unless Whitman errs in explicitly ascribing to the poet the power to destroy and remould, the phrase "What is past is past," cannot be taken in any direct Adamic way. Another interpretation must be found to complete the understanding of the passage. The coupling of "destroy" with "remould" suggests the possibility of treating the past in such a way that by "destroying" it the poet must "expose superior models." Whitman's use of the language of disclosure in the context of poetic destruction reinforces the interpretation that the authentic relationship to the past is one of "re-newal," "re-trieve," and "dis-covery."

In perhaps the most important passage in the 1855 "Preface," from which I have drawn the epigraph of this section, Whitman explicitly, but briefly, insists upon precisely this destructive, retrieving orientation toward the dead past. I quote the

entire passage here because it presents other issues which I intend
to discuss in the context of Whitman's poetics:

> Without effort and without exposing in the least how it is
> done the greatest poet brings the spirit of any or all events and
> passions and scenes and persons some more and some less to
> bear on your individual character as you hear or read. To do
> this well is to compete with the laws that pursue and follow
> time. What is the purpose must surely be there and the clue of
> it must be there . . . . and the faintest indication is the indica-
> tion of the best and then becomes the clearest indication. Past
> and present and future are not disjoined but joined. The great-
> est poet forms the consistence of what is to be from what has
> been and is. He drags the dead out of their coffins and stands
> them again on their feet . . . . he says to the past, Rise and
> walk before me that I may realize you. He learns the lesson
> . . . . he places himself where the future becomes present. The
> greatest poet does not only dazzle his rays over character and
> scenes and passions . . . he finally ascends and finishes all . . .
> he exhibits the pinnacles that no man can tell what they are for
> or what is beyond . . . . he glows a moment on the extremest
> verge. He is most wonderful in his last half-hidden smile or
> frown . . . by that flash of the moment of parting the one that
> sees it shall be encouraged or terrified afterward for many
> years. (LG, P, 718)

This passage brings together the ideas of poetic indirection, of
poetic "re-trieve," and of the necessarily temporal, historical consciousness and project of the poet. Because the past, present, and
future do not exist independently, the American poet who hopes
to build a tradition out of the present for the future must begin
by rediscovering what the now "defunct" tradition of Europe offers. The "lesson" the poet learns is of the failure of the past,
why it is no longer adequate, what America must do differently
to succeed. Whitman's temporal sense is acute. Indeed, he not
only insists upon the temporal awareness of past, present, and future, but claims that the American poet's success requires that his
poems, their forms, be "informed" by the laws of time which

Walt Whitman

govern nature. Since Whitman differentiates American from European verse by claiming "vista" as the essential element of a native poetry, his assertion in the quoted passage of the connection between time and poetry clearly indicates the close relationship which exists between the historical nature of man and the temporal laws of poetry. "Vista" indicates process, futurity, scope, change, ongoing dis-covery and exposure, and it recalls Heidegger's understanding of "sight" as retrieval. European poetry, on the other hand, is direct and descriptive; it illustrates, and "that finishes the verse." Thus, it can be argued that American poetry differentiates itself by never "finishing" its process.

In other words, for a native poetry to be successful it must be temporal, indirect—i.e., historically aware and destructive—and end-less. Not only can poetry never completely separate itself from its past tradition, but, in order to affect its audience, to change the character of its readers to give them some awareness of the temporal nature of their being, it must "compete with the laws that pursue and follow time." Poetry must have an essentially temporal structure which is marked by "vista," by open-ended discovery which is the structural and methodological equivalent of "America," as both reality and as metaphor for the vital world of poetic concerns. There are two points of focus then in the discussion of this passage, one is the poem as temporal event or action and the second is the poet as temporal, historical being. The two cannot be divided without violating Whitman's intent here, since the poem as process emerges only from the fact that human life is historical. Yet, the formal elements of the poem make a claim on the reader just as the fundamental temporality of existence makes claims on the poet.

Whitman's sense of the poet's "poetic" history, that is, of his place in relationship to the literary past, is crucial but not absolutely fundamental. There is a more basic temporal structure within the poet, within the Dasein, which in effect makes possible or requires an awareness of the literary past and tradition. Whitman insists upon the American poem emerging from the experience of the individual ego. Since the poem must follow the laws of time, it follows that temporality is for Whitman located essentially within the individual. The poet defines the potential not only for recording the present and examining the past to expose from within it the vital laws habit has obscured, but the poet functions as potentiality itself. He is the possibility for discovery and dis-closure. He is the means for opening up the future and demonstrating the nature of man's being as potentiality. The poet not only testifies to man's being present in the world, but "he places himself where the future becomes present," at the point where "sight" and "eyes" are retrieved from metaphysics and coercion.[15] In other words, the poet lives on the verge, on the boundary between what-is and has been within life and tradition and what is not yet; he creates in the gap between the actuality defined by the past and present and the potentialities which the future, growing out of the past and present with which it is conjoined, presents.

Yet, this word "presents" is out of place in Whitman's rhetoric. Indeed, the poet who sees the farthest, who reaches into the mysterious realms of death and Being is faced with the ineffable, with the "un-presentable." Indirectly, giving a "clue" here and there—and again "clue" can be read in terms of both Heidegger and Derrida's concept of the "trace"[16]—the poet "exhibits the pinnacles that no man can tell what they are for or what is beyond. . . ." As Heidegger's analysis of Stefan George's "The Word" makes clear, the poet ultimately is confronted by the failure of language to articulate his final vision of what the ordinary and habitual obscures.[17] In a similar way, Whitman's vision culminates in no Hegelian synthesis or positivistic *telos*. He discovers so much of what the vista reveals that he can only indirectly disclose those realms which are at the limits of his perception and language. Representation and signification both break down when the poet successfully destroys enough of the traditional habits to encounter this mysterious limit of articulation. Perhaps all that the poet does finally encounter in this way is the failure of language, which reduces him to gesture and bodily expression. Whitman seems to suggest this in the next passage: "[The poet] is most wonderful in his last half-hidden smile or frown . . . by that flash of the moment of parting the one that sees it shall be encouraged or terrified afterward for many years." The poet moves beyond, transcends what the ordinary or habitual defines as life and at that moment is reduced to a non-verbal being. The necessary shared basis of language, its common referents and significations, disintegrate. In a similar way, this passage can be seen as the moment of the poet's departure from life itself, i.e., of his physical and imaginative death. The ambiguity of the potential observer's interpretive response to the smile or frown reinforces the Heideggerean sense of death being forever my own. It also suggests the discomfort which the presence of death in the habitual society creates in its members. But most importantly, this passage indicates what effects the poet has upon the ordinary world when he exhibits something which is beyond that world's norm. Whitman's "Preface" contains a detailed attack on the bourgeois world's values and "desperate revolt at the close of a life" (LG, P, 725), which supports the idea that his poetry is meant to unsettle and disrupt the common life of the ordinary man and not merely to record the world of nineteenth-century America.

Because of the direct involvement of the historical poet in his poetry, his texts are intended to have historical, kinetic, affective value. Unlike the New Critical art which Stephen Dedalus describes, Whitman's poems reveal to the reader the radically temporal nature of his experience and being. Whitman's poems disrupt past texts to reveal what they have concealed in order to disassociate the reader from the ordinary world and habitual modes of poetry. Whitman's verse is designed to convert and unsettle the reader by destroying his habits and his literature. In place of a literature which is direct, descriptive, and finished, Whitman offers the indirect, the destructive, the unending, and the process-ional.

In an important passage warning his reader of the risk and

dangers inherent in reading *Leaves of Grass,* Whitman declares his intent to write antitraditional, temporal poems:

> A great poem is *no finish* to a man or a woman but rather a *beginning.* Has anyone fancied he could sit *at last* under some due authority and rest satisfied with explanations and realize and be *content* and full? To *no such terminus* does the great poet bring . . . *he brings neither cessation or sheltered fatness and ease.* The touch of him tells in *action.* Whom he takes he takes with firm sure grasp into *live regions previously unattained* . . . . *thenceforward is no rest* . . . . they see the space and ineffable sheen that turn the old spots and lights into dead vacuums. The companion of him beholds the birth and progress of stars and learns one of the meanings. Now there shall be a man cohered out of tumult and chaos . . . . the elder encourages the younger and shows him how . . . they two shall launch off fearlessly together till the new world fits an orbit for itself and looks unabashed on the lesser orbits of the stars and sweeps through the *ceaseless rings and shall never be quiet again.* (*LG,* P, 729. My italics)

*Leaves of Grass* is designed to jolt the reader out of his complacency, his "fat certainty." It is to unsettle his preconceptions which, once destroyed, appear only as habits. Most importantly, the poem is to have an emotional and ontological effect: it is to disorient and cause anxiety by revealing the basis of human being in a radically ungrounded sense of process, action, and endless, nonteleological time. The text emerges out of the process of a life in time, out of an awareness of literary history and the idea of destruction, and out of a recognition of the need to drive men and women out of their habitual life patterns in order to maintain life, to assure ongoing dis-closure which is the definition of truth and authenticity.

The poems assault the traditional ontological assumptions of presence, certainty, and rest as the ground of all being. They destroy the assumptions of *arché* and *telos,* while they deconstruct the Romantic metaphor of the journey and quest. In a way al-

[149]

Walt Whitman

most as completely and radically as the absurd dramatists of the
twentieth century, Whitman violently drives his readers into a
disorientation by breaking down their claims for rest and com-
posure, by writing a poetry without end and with intense kinetic
value. In Stephen Dedalus' terms, Whitman's art would be both
pornography and propaganda, since it is intended to attract and
repulse.

Perhaps Whitman's fundamental poetic insight for the new
American poetry lies in seeing it as a means of revitalizing the
awareness of basic human nature: life is process and change; man
is historical and temporal; literature becomes habitual and comforting and, therefore, only a semblance of itself. American literature must disclose this basic truth, indirectly, by opening up the
past to reveal the fundamentally temporal being of life and art
which the logocentric tradition's emphasis on *telos* and stasis has
obscured. In the act of this destruction, the new poems will
record these basic poetic imaginings while driving the audience
into a confrontation with them by creating an anxiety which the
audience cannot ignore. The forms of the poems will not end or
comfort, will not simplify, and will not provide aesthetically the
evidence for the assumed ontological security which habitually
grounds all "normative" worlds of ordinary experience.

Whitman's prose does not, however, seem to completely escape from the habitual and common to the degree that would appear to be necessary to his entire project. While his theory of indirection and his comments about the "clue" of poetic intention
caution a reader against misreading Whitman by literalizing his
work and suggest that even his most "obvious" myths might be
examples of his deconstructive, indirect rhetoric, there are elements of traditional language, usually associated with Emersonian idealism, which appear to ground and motivate the writing. These mystified linguistic structures and tropes are in direct
opposition to the destructive impulse I have been exhibiting in
the "Preface." The idea of historical interpretation could be used
to destroy the mystified elements in Whitman, and the theory of
indirection could be used to suggest that Whitman is not mys-

[150]

Walt Whitman

tified in these idealistic matters, but rather that he is employing such language against itself, in the context of the theory of destruction, in order to overcome the Emersonian version of traditional rhetoric. Yet, the all important "clue" to this destruction seems to me to be missing. It appears that Whitman undoubtedly is mystified about the possibility of re-presenting the "presence" of the "Soul," of the correspondence between this world and another spiritual realm. He seems unaware that such a belief in the centrality of a transcendent realm is in direct opposition to his discussion of ongoing dis-covery as "ceaseless rings," which he suggests are to dis-orient and unsettle the habitual.

   While the "Preface" is based upon a destructive theory that language becomes habitual and comforting because dead and unexamined, Whitman's own language of "presence," of "the unshakable order of the universe" (*LG,* P, 726), remains an unexamined trope derived most immediately from Emerson. Whitman denies the idea of *arché,* of any absolute beginning or first principle: "no result exists now without being from its long antecedent result, and that from its antecedent, and so backward without the farthest mentionable spot coming a bit nearer the beginning than any other spot." The absence of a stable origin ungrounds history and anthropology and the centrality of all causal systems. Yet Whitman does not question the idealistic myth which assumes the unity and integrity of "History" to be a whole that can be seen "all at once": "and if to [the poet] is not opened the eternity which gives similitude to all periods [. . .]—let him merge in the general run and wait his development" (*LG,* P, 728). While the attack on *arché* and *telos* destroys precisely the poet's privilege to see all of history at once, to recognize how history "is held by the ductile anchors of life" (*LG,* P, 728), Whitman does not, within the immediate context, in the place or moment of this statement, give any evidence for taking these statements "metaphorically." His seeming belief in the "truth" of the transcendental language is not undercut by its juxtaposition to the language of destruction.

   In a blinded rhetoric, peculiarly like the one in Husserl's

[151]

Walt Whitman

"Philosophy and the Crisis of European Humanity," which Paul de Man takes as the classic example of such rhetoric, Whitman too seems not to realize fully that the critique of habitual language which he insists is necessary to founding American poetry is self-referential (*BI,* 14ff). For example, in a statement which explains the significance of exact science as a deconstructive, demystifying force, Whitman writes: "The whole theory of the special and supernatural and all that was twined with it or educed out of it departs as a dream" (*LG,* P, 721). Yet, Whitman finds in this same science some "reason" to justify the transcendental ideal of spirit infusing all matter:

> What has ever happened. . . . what happens and whatever may or shall happen, the vital laws enclose all [. . . .] any miracle of affairs or persons inadmissable in the vast clear scheme where every motion and every spear of grass and the frames and spirits of men and women and all that concerns them are unspeakably perfect miracles all referring to all and each distinct and in its place. (*LG,* P, 721)

Fundamentally, this assurance of divine order undercuts the very possibility of writing a poetry which could in any way drive its reader into periods of unrest, into "ceaseless rings." In fact, the miraculous order Whitman proclaims here is the apotheosis of the traditional language of the West. It guarantees all action by providing a firm basis from which man can proceed out into the world. It becomes not only a center, a proposition and belief which is not involved in the play of the texts, but it acts as an *arché,* a beginning, a source, a first principle which conceals the real risk of the constant restlessness which Whitman himself describes.

Examples of Whitman's use of this traditional language of presence in the form of Emersonian transcendentalism could be mutliplied. Most importantly, however, a few examples provide evidence to indicate the opposite of what Paul de Man claims for poets in *Blindness and Insight:* not all writers are completely demystified. Some, like Whitman, require at least partial destruction. In fact, as the discussion of Heidegger has shown, only insofar as there is semblance can there be truth; only insofar as a writer errs can he destroy, can he insist upon the demystification of language. Whitman is not radical enough. He does not pierce through to the fundamental nothingness which all literary language conceals and reveals. But he has begun the American tradition, which in many ways has become the Modern and Postmodern one: an attempt to found a new tradition for the future cannot proceed from a naive belief in the possibility of absolute, new beginnings. Such ideals are hopeless and merely aesthetic, in Kierkegaard's sense of the term, i.e., an attempt to transcend actuality for a verbal world of infinite possibilities. Indeed, Whitman's "Preface" destroys the very myth of misinterpretation which was to grow up around him. He shows that the idea of the new, or what de Man using Nietzsche in *Blindness and Insight* calls the "Modern," is only a myth. As Heidegger proves, one's past lies in front of one and not behind. We are already our tradition and attempts to escape this fundamental fact by ignoring history, its consequences, and actuality itself are only mistaken attempts to become like God. Quite ironically, in many ways, Whitman's "Preface" can be said to be the manifesto of the tradition. For it is only by setting the past on its feet again by disclosing what it has concealed or forgotten that the new tradition can begin. Whitman's ideas parallel those of Heidegger on the "retrieve." Although Whitman seems hardly as self-conscious as Heidegger, his own program for American art—with its insistence upon this historicality of poet and poetry—certainly appears to foreshadow the more fully developed theories of "phenomenological destruction."


II


Whitman's poetry as well as his program are transitional in an important sense: his work represents the beginnings of the Modern and Postmodern attempt to deconstruct archetypes, the first sense that the tradition has failed and can no longer be seen as adequate to Modern life or art. But Whitman's poems, as I have tried to suggest in the context of the 1855 "Preface," are far from embodying the complete and radical deconstruction which one finds, for example, in Wallace Stevens. Whitman's deeply felt sense of the concrete historicity of the poet and his poems motivates his attack on a tradition which has become "ahistorical," which has not changed with the "dis-covery" of America and science. Yet, while Whitman feels liberated by the radical freedom which he enjoys as a result of this Modern de-traditionalization, his life and work are marked by a strong, unquestioned attraction to the idea and belief in some controlling center, some radically unalterable ground upon which the poem, the structure, and the poet's own self may be built.

Whitman's poetic deconstructions not only foreshadow in method Heidegger's phenomenologically destructive retrieve, but they are peculiarly similar to Jacques Derrida's "decenterings" of the ideas of beginning, end, and self. In versions of the tradition, these terms have functioned as privileged "centers" for philosophical and literary structures, but all betray a belief in a transcendent presence which lies outside the theoretical and ontological realm of doubt and questioning. Derrida's concept of center is of value in reading Whitman's poems in this context, so at the risk of some redundancy, I will reintroduce some material from "Structure, Sign and Play in the Discourse of the Human Sciences." In this essay, Derrida points out that what a "center" "is" is less important than how it functions:

> The function of this center was not only to orient, balance, and organize the structure—one cannot in fact conceive of an unorganized structure—but above all to make sure that the organizing principle of the structure would limit what we might call the *play* of the structure. By orienting and organizing the coherence of the system, the center of the structure permits the play of its elements inside the total form. And even today the notion of a structure lacking any center represents the unthinkable itself.

[154]

Walt Whitman

> Nevertheless, the center also closes off the play which it opens up and makes possible. As center, it is the point at which the substitution of contents, elements, or terms is no longer possible. At the center, the permutation or the transformation of elements (which may of course be structures enclosed within a structure) is forbidden. At least this permutation has always remained *interdicted* (and I am using this word deliberately). Thus it has always been thought that the center, which is by definition unique, constituted that very thing within a structure which while governing the structure, escapes structurality.[18]

The center of any structure (and a structure may be a building, a philosophical system, a group of myths, or a poem) is the un-questioned *a priori* about which all else circles. It guides change, but is itself free from change. In most traditional systems, especially in the West, it takes the form of transcendence. Despite its form, however, it always provides man with certitude, with the evidence of something beyond change which controls life and prohibits chance.

I will assume along with Derrida, for the purposes of this chapter, that Nietzsche must be pointed to as the definite point at which Modernism begins and the tradition of presence is brought into question. As both Derrida and Paul de Man argue, Nietzsche's major contribution to Western thought is an attack upon the forms and premises of that thought itself. In "Genesis and Genealogy in Nietzsche's *Birth of Tragedy*," de Man demonstrates that Nietzsche deconstructs the myth and metaphor of evolution and generation, that is, he discloses the discontinuities of literary structures modelled upon the generic construct.[19] Nietzsche si-multaneously de-creates the positivistic myth of historical prog-ress. In both critiques, Nietzsche attacks the concepts of *arché* and *telos* which dominate Western metaphysics. The concepts of beginning and end function, as Derrida argues, as "centers." The beginning, clearly, is a point of departure, a sound base from which all else emerges and back beyond which we cannot go. If we try to violate the beginning, we find only Aristotle's and Aquinas' infinite regressions. The end, or *telos,* of course, is a

[155]

certain, stable projection in the future toward which we travel. Like the ending of a well-made fiction,[20] like the paradisal goal of apocalyptic philosophies, such as the heaven of Christianity, any *telos* is a defined point of certain arrival about which all of human action and history centers.

Nietzsche, Heidegger, and Freud, according to Derrida, see this traditional Western center only as a means of eliminating anxiety and preventing risk. In each traditional system, whether poetic or philosophical, a center exists about which the rest of the structure is suspended. Therefore, all structures before the end of the nineteenth century are "centered structures." These exist until then because the need and faith for a center is so completely absorbing that its very "presence" as a primary assumption of thought is not made explicit. Exposure requires first a sense that the tradition has failed and then a deconstructive analysis to exhibit it fully. However, as Derrida argues, in the middle of the nineteenth century, Nietzsche comes to see that man always centers his structures for a reason, namely that he uses them as existential anaesthetics:

> The concept of centered structure is in fact the concept of a play based on a fundamental ground, a play constituted on the basis of a fundamental immobility and a reassuring certitude, which itself is beyond the reach of play. And on the basis of this certitude anxiety can be mastered, for anxiety is invariably the result of a certain mode of being implicated in the game, of being caught by the game, of being as it were at stake in the game from the outset.[21]

As Derrida defines the event, recognition of and release from the centered structures can issue in two reactions. Although the decadents, the symbolists, and ironists assume a world-weary, despairing attitude in the face of change and death unexplained by a centered myth—what Derrida calls "Rousseauist"—Nietzsche and Whitman joyously affirm the freedom to act and discover which this decentering gives them:

[156]

Walt Whitman

> Turned towards the lost or impossible presence of the absent
> origin, this structuralist thematic of broken immediacy is there-
> fore the saddened, negative, nostalgic, guilty, Rousseauistic
> side of the thinking of play whose other side would be the
> Nietzschean *affirmation,* that of becoming, the affirmation of a
> world of signs without fault, without truth, and without origin
> which is offered to an active interpretation. *This affirmation then
> determines the noncenter otherwise than as loss of the center.* And it
> plays without security. [22]

    The centerless nature of Whitman's art and the joyous de-
creative process which he employs in it are most visible in two of
his major preoccupations: the poet or man as child and the ever
ongoing, unending world of history imaged as journey. But before I begin a discussion of *Leaves of Grass* by examining these
items, I must briefly return to Whitman's still mystified, logocentric language.
    There is in *Leaves of Grass,* especially in the later poems, an
insistence upon the existence of god. As Louis Martz puts it: "his
tendency to make abstract assertions about the future grew, until
he weakened his essential poetic power, his ability to deal concretely and dynamically with the world about him. . . . His
'flights of a fluid and swallowing soul' may fly out too often
beyond the human horizon into a place where the air is too thin
for poetry." [23] I do not wish to argue that Whitman abandons his
early position of freedom to assume a safer stance in a world
guaranteed by a transcendence. Martz puts the case too simply.
Clearly, the problem of transcendence exists in the poem from
the very beginning, and indeed, the early radical freedom continues, although somewhat abated, to the very end. As Charles
Metzger argues, Whitman at times turns toward god for assurance, but he primarily, especially in his early poetry, relies on
self. [24] Whitman, as a transitional figure, knows the risks of misinterpretation he takes in carrying to its extreme the metaphor of
the New Adam. But, by assuming the Adamic myth as a rhetorical stance, he is able to destroy the habitual and mystified tradi-

[157]

tion throughout. As a result, the benefits, joys, and pleasures of the potential freeplay fascinate him. At the same time, however, he recognizes that he is losing surety when he pursues this programmatic destruction. Much of the best poetry of *Leaves* modulates dialectically between these two poles, and some of it is the direct result of tension between their associated antinomies.

The major impediment to seeing the fundamentally "centerless" nature of Whitman's poetry is the tendency of critics to see his insistence on "self" or "personality" as a new center. Robert Spiller's description of the relation of Whitman's self to the universe is typical of such ego-logocentric criticism:

> Given his idea of Personality—so close to Emerson's conception of the Over-Soul—Whitman's thought moves outward in concentric circles from a concentration on the abstract value of his own self. . . . this idea of self moves from its fully realized inner core to the extreme outward limits of cosmic unity.[25]

According to Spiller, the entire poem, at least as finally arranged, moves from a concentration on self to some sort of unity with suprahuman forces. The series of concentric circles would and does suggest a centered structure, and no doubt Whitman would have us see the similarity. Even Metzger thinks that Whitman's "conception of unity . . . centers around his personal identity."[26] This, of course, is only a narcissistic variation on the Adamic metaphor. The self is, in fact, frequently portrayed as radically separated from all firm bases, striking out *ex nihilo* upon the open road. Equally as often, self and nation appear as the "result" of an infinitely long and rich past to whose origin Whitman never tries to penetrate. He never confronts the universe from a panoptical position of transcendence, but only from his limited, projective "vista."

The critical "centering" of Whitman's self fails to consider his presentation of the self as an origin-less thing, unfounded on any secure basis, and it also ignores the open-ended quality of the poem's form and of the poetic journey. Furthermore, since Whitman identifies poet, poem, and nation, this centering process dis-

Walt Whitman

counts his presentation of the radical novelty of America. It is also crucial that when Whitman does speak of the past and its relation to self and America, it is often to emphasize the indeterminate number of states, cultures, and men who, in fact, lead up to his own self and the United States.

The self in this poem has no firm basis. One of Whitman's primary metaphors for this state is the romantic image of the innocent child. This metaphor is also a fine example of the deconstructive nature of Whitman's art. He uses the metaphor of the child-artist, which William Wordsworth typifies in the *Intimations Ode,* but he shows the inefficacy of Wordsworth's presumed relation of child to light by using the metaphor in a way which disconnects the child from any source:

> There was a child went forth every day,
> And the first object he look'd upon, that object he became,
> And that object became part of him for the day, or a certain
> part of the day,
> Or for many years, or stretching cycles of years.
>
> (*LG,* 364)

These lines introduce the typical romantic metaphor of the innocent child-poet-discoverer. If we assume Wordsworth's *Ode* to be paradigmatic, then Whitman's achievement becomes clearer. In Wordsworth's allegorical poem, of course, the child goes forth once, leaves light, the transcendent source of vision and understanding, and finds that the light fades as he grows older, until either death or the poetic renewal of light occurs by the agency of recollection.

Whitman's child-poet goes "forth every day;" his departure is not marred by the sadness of loss, by the sense of a growing lack in life; rather, this child sympathetically identifies everyday with every object which he encounters in this world. These identifications are not momentary events; they are not instants to be recalled in later life in hope of renewal; rather, they become part of the self by entering permanently into the self. Whitman's child grows; he is not a static, unchangeable creature. He expands his

[159]

self by filling it with encounters with the outside world. In Georges Poulet's terminology, we might say that Whitman is trying to fill the infinite void within himself by internalizing all of the exterior world.[27]

The movement in the poem follows this process of expansion as the child first internalizes the day and its events, and then, the commonplaces of nature, "The early lilies became part of this child" (*LG,* 364). His expansion continues as he experiences the seasons, the cycles of nature, and then the works of man. However, the quest metaphor of the Romantic hero is altered in "There was a child went forth." The poet-child's travel is not teleological, but process-ional. Regarding the "vista" reveals the limits of the horizon. Whitman's poem emphasizes the process of discovering objects in the world as well as the revelation that the questor himself is always in and of the world. This poem is a voyage of discovery by an "innocent" child into the "vistas" of life in nature, in America. The child's trip is always forward looking and he is never, like the persona of Wordsworth's *Ode,* attracted to the transcendent light lost in the fall into time.

Finally, the movement of the poem returns the child and the reader to home. In the same way, Wordsworth's *Ode* returns us to a source of light, to his child's transcendent "home."[28] Wordsworth's language and vision appear to be radically logocentric. The *Intimations Ode* begins by recounting, by recollecting, the past in which all elements of nature "did seem/ Apparalled in celestial light" (l. 4). And as the poet grows older, as he loses his "innocence" and falls further into the world of matter, he realizes that "It is not now as it hath been of yore" (l. 6). The divine soul of an infant which related the poet to godhead is covered over with the passage of time and the accretion of experiences gathered in life's journey: "The things which I have seen I now can see no more" (l. 9). The poet's life in this poem is lived facing backward, recollecting the eternal and idyllic moment of the past life, perhaps even the divine moment of a life in another world. In the *Phaedo,*[29] of course, Socrates lectures Simmias and Cebes upon the immortality of the spirit and the pre-

existent soul. Socrates hopes to establish the theory of knowledge based upon recollection which justifies his own method of
questioning as instruction.

Wordsworth, however, is certainly aware of Socrates' description of the immortal soul: "Then, Simmias, our soul existed
formerly, apart from our bodies, and possessed intelligence before they came into man's shape."[30] Philosophy is the process of
attempting to regain the knowledge and glory of the soul prior
to its reconnection with a human body. Indeed, life for Socrates,
as Kierkegaard points out about him quite frequently (*CI,* 121f),
is lived as a recollection, that is, as an attempt to regain the perfection of a nontemporal, nonworldly state. Such an attempt is,
of course, totally contrary to the ongoing process of uncovering,
of disclosing the new which occurs in Heidegger's philosophical
destruction and in Whitman's poems. The Socratic recollection
looks solely to the past while Kierkegaardian repetition and the
Heideggerean retrieve are directed towards the future by exposing what the past conceals.

Wordsworth tries in the *Intimations Ode* to articulate the
sense of the loss of this original presence:

> Not in entire forgetfulness,
> And not in utter nakedness,
> But trailing clouds of glory do we come
> From God, who is our home:
> Heaven lies about us in our infancy!
> Shades of the prison-house begin to close
> Upon the growing Boy
> But He beholds the light, and whence it flows,
> He sees it in his joy;
> The Youth, who daily farther from the east
> Must travel, still is Nature's Priest,
> And by the vision splendid
> Is on his way attended;
> At length the Man perceives it die away,
> And fade into the light of common day.

(ll. 62–76)

[161]

Walt Whitman

Just as Socrates realizes that as long as the soul is attached to the body (the philosopher should welcome death) recollection cannot be fully achieved, Wordsworth recognizes that he must look in the world for traces of what "exists" in the origin: ". . . find/ Strength in what remains behind" (l. 184). The Wordsworthian wanderer travels looking for revelations of the eternal moment in time. He turns not toward the things in nature for themselves, for the claims which their existences make upon his being, but to *see* in them the visionary evidence of the continued "existence" of that eternal, un-earthly, mode he has left behind. Wordsworth hopes to be able to go "home" again.

Whitman, in his poem, however, identifies his child's home and parentage as distinctly human:

> His own parents, he that had father'd him and she that had conceiv'd him in her womb and birth'd him,
> They gave this child more of themselves than that,
> They gave him afterward every day, they became part of him.
> (*LG*, 365)

This image of the poetic self's development and expansion, of its journey in experience, emphasizes the earthly roots of the self. It does not have its source in the transcendent nor in the certain. The poem refuses the language of presence. The poetic self is radically ungrounded in Whitman; there is no origin-al innocence lost in experience pursued by memory; rather, there is experience as absorption, the expansion of the self by generous sympathy as ideal. This process does not end in an integrated identity, a unified self, but rather in a clear perception that in the "fallen world" there are only "selves." Identity is not achieved through recollection; rather, difference remains in dispersal and delay. Furthermore, by insisting on the birth of this child, Whitman associates the image with the infinite regression of humanity into the past. The last lines of the poem make this clear: "These became part of that child who then went forth every day, and who now goes, and will always go forth every day" (*LG*, 366). The tripartite, temporal rhetoric of this passage clearly echoes the

Christian praise of Christ who "always was, and always will be, forever and ever." The submerged religious rhythm does not impart any note of divinity to the child. It only insists upon the never-ending "ek-static" process of encounter on the part of the artist–child who now and throughout history, from no beginning and to no final end, always "goes forth."

The lack of firm origin in *Leaves of Grass* is first suggested in "Song of Myself":

> I have heard what the talkers were talking, the talk of the
>     beginning and the end,
> But I do not talk of the beginning or the end.
>
> There was never any more inception than there is now,
> Nor any more youth or age than there is now,
> And will never be any more perfection than there is now,
> Nor any more heaven or hell than there is now.
>
> (LG, 30)

This is more than a declaration of intent to concentrate on the world for subject matter; it is a manifesto of Modernism. It announces Whitman's truly radical break from the past. The topic of poetry is the present, the constantly changing encounters of the self with the world. Poetry emerges from all this experience:

> Stop this day and night with me and you shall possess the ori-
>     gin of all poems,
> You shall possess the good of the earth and sun, (there are
>     millions of suns left,)
> You shall no longer take things at second or third hand, nor
>     look through the eyes of the dead, nor feed on the spectres in
>     books,
> You shall not look through my eyes either, nor take things
>     from me,
> You shall listen to all sides and filter them from your self.
>
> (LG, 30)

These lines prefigure not only Williams' "no ideas but in things" and the basic tenet of phenomenology, "to the things them-

Walt Whitman

selves," but also suggest Charles Olson's complex notions of history and vision which I will develop in my last chapter. Although Whitman announces in these lines from "Song of Myself" the "origin" of all poetry, he carefully shows that this "origin" is neither ultimately unchanging nor his own self. He is not the great "origin" through whose eyes we see all of experience. Each self looks independently and sees its own truth. Each strips away all that is dead or "spectral." Each self has a generous attitude, that is, each accepts every part of experience: "The American bards shall be marked for generosity and affection and for encouraging competitors" (*LG,* P, 720). And, as the etymology of "generosity" suggests, the "Bard" will remain in difference without reaching irritably after identity and unity.

In "Song of Myself," the persona declares his total and complete independence of all external sources which claim priority:

> These come to me days and nights and go from me again,
> But they are not the Me myself.

> Apart from the pulling and hauling stands what I am,
> Stands amused, complacent, compassionating, idle, unitary,
> Looks down, is erect, or bends an arm on an impalpable certain
> rest,
> Looking with side-curved head curious what will come next,
> Both in and out of the game and watching and wondering at it.
>
> (*LG,* 32)

The modern American, having revitalized old "systems," confronts all varieties of experience. Unlike all other "centers" which are free of the structure hung about them, Whitman as "center" of his own poetic structure partakes in the game. As a poet, he must maintain some minimal distance from an event, but it is not a detachment which ultimately separates him from the world. His responses are never cautious or meditative, but extravagant and impetuous: "I am satisfied—I see, dance, laugh, sing" (*LG,* 31).

[164]

Walt Whitman

Despite the novelty of these encounters, Whitman insists that they are not origin-al:

> These are really the thoughts of all men in all ages and lands,
>     they are not original with me,
> If they are not yours as much as mine they are nothing, or next
>     to nothing,
> If they are not the riddle and the untying of the riddle they are
>     nothing,
> If they are not just as close as they are distant they are nothing.
>
> This is the grass that grows wherever the land is and the water
>     is,
> This is the common air that bathes the globe.
>
> (*LG*, 45)

There are at least two elements of this passage which deny that the self is center in *Leaves of Grass*. On the one hand, the self's thoughts and perceptions are similar to those of other men. The idea of the shared experiences of people is the basis of Whitman's theory of democracy. On the other hand, they are not a source, not a beginning, but rather are in common with "the thoughts of all men in all ages." They are part of an unending regression in history and of an infinite projection into the future. This "progress," of course, involves the shared response of all mankind. Identity or universality is dispersed historically by cultural repetition of different peoples in different ages.

Democracy is a crucial part of Whitman's vision of an "ideal" world. The United States, as a democracy, is unique because of the generosity of its members toward one another and toward nature. In "The Base of All Metaphysics" Whitman's vision of love, of generosity, as a fundamental principle of unity is very explicit:

> A word I give to remain in your memories and minds,
> As base and finalè too for all metaphysics.

[165]

Walt Whitman

> . . . underneath Christ the divine I see,
> The dear love of man for his comrade, the attraction of friend
>     to friend,
> Of the well-married husband and wife, of children and parents,
> Of city for city and land for land.
>
> (*LG*, 121)

Whitman can identify himself sympathetically with all people, including the suffering, because of this loving generosity. He is not repelled, by horror, into flight. He does not attempt to abstract what is into some aesthetic and manageable fiction such as a nostalgic love for "universal humanity."

The self is identified with the nation from the opening when Whitman asserts that America is the greatest poem. The journeys of these two continue on a parallel course throughout the poem. In "Europe," the earliest written poem of *Leaves,* America is portrayed as the phoenix:

> Suddenly out of its stale and drowsy lair, the lair of slaves,
> Like lightening it le'pt forth half startled at itself,
> Its feet upon the ashes and rags, its hands tight to the throats of
>     kings.
>
> (*LG*, 266)

The nation is a democracy and springs origin-less from ruins in this poem. Just like the self, the nation is causally disconnected from a firm base.

The poem is oriented toward an infinite future. Although the millenium, the forming of all peoples into one unit is a desirable goal, the exuberance and joy of the poem, ultimately, emerges from the unknown, the incredible, the not-yet-dreamed. Whitman uses the language of Western *telos*-oriented structures to go beyond the idea that the pursuit of a knowable end is a totally adequate mode of life. Universal democracy and love, then, is no more a final center for the poem than the self.

Furthermore, when in some of his later poems Whitman does consider the nature of the soil out of which America grows, it resembles the infinite regression behind the child-poet. In

[166]

"Song of the Exposition," Whitman strongly asserts the need to put the past in a proper perspective:

> To obey as well as command, to follow more than to lead,
> These are also the lessons of our New World;
> While how little the New after all, how much the Old, Old
> World!
>
> (*LG*, 196)

Whitman recognizes how the accomplishments and vastness of the past dwarf the merely present moment. "Passage to India" treats the same theme more explicitly:

> The Past—the dark unfathom'd retrospect!
> The teeming gulf—the sleepers and the shadows!
> The past—the infinite greatness of the past!
> For what is the present after all but growth out of the past?
> (As a projectile form'd, impell'd, passing a certain line, still
> keeps on,
> So the present, utterly form'd, impell'd by the past.)
>
> (*LG*, 411–12)

Not only is the individual "impelled" by the past, but "present" culture is denied autonomy. It is only one instant, one flourish in the vastness of history. The past, however, is an infinitude of time, a "teeming gulf," and not any firm basis. "The sleepers and shadows" echo the ruins of "Europe." This passage not only denies the status of "absolute" to the present moment, but also to the traditionally autonomous, certain, and therefore comforting concept of "presence." Derrida, in fact, argues that the traditional matrix of centrality "is the determination of being as *presence* in all senses of this word." "Presence," of course, is not merely what we perceive as present: "It could be shown that all the names related to fundamentals, to principles, or to the center have always designated an invariable presence."[31] Whitman denies the self, the nation, and the present world the role of constant. All of these phenomena share in structurality and are not free of the structurality itself. In other words, they cannot be centers.[32]

Walt Whitman

Not only, then, does the poetic treatment of democracy show why the self is not a center in the poem, but it deconstructs the idea of an ending for the nation and the poem. Since the United States and the self follow parallel tracks in the poem, we can find examples of the self acting exuberantly in the world without a well-defined sense of an ending.

The journey is the major metaphor which Whitman uses throughout *Leaves of Grass* to dramatize the self's freedom from the restrictions of a future goal which controls the present. "Song of the Open Road" is one of the major poems which develops this journey motif:

> Afoot and light-hearted I take to the open road,
> Healthy, free, the world before me,
> The long brown path before me leading wherever I choose.
>
> Henceforth I ask not good-fortune, I myself am good-fortune;
> Henceforth I whimper no more, postpone no more, need nothing,
> Done with indoor complaints, libraries, querulous criticisms,
> Strong and content I travel the open road.
>
> The earth, that is sufficient,
> I do not want the constellations any nearer,
> I know they are very well where they are,
> I know they suffice for those who belong to them.
>
> (*LG*, 149)

The journey is naturally oriented toward the future, but this particular journey is destined for no final point. The only "object" determining this trip is the will of the self and not some *telos* toward which all else must be directed. Without this goal, the self is "free." He can travel wherever he will, disregarding all old parts and all public roles:

> From this hour I ordain myself loos'd of limits and imaginary lines,
> Going where I list, my own master total and absolute,
> Listening to others, and considering well what they say,
> Pausing, searching, receiving, contemplating,

[168]

Walt Whitman

> Gently, but with undeniable will, divesting myself of the holds
> that would hold me.
>
> (LG, 151)

The journey begins by announcing freedom and by casting off all
that might restrict or predetermine. This does not deny the
shared or old since the self still loves the "public road," but it
adds the unforeseen possibilities to the future of the self.

The poem goes on as a celebration of complete freedom
which follows the divestment of bonds, of center:

> Allons! the inducements shall be greater,
> We will sail pathless and wild seas,
> We will go where winds blow, waves dash, and the Yankee
> clipper speeds by under full sail.
>
> Allons! with power, liberty, the earth, the elements,
> Health, defiance, gayety, self-esteem, curiosity,
> Allons! from all formules!
> From your formules, O bat-eyed and materialistic priests.
>
> (LG, 154–55)

The seas and roads are previously untried and the journey not determined by the end. Therefore, the "pathless and wild" often
present events which appear to be undesirable or threatening.
Whitman confronts many of these throughout "Song of the
Open Road." The major one is death; the second is change. Neither of these overcomes the exuberance permitted by total free
play as it does, for example, in the early Yeats. Whitman's first
response to death remains essentially unchanged. In "Song of
Myself," he sees it and accepts it as part of the natural process
and therefore of the journey:

> And as to you Death, and you bitter hug of mortality, it is idle
> to try to alarm me. . . .
>
> And as to you Corpse I think you are good manure, but that
> does not offend me, . . .
>
> And as to you Life I reckon you are the leavings of many
> deaths,

Walt Whitman

(No doubt I have died myself ten thousand times before.)

(*LG*, 87)

The cyclic idea of life and death in "Song of Myself" is fairly
traditional in the poem, and the proud tone of these lines continues until section six of "Crossing Brooklyn Ferry."[33] Whitman confesses that his solution to the questions of evil and death
trembles at times:

> It is not upon you alone the dark patches fall,
> The dark threw its patches down upon me also,
> The best I had done seem'd to me blank and suspicious,
> My great thoughts as I supposed them, were they not in reality
> meagre?

(*LG*, 162)

In these lines, Whitman's whole achievement as poet is shaken.
This poetic dark night is one of the risks he runs as poet journey-
ing freely without a firm center. He feels his imaginative and natural life threatened. Yet, in "Crossing Brooklyn Ferry," he finally
overcomes this anxiety and continues onward. He accepts his
recognition of the priority of diversity and nature; he is generous
to all, and thus can go on as a poet:

> We receive you with free sense at last, and are insatiate hence-
> forward,
> Not you any more shall be able to foil us, or withhold your-
> selves from us,
> We use you, and do not cast you aside—we plant you perma-
> nently within us,
> We fathom you not—we love you—there is perfection in you
> also,
> You furnish your parts toward eternity,
> Great or small, you furnish your parts toward the soul.

(*LG*, 165)

He recognizes even these crises as things in themselves, admits
their necessity as parts of the whole of existence, and adds his experience of them to his own multiple "self."

In "I Sit and Look Out," Whitman observes horror, disease,

and death, and yet he allows them: "All these—all the meanness and agony without end I sitting look out upon,/See, hear, and am silent" (*LG, 273*). He no longer protests against these things, which seem frightening. He accepts them as part of his living. This acceptance does not, however, imply that Whitman is now proof against the doubts and anxieties he sees in "Crossing Brooklyn Ferry." In "Out of the Cradle Endlessly Rocking," for example, written by Whitman upon the death of his brother, loss and "unsatisfied love" disrupt this acceptance. Despite its menace to his art and his security, Whitman examines the implications of death and grief, and then continues on his journey without a sense of despair or recourse to a god:

> O you singer solitary, singing by yourself, projecting me,
> O solitary me listening, never more shall I cease perpetuating you,
> Never more shall I escape, never more the reverberations,
> Never more the cries of unsatisfied love be absent from me,
> Never again leave me to be the peaceful child I was before what there in the night,
> By the sea under the yellow and sagging moon,
> The messenger there arous'd, the fire, the sweet hell within,
> The unknown want, the destiny of me.
>
> (*LG, 252*)

The self experiences the loss of the loved other but does not try to escape or lessen the sadness, the pain, or feeling of lack. In fact, the self calls out for the complete revelation of the "destiny":

> O give me the clew! (it lurks in the night here somewhere,)
> O if I am to have so much, let me have more!
>
> A word then, (for I will conquer it,)
> The word final, superior to all,
> Subtle, sent up—what is it?—I listen;
> Are you whispering it, and have been all the time, you sea-waves?
> Is that it from your liquid rims and wet sands?

[171]

Walt Whitman

Whereto answering, the sea,
Delaying not, hurrying not,
Whisper'd me through the night, and very plainly before day-
  break,
Lisp'd to me the low and delicious word death, . . .

(*LG,* 252)

He asks that the night, the darkness, the doubt, not hide any of
itself from him. He dares to ask for the revelation of annihilation
behind darkness. He is not attempting to protect the self from
the void. He prays to be "laved" by the word itself: "Death,
Death, Death, Death, Death" (*LG,* 252). The inevitability of
death is accepted, but now not merely intellectually. Death is totally revealed. Its truth "flames out" to use W.C. Williams'
image in "Tract"; it manifests itself fully. There is no retreat on
Whitman's part, no despair.

   Despite the impressive victory of "Out of the Cradle,"
however, Whitman's journey remains potentially horrible and
frustrating. In 1860, the year after "Out of the Cradle," the balance and harmony of unconsciousness tempts Whitman away
from confrontations with contingency:

   Me wherever life is lived, O to be self-balanced for contin-
     gencies,
   O to confront night, storms, hunger, ridicule, accidents, re-
     buffs, as the trees and animals do.

(LG, 11)

Needless to say, Whitman resists this temptation and continues
on his endless way. In other words, Whitman does not rest in a
poetic "victory" over the outside world and over time, both of
which threaten him in this poem. There is no sense of his poetry
or of his journey having come to an *end,* to a *conclusion* which
*sums up* the entire enterprise and contains it. There is no "concrete universal" in this poem. There is merely the continuing
process of discovering and creating along the way of Whitman's
daily encounters with things in the world. His poetic project is,
quite simply, a repetition of itself and of that of other poets.

[172]

Walt Whitman

For another crucial aspect of this journey-metaphor reveals the impossibility of ever reaching ultimate foundations, whether past or future. Whitman, of course, puts off all hope of doing so in "Song of Myself," and at other times he shows that any "center" is always beyond human reach. The best the self can do in any quest for a center is "to leap beyond" (*LG*, 77) and try to bring it nearer, although never into immediacy, into "presence." In "Song of Myself," just as the past is an infinite gulf, the future is an unending procession. Whatever appears at a given moment as a god, a *telos* or *arché,* is always actually hiding something more remote behind it:

> There is no stoppage and never can be stoppage,
> If I, you, and the worlds, and all beneath or upon their sur-
> faces, were this moment reduced back to a pallid float, it
> would not avail in the long run,
> We should surely bring up again where we now stand,
> And as surely go as much farther, and then farther and farther.
>
> A few quadrillions of eras, a few octillions of cubic leagues, do
> not hazard the span or make it impatient,
> They are but parts, anything is but a part.
>
> See ever so far, there is limitless space outside of that,
> Count ever so much, there is limitless time around that.
> (LG, 82–83)

The infinitude of space and time images the inaccessibility of finality. In fact, there is nothing which is not a part, nothing, that is, free of being part of the structure, nothing constant. The same idea appears in "A Song for Occupations":

> I do not affirm that what you see beyond is futile, I do not ad-
> vise you to stop,
> I do not say leadings you thought great are not great,
> But I say that none lead to greater than these lead to.
> (LG, 218)

Whitman does not stop the quest in despair; he advises pursuit, but he knows that beyond each object is another, *ad infinitum,*

[173]

and that none is "greater," that is, more free and independent than any of the more immediate. The ultimate goal always evades; the final center does not exist.

There is no further need to multiply examples of Whitman's deconstructions of the "center" and the language of presence. I must, though, show that Whitman's very Modern attitude modulates with the more traditional attitude toward the universe, that is, one which sees a center. There are essentially two ways in which this happens. These can be discussed more briefly than I did the lack of a center because Whitman's critics have made this aspect of *Leaves of Grass* more readily available.

Initially, it must be repeated that even from the beginning, god and transcendence are in *Leaves*. However, what I have already done shows, I think, how this theme, particularly in "Song of Myself," is more than counterbalanced by the unavailability of any center:

> I have said that the soul is not more than the body,
> And I have said that the body is not more than the soul,
> And nothing, not God, is greater to one than one's self is, . . .
>
> And I say to mankind, Be not curious about God,
> For I who am curious about each am not curious about God,
> (No array of terms can say how much I am at peace about God
>     and about death.)
>
> I hear and behold God in every object, yet understand God not
>     in the least,
> Nor do I understand who there can be more wonderful than
>     myself.
>
> Why should I wish to see God better than this day?
> I see something of God each hour of the twenty-four, and each
>     moment then,
> In the faces of men and women I see God, and in my own face
>     in the glass . . . .

(LG, 86–87)

In "Song of Myself," Whitman is conscious of divinity but unwilling to admit its absoluteness or even its superiority to self.

Walt Whitman

Furthermore, God's "divinity" is shared; it is de-centralized; it exists in human and natural objects. This is not pantheism, which sees god as coextensive with nature, but an attempt to banish god from human consideration as a goal. God exists only in the manifestations of things to people, to selves who are more wonderful than god.

Yet a transcendent presence does emerge in the poem, and there are at least two ways in which this presence emerges from Whitman's center-less world. The first occurs occasionally throughout Whitman's journey and usually demonstrates the poet's desire for a god when confronted by horror or anxiety. God appears to alleviate horror and suffering more and more often in the poems following the Civil War and "Drum-Taps."

In "Passage to India," this rather traditional reason for calling on a god blends with the second, which, in fact, emerges from Whitman's own free play. The last stanza of "Passages to India" demonstrates God in his role as guarantor of safety:

> Sail forth—steer for the deep waters only,
> Reckless O soul, exploring, I with thee, and thou with me,
> For we are bound where mariner has not yet dared to go,
> And we will risk the ship, ourselves and all.
>
> O my brave soul!
> O farther farther sail!
> O darling joy, but safe! Are they not all the seas of God?
> O farther, farther, farther sail!

> (LG, 421)

Significantly, the wild seas of the earlier poems are safe now since God has returned; the journey is without radical risk since the deep seas are God's, that is, are founded on a firm basis. This changed attitude toward risk is typical of some of the late poems. Earlier in the same poem, God is shown as the force which constantly recreates the universe:

> Thou pulse—thou motive of the stars, suns, systems,
> That, circling, move in order, safe, harmonious,
> Athwart the shapeless vastness of space,

[175]

Walt Whitman

> How should I think, how breathe a single breath, how speak,
>   if, out of myself,
> I could not launch, to those, superior universes?
>
> (LG, 419)

God, hovering over the shapeless universe, makes possible the journey into endless space.

The second reason for the appearance of God so frequently in these last poems results from the idea of free play itself. The self, once it achieves its own identity, that is, the unity of body and soul, goes on an endless journey through the universe acquiring experience directly and vicariously by sympathetic identification. When the self confronts God in "Passage to India," it swells itself to the sublime vastness of the infinite to "cope" with God:

> Swiftly I shrivel at the thought of God,
> As Nature and its wonders, Time and Space and Death,
> But that I, turning, call to thee O soul, thou actual Me,
> And lo, thou gently masterest the orbs,
> Thou matest Time, smilest content at Death,
> And fillest, swellest full the vastnesses of Space.
>
> (LG, 419)

All experience accretes in the self to infinitude so that it becomes a homologue of God. In Georges Poulet's terms, the self brings the infinite exterior into the endless spaces of the interior and fills the self until it becomes the equal of God, until it achieves a *totum simul*.[34] The self comes to hold all simultaneously just as God does. In this capability, the poet is "The true Son of God" (*LG*, 416).

In these later developments in Whitman's poetry and vision, the free play and exuberance continue to exist, but now contradictorily with a feeling of certitude. God and self are equivalents; they are "centers" in the late verse as they are not earlier in *Leaves of Grass*. The earlier analogy of the poet and spider is denied:

[176]

Walt Whitman

A noiseless patient spider,
I mark'd where on a little promontory it stood isolated,
Mark'd how to explore the vacant vast surrounding,
It launch'd forth filament, filament, filament, out of itself,
Ever unreeling them, ever tirelessly speeding them.

And you O my Soul where you stand,
Surrounded, detached, in measureless oceans of space,
Ceaselessly musing, venturing, throwing, seeking the spheres
   to connect them,
Till the bridge you will need be form'd, till the ductile anchor
   hold,
Till the gossamer thread you fling catch somewhere, O my
   Soul.

(LG, 450).

There is no more uncertain extension into the void; the self is now firmly anchored and the bridge is more substantial than mere filament. There is no risk once a god makes sailing safe and once the self discovers itself the equivalent of god containing all experience.

Many critics, like Martz, complain of the decline of Whitman's late poetry. It not only becomes "abstract assertion," but it becomes in some ways fraudulent. The existence of a center denies absolute free play as Derrida argues. The strained assertion of the late poems is a result of the loss of complete free play. Whitman maintains the tonal exuberance, but the real excitement of the early poetry is lost because the enticing "risk" of playing without a center is missing.

III

Whitman's *Leaves of Grass* and his various prose Prefaces provide important poetic evidence of the inadequacy of the entire New Critical description of the tradition of American, and especially Modern American poetry. Whitman writes poetry of the first order which does not fit the spatialized preconceptions of ironic form. The openness of his poetry, its process, its refusal of strict "aesthetic" boundaries, makes it a threat to the New Critical sense of order and tradition through which the ironists cover-up the temporal nature of poetry and reading. Whitman "begins" an American tradition not by articulating in verse the "visionary" program Emerson imagines and, thus, making it available to succeeding poets. Rather, Whitman presents the American poets who come after him with the re-discovery of that temporality, of essential poetic "generosity" toward nature and the self which does not attempt to reify both these objects along preconceived and predetermined lines.

In summary, I think it can be said that Whitman provides essentially two fundamental possibilities to American poetry: first, the possibility of re-newing the tradition by turning it against itself so that what it obscures can be re-discovered and re-vitalized as an issue of human interest; second, *Leaves of Grass* suggests a nominalistic aesthetic and theory of language which requires each poet to look for himself, to go back himself to the thing itself and not be satisfied with the words which have built up in tradition to "re-present" those things. No major American poet since Whitman has not manifested both of these interests, but Wallace Stevens appears to be paradigmatic of those—including the Eliot of *The Waste Land* and *The Four Quartets*—who have extended the first possibility to an extreme. Stevens, as my next chapter will show, breaks open hardened past forms and frustrates the habitual responses associated with those forms to reveal the fundamentally fictional nature of all poetic statement. Stevens, like the Rousseau described by de Man in *Blindness and Insight,* is totally aware of the fact that language rests upon nothingness. "Fiction" merely offers itself as the illusion of a presence "covering" this abyss of emptiness underlying poetry and everything else.[35]

Charles Olson, on the other hand, although interested in destroying the tradition, hopes to articulate the issues it covers-up in a language drawn from another lexicon, from those men

and civilizations, like the Maya, that Western tradition has failed
to examine authentically. For Olson, the key to poetic authenticity is the second possibility Whitman reveals. Olson's language
can be an alternative to the reified New Critical tradition and to
the bourgeois "pejoracracy" only because it is nominalistic.
Words do not exist prior to things for Olson. He cannot accept
"hearsay" or the "idle talk" of the crowd. Like the historian
Herodotus, Olson feels he must go out beyond the veil of "discourse," the accepted linguistic equivalents of things, to the
things themselves.

The next two chapters will develop these ideas regarding
each of these poets. Compared to Whitman, whose own values
and attitudes are ambiguous, their achievements seem extreme
and much more "Modern"—even, perhaps, Postmodern. Yet,
Whitman is a pioneer. He re-discovers the way. He finds for
American poetry the stance toward the past which is really
directed to the future. He suggests the fruitful imaginative use of
the American continent and its awesome physical newness. He
insists upon the absolute and devoted attention to the world first
and to the Word last which has helped to move American poetry
away from the barren logocentric tradition of metaphysics to a
more temporal poetics of discovery.

# Chapter Five

# Fiction, Risk, and Deconstruction: The Poetry of Wallace Stevens

"Fiction" is, of course, one of the most crucial elements of Wallace Stevens' poetry and poetics. Despite the critical attention which it receives, no one has commented upon its radical implications for Stevens and for Modern poetry in general. In *Opus Posthumous,* Stevens emphasizes his vision of the world and of all interpersonal and intrapersonal relations as fiction: "The transition from make believe for one's self to make believe for others is the beginning, or the end, of poetry in the individual." [1] Not only is the self and the other defined as fiction, but "empirical reality" is seen to be finally devoid of transcendent certitude; in the last measure, we are left with nothing but "fiction": "The final belief is to believe in a fiction, which you know to be a fiction, there being nothing else" (*OP,* 163).

Although these "Adagia" are largely undatable and may stem from Stevens' late period, this idea of "fiction" exists throughout his poetry from *Harmonium.* His titles clearly show that he thought of even his early poetry as "fiction": *"Metaphors* of a Magnifico," "Earthy *Anecdote,"* "The *Apostrophe* to Vincetine," *"Fabliau* of Florida" (my italics).

While all readers admit at least implicitly that literature is in some way "fiction," there is little if any agreement on what this means and implies. The argument usually divides along two lines. On the one hand, the worshippers of the constitutive imagination would have it that "reality" is the result of perception transformed by self into a coherent order which might take many forms. In its severest forms, this results in *Symboliste* works which are so personal and impenetrable that they appear the products of virtually solipsistic minds. On the other hand, the "realists" discount the independence of the imagination from so-called empirical reality which is "out-there." In its purest forms, this leads to photographic realism which is committed to the primacy of matter over mind. And, of course, the *Symbolistes,* like the Modern ironists epitomized by Brooks, are rebelling against realism and naturalism for complex reasons.

Because of his own propensity to use the language of this tradition, Stevens' critics discuss his concept of "fiction" in exactly these terms. Scholars ignore the truly radical notion at the "center" of his "fiction," keep him in the mainstream of the Romantic and dualistic metaphysical tradition, and obscure his most salient Modern characteristics.

Roy Harvey Pearce's fine essays on Stevens are paradigms of this problem.[2] Although Pearce defines himself in opposition to the New Critics, his language of continuity keeps him in essentially the same tradition. Pearce begins from the assumption that Stevens continues in the tradition of Romantic and American dualism and proceeds to argue that he brings it to culmination by achieving a kind of Kantian synthesis which posits reality in a "third term": the conjunction of self and outside world in an active perception of empirical reality:

> Thus the world in which Stevens' history unfolds is one characterized above all by an extreme vision . . . of that radical opposition which has obsessed so many major American poets. It is the opposition between the poetic and antipoetic—between the self (or in Stevens' more usual terms, the imagination, or the mind) and a reality which is not part of that self but must be brought into its purview, composed, and so (as it were) re-created.[3]

Wallace Stevens

The developmental metaphor of nineteenth century organicism and positivism dominates Pearce's discussion of Stevens. He sees Stevens' career as a movement from a clear beginning to a definite end which achieves synthesis and thereby eliminates the tensions which the unresolved conflict arouses. Pearce concludes that in Stevens' final poetry "the Imagination may be defined as at once the use which the Reason makes of the material world and the use which the material world makes of the Reason."[4]

Pearce is certainly not alone in maintaining this position. Bernard Heringman, in "Wallace Stevens: The Use of Poetry," argues that for Stevens, "the final development of the fictive process" is a synthesis, an intersection of reality and imagination. Poetry for Stevens is a "means of escape from reality, a means of ordering the chaos of reality, a means of finding a good in reality." This constitutes, according to Heringman, "a shift toward the *center, toward the balancing point* between the two members of the dichotomy."[5]

These two essays are typical of two streams of Modern criticism. The Romantic desire both for synthesis by dialectic and for the developmental metaphor underlie the perspective which causes these critics to look for a "final" position in Stevens. The New Critical influence allows them to *see* this "final" stage as a *telos* which completes the activity of the poet and, ironically (that is, by means of a pervasively ironic stance), reduces tension and existential anxiety as well in a "balancing point" of *stasis*. However, as I have pointed out in chapter one, Paul de Man's readings of Nietzsche's destruction of the metaphysical tradition lets the myth of development, progress, and *telos* emerge in its Being as fictional discourse. Nietzsche shows that discursive structures "centered" around metaphors of evolution and generation contain no priority within themselves. The concepts of beginning and end function, as Derrida argues,[6] as "centers" which are variations of the myth of presence.

Joseph Riddel's critique of Helen Vendler's *On Extended Wings* shows the effects of this "blindness" in reading Stevens which results from the dialectical, New Critical bias, that is,

[183]

from the pervasively ironic stance of formalist criticism of Modern texts: "Mrs. Vendler insists that Stevens' long poems, like his long career as a poet, reveal a dialectical dissolve that gathers beginning into end in a select harvest of poems not only seeking but achieving purity." Mrs. Vendler wants Stevens' poetry to have not only a "teleological refinement," but also, echoing both Brooks and I.A. Richards, "internal resolutions" so that " 'poetry can save us.' " [7] In his last stage, according to Vendler, Stevens "has gone beyond crying out to Jerusalem, beyond crying out even to a living name or place or thing, beyond all directed cries at all. Utterance is utterance, and the exertion to make it something more has disappeared." [8] Vendler's view of Stevens' poems as circles gathering "beginning into end" and apotheosizing themselves as Absolute Images of verbal purity is the result of a circular argument which stems from the sedimented, reified, covered-over habits of reading Modern texts from a New Critical point of view.

As I have suggested in chapter one, Heidegger demonstrates that "interpretation" is a structure of "understanding" and, therefore, that it is "projective," that is, fore-sightful and fore-having. Thus, all interpretation, whether it be the primordial articulation of what is ready-at-hand and disclosed to understanding in Being-in-the-World, or the derived mode of direct assertion, is necessarily "circular." However, since the "ontological circle" of interpretation is not the vicious circle of logic and first principles, Vendler, like the New Critics, is mistaken in attempting to avoid the circle. Rather, the problem becomes one of *getting into the circle in the right way* (*BT*, 27–28; 193–95; 362–64). For Heidegger the authentic way into the circle must be phenomenological, i.e., not coercive and teleological, but rather a "letting" the entity disclose itself from itself as a phenomenon. The similarity between such phenomenological interpretation and "phenomenological destruction" (*BT*, 63) demands that historiological interpretation, such as literary criticism, be seen by critics as destructive. As I argued in chapter two, insofar as a poem is discourse and therefore is interpretation, a projection of Being-in-the-World, it too must be recognized as destructive.

[184]

Wallace Stevens

Ironic criticism, which in its desire for infinitude and godlike hovering tries to deny what Kierkegaard calls "actuality" and Heidegger "existence," naturally cannot help but be blind to the interpretive, i.e., destructive, aspects of poetic discourse and structure. Its traditional metaphysical dualistic myth which is often the ground of more particular "fictions" of presence—self, transcendence, intuition, finality, center—is itself the frequent object of the destructive discourse, not only of Whitman, but of that archetypal "ironist," Wallace Stevens, as well.

Riddel bases his criticism of Vendler on certain generalities about Heidegger's destruction of onto-theological metaphysics and on Derrida's interpretation of Heidegger and others in "Structure, Sign, and Play in the Discourse of the Human Sciences." Although Riddel is restricted by the format of a review-article, he is able, nonetheless, to turn traditional discourse back upon Vendler just as Stevens turns it back upon itself. Riddel attacks Vendler's Romantic notions of *arché* and *telos* and concludes in opposition to Vendler that "there is no more a consummated arrival in later Stevens than there was a meaningful departure in the earlier."[9] Stevens, Riddel argues, uses poetry to scrutinize its own origins until he finds that at the "center" of poetry and all reality there is no "presence":

> For in both his poetry and his prose, Stevens is engaged in an "act" of decreation, one dimension of which is the turning of language, and in certain instances a familiar or even banal concept back upon itself, by way of pursuing some origin at the heart of utterance—or to put it in terms of one of his poems, to seek the unspoken word of the "central poem" that is at once proved and disproved (and thus displaced) by "lesser poems." In short Stevens seems to sense a presence at the origin, a discoverable presence, but every penetration to that presence only reveals that the place is a fiction, an interpretation, and thus not an ultimate or supreme or central poem but only another lesser poem.[10]

In language, which is perhaps more immediate in the context of Heidegger, Riddel's claims may be interpreted by saying that Stevens is aware that all discourse is interpretation, that is,

[185]

fiction, and that this fundamental truth is obscured by the reification of certain concepts into a pattern of habits, a "natural standpoint." Like Heidegger, Stevens senses the necessity for all interpretation which hopes to redeem the truth of fiction and nonhabitual, nonmythic ways of confronting "Not Ideas about the Thing But the Thing Itself," to be violent, destructive, discoverings of Being and of the original "truth" (in Heidegger's sense of *aletheia,* of course) which is lost in the now solidified linguistic assertions about what in the past originally dis-closed itself.

Riddel's seems a very reasonable description of Stevens' poems, especially of those which employ the primary metaphors of quest, journey, and meditation. Although the poems seem, as Pearce and Vendler testify, to progress to a final point of formal integration and philosophical harmony, they actually bring into question the centrality of such concepts as these as well as such formal achievements. The problem with Riddel's essay, however, is his literal usage of the metaphor of discovery. He would have it that Stevens really searches for a "center" in his poetry and ultimately finds that nothing is there:

> It is a search, of course, that must repeatedly bring into question all other centers, and thus all myths, and ultimately bring into question the idea of center itself, until in the centerless center of imaginative activity, of the poem speaking itself, we understand the significance of the poetry of "play," the freedom of its activity within the space of language.[11]

In maintaining this position, however, Riddel is inconsistent. Had he carried to completion the insight that this poetry scrutinizes itself by looking for its origins, he would recognize that the very metaphor of search, which he employs to describe Stevens' works, is also being turned back upon itself. It is by virtue of the awareness that there is no center that Stevens is able to rethink specific centered myths and metaphors and show them to be fiction in a radical sense in the early poetry. The rethinking of the quest-search metaphor and its decentering is perhaps clearest in "The Comedian as the Letter C" which I shall discuss later.

It can be said now, however, that Stevens does not learn by a failed quest for a center that center and therefore quest are meaningless. Rather, he actively employs the *telos*-oriented quest metaphor against itself not merely to show that there is no center but to test in fiction various poetic and personal myths and metaphors in a world with no firm point of reference. Herein lies the radical risk of Stevens' poetry.

Although he knows from the beginning that there is nothing at the "center" and consequently that all is "fiction," he nonetheless writes poems, creates "fictions." To do so, he avails himself of all that he has as a person and as a poet. He marshals one metaphor, belief, and interpretation after another in tests of value of received and acquired "truths." He does this in order to destroy their hardened existence, to discard what is now useless and obscuring, and to release what had long ago disclosed itself and become the origin of the particular myth or metaphor.

He de-centers and destroys the various structures which had acclimated man in the world and which had covered over his previous existentiality and finitude as well as the actual metaphoricity of his linguistic structures. Poetically, Stevens goes beyond experiencing the anxiety and dread which results from confronting the world stripped of what makes it human. He risks the linguistic structures and tropes which had anthropomorphized and reified disclosure. He frees poetry's possibilities by breaking away from the traditional "poetry" at-home in the inherited language and structures of a metaphysical "tradition."

Harold Bloom argues that in the American poetic dialectic "Freedom," which for Emerson is "Newness," "Influx," and "Wildness," *is* the nature of the "Poet" himself. Yet "Fate," which might be called "Destiny" or "necessity," limits Freedom, so that the poet must settle for second best, the "surprise" afforded by the "pathos of power" (*WS*, 3, 6). Here is Bloom on the interplay of Freedom, Fate, and Power as he prepares his meditation on Stevens:

> Fate is a reseeing series of tropes, but Power is a reaiming. Fate is taboo, but Power is transcendence. In between, in the realm

of Freedom or meaning, revision is neither a reseeing nor a
reaiming but only a re-estimating, and such freedom to esteem
again is neither taboo nor transcendence but transgression, or
the threshold-state proper. (*WS*, 17)

Within his general theory of poetry and criticism and given
his special sense of Emersonianism, that is, of American repression, we are not surprised when we find Bloom announcing that
Stevens' poetry can be most profitably read as a series of tropes
and crossings resting on the "anxiety of influence." Stevens is
taken up into the Bloomian apparatus and the significance of his
poetry is restricted to the realm of Gnostic subjectivity: "Freedom or the second chance, the saving blend of Vocation and
Temperament, has been discovered in the dance of substitutions,
not in the substitutions themselves" (*WS*, 22). As I have already
suggested, this "free play" of substitution upon a given ground
which limits that free play is an aspiration to godhead, as one can
see by reading Cleanth Brooks through the achievement of
Heidegger and Kierkegaard. It is an aestheticization of poetry
which, of course, denies to poets and poetry the cognitive power
of the critical will. But, as the case of Riddel's fine essay makes
clear, and as de Man generally argues, the poet precedes the critic
in his belated demystification or revisionism. This is certainly
true in the case of the relation between Bloom and Stevens. Although I will not attempt to specify all of the ways Stevens'
poetry preempts Bloom, I will suggest both that Stevens begins
with a more complex sense of the issues at stake in reducing
poetry to the free play of substitutions resting on a sure
ground—Stevens, unlike Bloom, seriously questions his own
"first idea"—and that Stevens' poetry is often a destruction of the
sublime as Bloom describes it.

It is not accidental that Bloom chooses to describe Stevens'
"sublime" in metaphors of "hovering" which are central to New
Critical ironic and aesthetic plays for power: "There is a Sublime
chill in *Of Mere Being,* but there is also an increasing or heighten-
ing that is of the nature of the American Sublime" (*WS*, 374).

Wallace Stevens

Stevens continually deconstructs privileged metaphors of presence related to these figures of height and sublimity. He turns toward these traditional figures to demystify them so that he can use them to dis-close "truth," rather than either being used by them or misusing them merely in the service of the subjective powers of an aggressive defense.

Stevens' problem is analogous to Kierkegaard's. How, when language has been usurped by the ironists and positivists, by the reifers and coercers, can an artist hope to use language without being himself mastered by that language and the interpretations embedded within it? How to repeat and not simply replicate? His answer, like Kierkegaard's, is to use mastered irony as a weapon in destruction. Proceeding from the disclosure of fiction—which my analysis of "The Snow Man" will develop more fully— Stevens is free of the coercive genealogical myth of progress and the aesthetic myth of ironic hovering. Consequently, his "tests" of various tropes and metaphors against the absence of center to reveal what is still positive and redeemable within the sedimented tradition are, as Kierkegaard says of Goethe, ways of "making his existence as a poet congrue with his actuality. . . . The truth is that the particular poetic production is simply a moment" (*CI*, 337). Thus, the result of phenomenological destruction and interpretation is a return to actuality, to an acknowledgment of Being-in-the World as a fundamental temporal constituent structure of Dasein. Since the poet is free to blast away the "aesthetic" interpretations in language by "re-thinking" the "centers" and revealing their Being as fiction, he performs and discloses movements which are possible only in the medium of life and not in art. He does not dualistically cordon off World from Word in a reversal of the ironists' position; rather, he dis-covers the inevitable being of language as human act, what Heidegger calls both *logos* (*legein*) and *Rede,* as occurring in-the-World and existing as the agency to let phenomena appear as such in themselves and from themselves (cf. *BT,* 55–58). Both poetic and critical activity have such discourse as their ontological ground.

"The Snow Man" is the earliest certain demonstration of

[189]

Wallace Stevens

Stevens' knowledge of the nothingness at the heart of fiction. The poem reveals two attitudes toward nothingness; it rejects one and accepts the other as primordial and original:

> One must have a mind of winter
> To regard the frost and the boughs
> Of the pine-trees crusted with snow;
>
> And have been cold a long time
> To behold the junipers shagged with ice,
> The spruces rough in the distant glitter
>
> Of the January sun; and not to think
> Of any misery in the sound of the wind,
> In the sound of a few leaves,
>
> Which is the sound of the land
> Full of the same wind
> That is blowing in the same bare place
>
> For the listener, who listens in the snow,
> And, nothing himself, beholds
> Nothing that is not there and the nothing that is.[12]

The poem works in essentially two movements. The first requires the reduction of the perceiving self to the point where he can see Nature without the intruding veil of a symbol or a correspondence which metaphorically transforms the other into an appendage of the self. The second movement, culminating in the last stanza, describes the new way in which the self beholds the other after becoming "nothing himself." He sees "Nothing that is not there . . ."; he can no longer impose human emotion, "any misery," on "the sound of the wind." Generally speaking, the poem has destroyed the pathetic fallacy. In fact, the nature of perception itself is changed. The pointed repetition of "behold" in lines five and fourteen emphasizes the change.

In the state *prior* to the reduction traced in this poem, "the listener" could only respond to the nothingness which exists by making it meaningful, by adding to it a sense of depth which makes it less "other." He refuses to let the "other" stand as it really is, as a mystery he cannot understand. He demonstrates no "Negative Capability," but, instead, transforms the "other" into something possessing "human" qualities, that is, readily interpretable along the lines of habitual, anthropocentric patterns of expectation which reflect the "listener's" own image back upon his senses. As a result, man as "the listener"—of course, an extremely ironic name since he no more listens to the wind as such than any systematizer allows an incongruent detail to disrupt the order of his grand scheme—cannot consciously "see" "the nothing that is" in which all of "what-is" exists. Whitman's horizonal vista is closed to the listener.

The first attitude to the external world obscures "truth" and maintains a comforting delusion. After reduction, the listener "beholds" more clearly that his pathetic identification with a seemingly concrete other is a fiction at the root of which lies "nothing." As well, he learns of a more profound relation between himself and the other. He is "nothing himself," that is, he is ontologically identical with the other insofar as they are both part of "what-is" existing in and by virtue of "nothing." Just as Sartre's Roquentin knows that the nausea is at the base of his own being as well as that of the chestnut tree in the public garden, the listener—finally properly named—recognizes the universality of the "nothing that is." He senses the falsity of the dualistic separation of *res cogitans* and *res extensa* and sees the primordiality of Being-in-the-World, alongside the World, as a structure of his own Being.

This poem reveals the untruth, the illusion, the fiction of all attitudes toward reality which ignore the nothingness at their base, their center. It suggests, for example, that the idea of the self, of the individual, is a fiction, a metaphor; reduction shows the listener to be "nothing himself." When fictions are demystified and the questor pierces to the center, he finds nothing. Stevens knows this and he risks the soothing concepts of the transforming sympathetic imagination and of the unique self to demonstrate it. He reveals that even these highly valued, yet unexamined, ideas or myths conceal the nothing which lies at the

## Wallace Stevens

heart of all utterance. In fact, this poem, as an *ars poetica,* shows
how literally poetry, linguistic discourse of the highest order, is a
metaphysical fiction based on nothing. It might be called, from a
traditional perspective, an "anti-poem" since it militates against
the naming of the center. Unlike all poems which might be written by anyone analogous to the listener before his reduction, this
one refuses analogy, metaphor, and correspondence to define
what the poem "really" or "finally" reveals. That is to say, the
poem is not even an allegory of the failure to name the center.
"The Snow Man" shows that all poems have nothingness at their
center and that other poems and poets, unconscious of this, while
delusively trying to name the center and thus to obscure the
nothing of what is, always disclose the omnipresence of mere
metaphor in poetry. This "anti-poem" is thus the archetypal
poem—if such a paradox may be invoked here. It presents itself
as an already deconstructed fiction. It not only acknowledges that
nothingness as "center" is the "source" of all poetry, but that it
is also the "origin" of all allegorical interpretation as well. This
means not only that all such interpretation is radically ungrounded and vulnerable, but that it has actively tried to forget
its own "source" in the *Ab-grund* of nothing.

As I have already suggested in my discussion of Whitman,
Derrida illustrates perfectly for my purposes here how the illusion of a centered structure provides a reassuring certitude by offering, as it were, a still point which identifies all the play of differences in the turning world of text and Being. The reader who
interprets not allegorically but destructively exchanges a *Grund*
for an *Ab-grund.* He *interests* himself in the metaphoricity of existence, refuses to hide behind aesthetic disinterest and systematization and, in fact, counterposes all he inherits, all he has—
myth, truth, and value—against the abyss of metaphor, of absence which is the being of the poem. This risk results from
being implicated in the game and it defines Stevens' difference
from the unmastered ironists. He exposes conventional and personal myths and beliefs to a poetic procedure radically "rooted"
in nothing.

[192]

## Wallace Stevens

The element of risk is critically underestimated in Stevens because his tone is not rhetorically sublime nor hysterical over loss. Yeats knows that "center cannot hold" and he shouts to us that "the blood-dimmed tide is loosed" and that "the ceremony of innocence is drowned" as he evokes the horrific, yet potentially pleasing sights and sounds of apocalypse. Stevens' interpretations of human fictions are metaphorical meditations upon their potential value for humanity as a way of becoming aware of the radical precariousness of absence which lies concealed behind each structure. Although his tone is quieter than that of Yeats and others, and consequently the degree of his risk is unrecognized, as "The Snow Man" shows, Stevens is willing to decenter even the most assuring myths of self, of the ability of poetry to reach some final position which will give it a unique value, and of the comforting aesthetic possibility of reading a poem simply as a narrative allegory of its own failed, fictional nature.

As Derrida points out, the absence of the center allows a greater amount of free play. No idea or metaphor is any longer an unquestioned value around which all else revolves. For Stevens this means that no element of the tradition, no relation to reality, no metaphysical or ironic strategy, can be left unexamined and be accepted in an unqualified way. In effect, then, Stevens' poetry is a process of meditative thinking like that of Heidegger in Gelassenheit, which re-interprets previous interpretations of Being following the "projection" of nothing which "The Snow Man" makes so explicit as the "fore-having" of Stevens' understanding. It is also a proleptic meditation; it anticipates and prevents all attempts to allegorize it by always asserting its own self-evident, metaphorically discontinuous status.

Stevens' poetry concentrates thematically on the way in which these interpretations emerge from a human's, that is, *Dasein*'s, Being-in-the-World. His poems engage the traditional metaphysical language of the dualistic imagination-reality conflict to destroy it; such destruction, of course, is not merely a privative function, but an attempt to regain whatever is positive within the tradition. He allows what the tradition covers up to

[193]

emerge primordially. This is the pervasive concern of his art. It
assumes many variations as Stevens deals with one major motif
after another. For example, his earliest book of poetry adopts the
language and attitude of the English decadents and some of the
French symbolists, and his style shows a corresponding lushness
and hypersensuality. Stevens turns his poetry against this early
achievement in such explicit poems as "Farewell to Florida."
This poem does not stand in a merely ironic and timeless relation
to what precedes; it does not embody suspended choices the poet
refuses to make. As a change, a seized-upon possibility in which
the "act of the mind," the poem, in the moment corresponds to
the life of the poet, it marks a movement away from his "aesthetic" stage. Although "A Farewell to Florida" is a rather obvious statement of his decision to abandon the fictions of *Harmonium* by abandoning the lush imagery and rhythms of death
and beauty, it points to the more sophisticated methods of re-interpretation like "The Comedian as the Letter C."

In his more ambitious long poems, there is a process of re-
thinking a traditional situation and language so that the potential
of the given idea may be heard and made newly manifest. Formally, these long poems employ traditional structural devices in
which the poet *might* think. The poem is not "made" to work itself out according to an idea conceived in advance. Rather, in the
process of developing the poem, the poet rarely brings the form
to the kind of fruition which its poetic lineage would lead a
reader—even an ironical one—to expect. The poems refuse all
sense of finality or simple reversal. Instead, they remain open to
whatever may appear as the poem itself subverts habitual structures and expectations.

"The Comedian as the Letter C" is the best early example of
Stevens' deconstructive poetry. The poem is modelled on teleological structures centered upon metaphors of genetics and quest,
more specifically, on the Wordsworthian model of the growth of
the poet's mind. Like Marcel Proust, the young Wordsworth,
having *lived through* the experiences of *The Prelude,* having *learned*
that "spiritual Love acts not nor can exist/ Without Imagina-

tion," [13] writes *The Prelude* with the end in mind as a goal for the poem, a *telos* known from the beginning. Just as the experience and knowledge gained by the end of the poem prepares Wordsworth to write the poem which we read, so the sudden illumination the ending affords to the reader of the rest of the poem and of its organization and guiding impulse betrays that the poem has not been allowed to emerge from the process of creation, from itself, but has been throughout written from the end to correspond with a *final* concept arrived at beforehand in Book XIV.

In his masterful *Natural Supernaturalism,* M. H. Abrams, in a chapter knowingly entitled, "The Idea of '*The Prelude,*' " reaches the same conclusion:

> In the course of *The Prelude* Wordsworth repeatedly drops the clue that his work has been designed to round back to its point of departure. . . . *The Prelude,* then, is an involuted poem which is about its own genesis—a prelude to itself. Its structural end is its own beginning; and its temporal beginning, as I have pointed out, is Wordsworth's entrance upon the stage of his life at which it ends. The conclusion goes on to specify the circular shape of the whole. [14]

Other versions of such teleological structures abound both in the Romantic Tradition and in the Modern movement. In Romantic poetry a similar impulse is to be found in the quest figures of the *Solitary* (*The Excursion,* Bk. II) [15] and of Shelley's *Alastor.* In both poems, the questors urge themselves on toward an Absolute; they are never satisfied with nor do they meaningfully confront what is ready-at-hand. They try instead to pierce the penetralium and cannot rest, as Keats first pointed out about Coleridge, in Negative Capability. They need a visionary goal, an end which will be a *final* truth or idea toward which they can read and write comfortably, secure in the knowledge that they have found or will find the still-point outside the game. Of course, both Wordsworth and Shelley frustrate the quests of their personae and return them harshly, in death, to the World of the here and now, to a confrontation with the unintelligible. Yet, in *Alastor,* there is a specific tone of regret that it is poetically necessary to show that the desired vision is not in the World and that one who devotes himself wholly to it must inevitably fail in the embrace of death.

In both poems, the questors' goal is an Absolute, Infinite Image which, especially in the case of Alastor, is "aesthetic" or "ironic" in Kierkegaard's sense of the terms. In *The Excursion,* the Solitary's momentary vision of a "mighty city" (l. 835) is so painfully pleasurable that he longs to die. Of course, his death-wish is immediately and subtly undercut by the actual death of the "Sufferer," (ll. 890–95) and the efficacy of the Solitary's Imaged Ideal is reduced. At the same time, however, as the vision is qualified by death, it becomes more desirable. It offers a flawless, Absolute, Infinite "World" of *stasis* and beauty where there is no death because there is no life. In other words, as Image, the vision is a *telos* for the persona, which the poem shows is "possible" only in art and not in life, in a finite World.

In *Alastor,* of course, the young questor becomes dissatisfied with the variety and beauty of the World and of human thought, and, as a result, as Shelley says in the "Preface" to the poem, "He *images* to himself the Being whom he loves." The picture of this Being is composed from all the wisdom, poetry, and philosophy the young man can gather and "The Poet is represented as uniting these requisitions, and attaching them to a single *image.*" Unable to find in the World or to project upon it the equivalent of the Absolute aesthetic Image he has created, Alastor dies: "He seeks in vain for a prototype of his conception. Blasted by his disappointment, he descends to an untimely grave." [16]

We can draw from Abrams' "interpretation" of this basic quest-journey structure of various Romantic texts—poetic and philosophical—some of the fundamental issues, values, and facts which are at stake in the imaginative exercise of this discursive structure. The metaphorical model of this form is, of course, "biological genesis, growth, and development" which the Romantics conceive "as a circuitous journey back home" (*NS,* 191). This metaphor becomes a clearly defined plot: "the painful education through ever expanding knowledge of the conscious subject as it strives . . . to win its way *back* to a *higher* mode of the *original unity* with itself from which, by its primal act of consciousness, it has inescapably divided itself off" (*NS,* 190–91. My italics.) In purely literary terms, this movement "tends to be imagined in the story form of a *Bildungsreise* whose end is its own beginning" (*NS,* 191). The teleological organization of this structure is designed to move both the questor and the reader of the text away from the disintegrated, vacuous uncanniness (*Unheimlichkeit,* "not-at-home-ness") of this fallen world of metaphorical difference, *back* to a mythic state of unity which is concealed by "consciousness." The *cogito,* in the classical Cartesian heritage of German Idealism, separates us from the extended world and its correspondences; this dissociation of the sensibility divides us from our home, our true center and goal to which we must return. We must come again into the "presence" of this "higher integration" (*NS,* 193), and transcend our "fallen state."

Although as Abrams points out, and as the *Solitary* and *Alastor* make clear, many writers qualify this "fortunate fall." When they realize that "the goal is an infinite one which lies forever beyond the reach of man, whose possibilities are limited by the conditions of a finite world," they are often willing to substitute "approximation for attainment, making success in life depend on man's sustaining his infinite aspiration throughout the course of his finite existence" (*NS,* 194–95). In other words, when confronted by the essential failure of a circular, teleological strategy to return them to the original presence of the center, they adjust their desires in the face of what many Freudian critics of Romanticism call the "reality principle." Rather than radically examine the assumptions behind their projection of a return, they compromise to accommodate their vision. Thus, in the moment of their greatest "insight," that is, of the necessary failure of the quest form, they are, as de Man would put it, necessarily "blind" to it. Their works show but they cannot see that their end-oriented structure reveals the absence of a center and that it performs its own destruction, that is, it manifests itself as a "fiction," as an "interpretation" determined beforehand by the "fore-sight" that there "is" a "center" out of the game. By destroying the Romantics' own and their descendents' view of the structure, de-struction, that is, phenomenologically interpretive art, can reveal what habit has covered over, what the quest motif proves despite its users' desires—that you cannot go home again, because there is no home to go to.

In Wallace Stevens' "The Comedian as the Letter C," Crispin strives for such a *telos,* such a return. The poem possesses the same basic structure of quest and growth as the Romantic poems I have mentioned. However, neither the poem nor Crispin arrives at a vision or an end to his "growth." Furthermore, unlike Wordsworth and Shelley, Stevens is not satisfied merely to describe a frustrated quest and to suggest the "opposition" between the desired image and the real world. Stevens actually rethinks the trope and destroys the hardened pattern of the quest-figure itself while at the same time anticipating Pearce's, Vendler's, and even Riddel's reading of his own poetry.

The opening of the poem establishes Crispin's connection with the Romantic tradition of the questor:

> Crispin at sea
> Created, in his day, a touch of doubt.
> An eye most apt in gelatines and jupes,
> Berries of villages, a barber's eye,
> An eye of land, of simple salad-beds,
> Of honest quilts, the eye of Crispin, hung
> On porpoises, instead of apricots,
> And on silentious porpoises, whose snouts
> Dibbled in waves that were mustachios,
> Inscrutable hair in an inscrutable world.
>
> (*P,* 58)

This Crispin is "the Socrates/ Of snails, musician of pears, principium/ And lex." He is an incongruous hero; his vision is limited, based on mundane objects of village life. He pretends to be a "lex" unto nature, whereas he is nothing but a "nincompated pedagogue" who now leaves his home on the land to try to be a

"Preceptor to the sea." Once "at sea" he creates doubt, that is, the comforting elements of his everyday life are left behind as he enters on a quest for a knowledge and a state of art which is beyond that available to him at home.

Stevens' decreation begins, however, in the very same lines as the introduction of the quest motif. In this case, the re-interpretation is accomplished largely by the language itself. Crispin's land perceptions are reduced in the richly sensual language which echoes the effete decadence of Stevens' early "Florida" style. In "Sunday Morning," for example, there are numerous instances of Stevens' attraction to a lush language which represents the peak of sensual perfection preceding decline and corruption:

> Death is the mother of beauty; . . .
> She makes the willow shiver in the sun
> For maidens who were wont to sit and gaze
> Upon the grass, relinquished to their feet.
> She causes boys to pile new plums and pears
> On disregarded plate. The maidens taste
> And stray impassioned in the littering leaves.
>                                      (P. 7)

Crispin's eye is at home with apricots and not plums, but clearly Stevens establishes enough of a verbal connection between Crispin and his own decadent fictions that examination of Crispin should be seen to involve Stevens' evaluation of his own early style and poetic preoccupations.

At the same time, Stevens undercuts the degree of seriousness which should attend to Crispin's quest. In the Romantic tradition, the poetic search for vision is the most crucial of all concerns and demands a very serious response. For Stevens, beginning with the knowledge that ultimately the Romantic quest is self-deluding, there is a corresponding reduction in the amount of seriousness ascribed to Crispin's search. Another way of saying this would be that Stevens, free of the compulsion to find a center, may completely indulge the poetic instinct to

Wallace Stevens

play. He adopts a tone of excess, of tongue-in-cheek, which parodies not only his own sensual fiction in *Harmonium,* but that of the Romantic quest. In the last lines of the paragraph quoted above, Crispin's vision shifts to porpoises and away from apricots. Clearly this exotic fish replaces the exotic fruit and represents the new vision which Crispin as Romantic voyager needs to accommodate. In these same lines, however, these porpoises are transformed into "snouts" which create figures in waves by "dibbling" and these waves are metamorphosed into "mustachios" which come to represent the "inscrutable hair" of an "inscrutable world."

The Romantics and, of course, the *Symbolistes* are questing for correspondences, for sets of meaning, some of which are transcendent, which exist behind or below the surface veil of things. In these lines, this veil which the symbol-making imagination is always trying to pierce is comically reduced by the excessive particularity of the image into the "inscrutable hair," the foam of an ocean wave. Crispin's journey begins in a most serious and, for many poets, still viable tradition. Stevens, however, reduces the viability of the quest by the humor of the imagery, which de-creates or masters the Romantic metaphor of the veil and of the idea of correspondences.

As a result of this sort of de-construction, the following thematic statement which undercuts Crispin as heroic, poetic questor not only comes as no surprise but resonates in ways beyond the merely thematic:

> What word split up in clickering syllables
> And storming under multitudinous tones
> Was name for this short-shanks in all that brunt?
> Crispin was washed away by magnitude.
> (P, 58–59)

By this point, the expectation that Crispin will come to a successful conclusion of unquestionable value, in the way of his ancestors, is in serious doubt. Stevens not only is thematically discussing Crispin and his identification with Stevens' own preoccupations in *Harmonium,* but, as Riddel would say, is using the form and language to think about, to re-interpret, the possibilities of Crispin and the quest motif as a fiction.

Crispin is "unnamed." There is no longer any clear "word" to define him. Not only has he been poetically reduced to "nothing himself" but the fictions which surround him, those that would establish the nature of the Crispin-questor figure, have been decreated and their efficacy put in doubt. Stevens can no longer write about Crispin using the poetic quest metaphor in any traditional way. He must create the poem by destroying the myth with which the poem begins. He disrupts the modern reader's expectation that the myth would structure the poem by harmonizing all the poem's metaphors in a traditional resolution.

Stevens' reduction of Crispin's self parallels that of the listener in "The Snow Man":

> The dead brine melted in him like a dew
> Of winter, until nothing of himself
> Remained, except some starker, barer self
> In a starker, barer world, in which the sun
> Was not the sun because it never shone
> With bland complaisance on pale parasols,
> Beetled, in chapels, on the chaste bouquets. . . .
>
> Here was no help before reality.
> Crispin beheld and Crispin was made new.
> The imagination, here, could not evade,
> In poems of plums, the strict austerity
> Of one vast, subjugating, final tone.
>
> (P, 59–60)

In this passage, the direct echoes of "The Snow Man" and of "Sunday Morning" disclose Stevens' poetry of re-interpretation. Crispin is reduced, like the listener, to "nothing himself." The key word of "The Snow Man," "behold," is repeated here in its past tense. The decadent plums of "Sunday Morning" are banished by a vision of austerity which is analogous to the vision of the "nothing that is" at the end of "The Snow Man." The quest figure and the re-interpretation of the sensual metaphors of Florida bring the reader to see that the reduction of all semantic fictions reveals the nothingness at the heart of verbal structure and literary competence.[17]

This is not to argue, however, that this is in any way the discovery of a "final" truth or value for Crispin. The point of finding a lack of center is that this is an uncomfortable discovery which leaves the "poet" unsatisfied and still questioning: "What was this gaudy, gusty panoply?/ Out of what swift destruction did it spring?" (P, 60). And Crispin continues on his search made "vivid by the sea." In the traditional terms of the reality-imagination conflict, he learns that the human imposition of romance is distortion and that he needs "an aesthetic tough, diverse, untamed,/ Incredible to prudes, the mint of dirt,/ Green barbarism turning paradigm" (P, 61). "The affectionate emigrant found/ A new reality in parrot-squawks" (P, 62). He joins the reality side of the controversy and he becomes himself a mere observer, a "connoisseur of elemental fate" (P, 63). His reduction to "nothing himself" does not in any way lead to comfort. When the storm strikes, he, like all the rest, takes refuge in the cathedral and is driven to search further.

Crispin then exchanges his southern habitat for Carolina and, traveling there, envisions it a cold and dimly lit scene. The moon replaces the sun in Crispin's imaginative vision of his promised land. Upon arrival, however, "he saw that it was spring,/ A time abhorrent to the nihilist/ Or searcher for the fecund minimum./ The moonlight fiction disappeared" (P, 65). Crispin had been projecting an image of himself upon Carolina as if he had never undergone the reduction of Part I. The thing outside in the world, however, manifests itself to him with such force that the self-satisfying projection is disrupted: "It purified. It made him see how much/ Of what he saw he never saw at all" (P, 66). Crispin again learns the lesson of "The Snow Man." His ability to "behold" is distorted by the imagination which creates comforting fancies of final paradises.

Wallace Stevens

Yet even at this point in his quest, Crispin believes that he can work through the distortion to a source, an essence:

> He gripped more closely the essential prose
> As being, in a world so falsified,
> The one integrity for him, the one
> Discovery still possible to make,
> To which all poems were incident, unless
> That prose should wear a poem's guise at last.
>
> *(P, 66)*

This is one of the clearest examples of Stevens' use of what Riddel, following Derrida, calls the language of presence. If, as Derrida argues, the concept of center or source always implies "presence" then in this case the inverse is also true. The language here clearly shows that Crispin wants an unchanging, transcendent center to be the result of his quest and the origin of all his poetry: essence, Being, unity, *integritas*. The "at last" betrays Crispin's intention most thoroughly. He wants an end to this quest which so far has only brought him through the uncomfortable destruction of various of his own cherished fictions.

In Part V, Crispin seems to have stopped his wanderings and to have found a viable and permanent aesthetic. His imaginative powers stop imposing on the other and he looks at "things within his actual eye" (P, 70). He is about to arrive at an aesthetic which gives priority to the "external world" and, paradoxically, finds transience in the fictional world of the imagination. Before this is even clearly stated, however, Stevens tells us "It seemed haphazard denouement." (P, 70) By now the reader is in on Stevens' game and knows the significance of a Romantic quest which "ends" by chance. The very idea of an "ending" in this poem contradicts the burden of the poetry. Nonetheless, Crispin seems to come to rest in an aesthetic which echoes that of the end of "Peter Quince at the Clavier":

> He first, as realist, admitted that
> Whoever hunts a matinal continent

[203]

Wallace Stevens

May, after all, stop short before a plum
And be content and still be realist.
The words of things entangle and confuse.
The plum survives its poems. It may hang
In the sunshine placidly, colored by ground
Obliquities of those who pass beneath,
Harlequined and mazily dewed and mauved
In bloom. Yet it survives its own form,
Beyond these changes, good, fat, guzzly fruit.
So Crispin hasped on the surviving form,
For him, of shall or ought to be in is.

(P, 70)

Crispin thinks that he has found a compromise position between his commitment to reality and his desire for a permanent center which will let him "be content." The re-interpretation of the possibility of arriving at any such point in this poem, as well as Stevens' prefatory disclaimer, undercuts Crispin's desire and seeming discovery. The similarity of Crispin's position to that of Peter Quince reemphasizes the way in which Stevens reevaluates himself and his own early poetry. This is a trait which emerges from the centerless nature of his vision and which he never abandons.

Crispin desperately holds onto the possibility of comfort in this new fiction. In this "surviving form" he not only finds what-is, as does "the listener" of "The Snow Man," but he abandons the future and time itself in the *presence* of being as well. The "shall or ought to be" point to the future. They point to willful action, to change, to moral situations—all things which might disrupt the comfort brought by an aesthetic based on a static, or at least cyclically recurring, vision of external nature.

In the last section of the poem, Crispin settles into domestic *stasis,* which is analogous to his aesthetic vision of nature. As a result, his imagination and all vitality are worn away. He creates off-shoots of his own slumping self and recognizes his trap. He then comes to a "position" which is final insofar as it is the literal end of the poem on the page; but even this is surely not final or

Wallace Stevens

"true." He accepts his last social and artistic fiction as his fate. He adopts the posture of the long-suffering Romantic poet, forced to abandon his world of dreams and imaginative ease for the sake of social obligation, for the ease of his "reality principle":

> Crispin concocted doctrine from the rout.
> The world, a turnip once so readily plucked,
> Sacked up and carried overseas, daubed out
> Of its ancient purple, pruned to the fertile main,
> And sown again by the stiffest realist,
> Came reproduced in purple, family font,
> The same insoluble lump. The fatalist
> Stepped in and dropped the chuckling down his craw,
> Without grace or grumble.
>
> (P, 74)

Crispin must "concoct" a value, a final message from his journey for the sake of success and comfort. He writes as though he has never learned the truth of the reduction to the state of nothing, that is, that all structures are fictions and man-made for the relief of tension and anxiety. Stevens' narrative comment upon Crispin's position is heavily ironic. He describes the journey and the poem as "anecdote" thereby reducing its significance and reinforcing the fact that it is after all a fiction based, like all poems, on nothing.

This last section is filled with hypothetical sentence structures from which a tentative "conclusion" might be drawn:

> Or if the music sticks, if the anecdote
> Is false, if Crispin is a profitless
> Philosopher, beginning with green brag,
> Concluding fadedly, if as a man
> Prone to distemper he abates in taste,
> Fickle and fumbling, variable, obscure,
> Glozing his life with after-shining flicks,
> Illuminating from a fancy gorged
> By apparition, plain and common things,
> Sequestering the fluster from the year,
> Making gulped potions from obstreperous drops,

[205]

Wallace Stevens

And so distorting, proving what he proves
Is nothing, what can all this matter since
The relation comes, benignly, to its end?
(*P, 75*)

According to Vendler, Stevens' use of "ifs," questions, and sub-
junctives is designed to display uncertainty, a "diffident didac-
ticism." [18] In this poem, though, the effect is exactly the opposite. Mrs. Vendler has been "deceived" by the comedy.
Crispin is, *in fact,* a failure in the quest. He can exist in the quest
form only as a means of destroying it. As a result, the hypothetical clauses of the last stanza continue the deconstruction by
ironically suggesting all of Crispin's failures in a speculative
frame. Stevens exaggerates his own "syntactic uncertainty" [19] at
Crispin's expense, and those of us who fail to laugh along with
Stevens fail to understand the playfullness of the poem.

The result of this decreation of the quest figure and of some
elements of Stevens' own early style is very serious. Crispin does
distort because he creates fictions which he fails to see rest on an
uncertain base. He has proven that "what he proves/ Is nothing,"
but he, of course, is blind to his own insight. The rhetorically
unstressed "nothing" of the final stanza easily escapes any significance unless we understand the end of the poem in terms of
Stevens' radical interpretation of fiction. Crispin proves himself
to be nothing. He proves nothing to be at the center. Most importantly, as a poetic device, he proves nothing in two senses: he
shows no finality in the working out of his story—as a poetic
device he proves to be nothing of final value; yet, as a device,
what he does positively prove or confirm "Is nothing." He demonstrates to the reader and poet the truth of "The Snow Man."
All of what-is shares in nothingness, which is the originless origin.

Thus "The Comedian as the Letter C" is not, as Vendler
says, a failed attempt by Stevens to make himself "into a ribald
poet of boisterous devotion to the gaudy, the gutsy, and the
burly"; nor is it a "verbal mimetic reproduction . . . of the ac-

tual density of the physical world."[20] The poem is a sophisticated use of a traditional poetic device whose value for modern poetry and modern man is no longer obvious until destroyed. Vendler ignores Stevens' claims that all structures are fictions and ignores the conscious use of convention, motif, and idea which this implies. Instead of seeing the poem as an "interpretation" of its own language which makes manifest what is "covered-up" by the quest, Vendler insists on writing about the poem as if it were using language free of tradition and social situation. As Roland Barthes argues in *Writing Degree Zero,* modern writers are preoccupied by the realization that their language does not come to them fresh; it has been used before, made into shapes which they cannot use. As a result, when the modern poet creates, he must and does do so with a fully developed awareness that he must re-interpret the language he uses in the process of making something his own.[21]

This process of re-interpretation goes on throughout Stevens' career. He continues to use the traditional language of the imagination-reality conflict in his poetic thinking. Most importantly, though, he thinks about, he re-interprets, the "fiction" that there is nothing at the center. The theme of "The Snow Man" recurs again and again and is most exhaustively questioned in the very late poetry.

There is in Stevens' poetry a curious alternation of opposites which critics ascribe to his "Romantic heritage." Like Roy Harvey Pearce, they claim that Stevens' alternating sympathy in the reality-imagination conflict is a dialectical movement which will lead to a synthesis. This is, of course, a convenient and comfortable way of justifying, and thereby eliminating by resolution, the "simultaneous" existence of opposites in Stevens. Since Stevens comes to no conclusion, to no balancing point between the elements of the dialectic, a more profitable way to look at these contradictions arises from Stevens' centerless vision. If all poetic structures are fictions with only partial value for humanity and if there is no privileged point of reference against which ideas may be measured, then the idea of contradiction which in itself

[207]

Wallace Stevens

emerges from the language of "presence," of onto-theology, is a fiction which should not be granted any superior metaphysical status.

Two late poems, "Not Ideas about the Thing but the Thing Itself" and "The Rock," are good examples of Stevens' sympathy for "unreconciled" antitheses. "The Rock" questions the primacy of matter over imagination, whereas "Not Ideas" asserts the certitude of objects' existence independently of the mind. "The Rock" opens with a radical statement of the priority of imagination over reality:

> It is an illusion that we were ever alive,
> Lived in the houses of mothers, arranged ourselves
> By our own motions in a freedom of air.
>
> Regard the freedom of seventy years ago.
> It is no longer air. The houses still stand,
> Though they are rigid in rigid emptiness.
>
> Even our shadows, their shadows, no longer remain.
> The lives these lived in the mind are at an end.
> They never were . . . The sounds of the guitar
>
> Were not and are not. Absurd.
>
> (P, 362)

The passage of time calls duration into doubt and the seemingly permanent existence of objects is seen as illusion. On the one hand, the reality which these objects has is seen from the present perspective as a product of the human imagination. On the other, the sounds of the guitar, that is, the "fictions" which the imagination produces and which are considered real, fade and reveal their fundamentally illusory nature. They rest on no firm center and therefore have no permanence. These objects and events are all "An invention . . . a queer assertion of humanity" (P, 362). They are "proposed" "As if nothingness contained a métier" (P, 363). In the face of emptiness and of change in the world, the imagination puts forth, proposes these fictions as real

Wallace Stevens

objects which exist "out-there" and which are comprehensible to man:

> A vital assumption, an impermanence
> In its permanent cold, an illusion so desired
>
> That the green leaves came and covered the high rock
> That the lilacs came and bloomed. . . .
>
> (P, 363)

The force of the human will compels the creation of these fictions. The self so wants a comforting illusion that it creates a soothing, yet impermanent illusion to populate the cold emptiness which truly endures. The flowers cover the barren rock and satisfy the self by putting sight of something in the place of a vision of nothing.

"The Rock" image itself, throughout the poem, is not identified with any finality, any ultimate source, but rather, paradoxically, with "barrenness," "the air," and "The step to the bleaker depths of his descents" (P, 364). The rock is an image of the nothingness of what-is. It represents a complete barrenness, an ultimate progression downward toward no goal. The traditional usages of this metaphor are thus inverted and what the trope always hides is made clear. Nonetheless, the poem goes on to establish a new fiction of relation between the self and the other (the rock), which seems to commit Stevens to the "imagination" side of the "traditional" controversy:

> It is the rock where tranquil must adduce
> Its tranquil self, the main of things, the mind,
>
> The starting point of the human and the end,
> That in which space is contained, the gate
> To the enclosure, day, the things illumined
>
> By day, night and that which night illumines,
> Night and its midnight-minting fragrances,
> Night's hymn of the rock, as in a vivid sleep.
>
> (P, 365)

[209]

Wallace Stevens

The mind of imagination will contain all of what-is; space and the mind will be coextensive so that all of what exists does so only by the grace of the imagination. This "reality" "exists" only in the dreamlike state of vision. The complete primacy of the imagination to the world outside only occurs *"as* in a vivid sleep." In this poem, what Vendler calls Stevens' "uncertain syntax" is relevant, because this imaginative perception shares only some qualities with the dream state; the daylight vision nonetheless remains different because it pretends to be real.

"Not Ideas about the Thing but the Thing Itself" questions this power of the mind to intrude into what exists out-there in any meaningful way:

> At the earliest ending of winter,
> In March, a scrawny cry from outside
> Seemed like a sound in his mind.
>
> He knew that he heard it,
> A bird's cry, at daylight or before,
> In the early March wind.
>
> The sun was rising at six,
> No longer a battered panache above snow . . .
> It would have been outside.
>
> It was not from the vast ventriloquism
> Of sleep's faded papier-mâché . . .
> The sun was coming from outside.
>
> That scrawny cry—It was
> A chorister whose c preceded the choir.
> It was part of the colossal sun,
>
> Surrounded by its choral rings,
> Still far away. It was like
> A new knowledge of reality.

(*P,* 387–88)

The poem begins with a perception and with the mind's attempt to bring that perception within itself and make a mental con-

[210]

struct of it. The triple repetition of "outside" prevents the reader, and the persona, from obscuring the separation between self and bird. Although the persona comes to know a truth, that is, that the cry exists independently of the perception of it, he also learns that this involves a constant separation of self and other which cannot really be bridged. The fiction that the imagination creates significance is de-created by the second stanza. In the third stanza, in fact, there is an explicit denial of the concluding fiction of "The Rock." In that poem, reality resides in the mind's active perception in a moment of "vivid sleep." In this poem, the "source" of the bird's cry is most emphatically taken away from the realm of the mental. The type of imagination which the persona praises in "The Rock" is here derogatorily classified as a "vast ventriloquism." The point of this metaphor, of course, is the denial of primacy, of origin, to the imagination which functions only as a mouthpiece, as it were, of something else, beyond human creation. For the persona of this poem, the other exists independently in reality. It does not depend on any source for its being, nor does it take part in any questionable ontological state like "sleep's faded papier-mâché."

In this poem, then, the primacy of the imagination is temporarily replaced by the fiction of complete immanence, which holds that the other can completely manifest itself and its Being so that its "meaning," its "nature," can be understood primordially. The poem certainly moves in that direction and, in fact, seems to arrive at this "final" position. The simile of the last two lines, however, points out that this idea of the revelation of the other and the gathering of new knowledge is also fiction.

By comparing "The Rock" and "Not Ideas," it becomes obvious that Stevens is not attempting any synthetic resolution of the elements of a dialectic. He is not trying to establish within each poem a final paradox which resolves tension in a literary figure. He continues to demonstrate that all fictions are just that and that the idea of final harmony is an impossibility. Critics who are disturbed by his seemingly contradictory ideas fail to see

Wallace Stevens

that they are victims of their own blindness, which makes non-contradiction and achieved harmonies privileged, centered positions based on what they think is "presence."

Stevens could only be accused of inconsistency if he failed to turn his poetic "destruction" back upon the vision of "The Snow Man." "An Ordinary Evening in New Haven" is concerned with the interpretation of "The Snow Man." After a thorough examination of the idea of nothingness and of the form of the meditation Stevens claims:

> This endlessly elaborating poem
> Displays the theory of poetry,
> As the life of poetry. A more severe,
>
> More harassing master would extemporize
> Subtler, more urgent proof that the theory
> Of poetry is the theory of life,
>
> As it is, in the intricate evasions of as,
> In things seen and unseen, created from nothingness,
> The heavens, the hells, the worlds, the longed-for lands.
>
> (P, 349)

The poem decreates the poetic meditation which it takes careful pains to parallel from its initial composition of place. Unlike traditional meditations, however, this poem does not end in an order "found by the poet in moments of supreme awareness . . . by an integrated mind and sense." [22] This poem is open-ended; it never arrives at the sort of final vision which Louis Martz claims for the meditative poem. Furthermore, "An Ordinary Evening" establishes, explicitly, a correspondence between the nature of poetry and of life; both elaborate endlessly. His poetry, then, is "created from nothingness," just as all human achievement, just as all of what-is shares in nothingness. The traditional conflict of imagination and reality is surpassed in Stevens' poetry. He realizes that both sides of the controversy are fictional discourses, strategies to comfort their respective adherents in the face of the nothingness which is at the root of all. Just as poets and other men hide behind fictional structures, so Stevens allows his poetry to create through "the intricate evasions of as." This is, of course, no simplistic escapism; rather, it makes poetic re-interpretation possible. The existence of all traditional fictions becomes the subject for Modern poetry.

In the very late poem, "As You Leave the Room," Stevens develops the most explicit reconsideration of "The Snow Man" vision. This poem invokes fictions which demonstrate the primacy of imagination over reality and it asks, "I wonder, have I lived a skeleton's life,/ As a disbeliever in reality" (P, 396). If Stevens were a merely dialectical poet in the Romantic tradition, he would then move on in the poem to an assertion of the source of reality in the outside world. This pattern is, of course, expected by the reader. Stevens, however, proceeds to a more complex position which is neither an assertion of the primacy of the external nor an attempted synthesis:

> Now, here, the snow I had forgotten becomes
>
> Part of a major reality, part of
> An appreciation of a reality
>
> And thus an elevation, as if I left
> With something I could touch, touch every way.
>
> And yet nothing has been changed except what is
> Unreal, as if nothing had been changed at all.
>
> (P, 396)

These lines open with an emphasis on the current time and situation of the poem, surely to point out that this is a reconsideration of a previous fiction and also to verify that each poem is the cry of its own occasion, that it is rooted in a particular historical and dramatic context. The snow starts to be transformed in these lines as it reappears in the poet's active thinking. The metamorphosis, of course, occurs not by virtue of the poet's imagination alone, but also by reason of the changed time and place of this poem which necessarily must be a different fiction than one of thirty-five years earlier.

The snow seems to become part of a reality out-there when

he says that it is part of a "major reality," but this appearance is corrected in the next phrase which further refines the nature of this "reality": "part of/ An appreciation of reality." Snow, which in the earlier poem reveals nothingness and destroys the veil which hides this nothingness, is now part of a "reality" which is constituted by virtue of poetic appreciation. "Appreciation" may be used with etymological preciseness as Pearce, in his misreading of this poem, would have it and, if so, it does imply that "major reality" does grow or "become" by virtue of accretion.[23] Experience then piles up or accretes and elevates the poet to a point of final perception. This is strikingly like the Romantic quest to return to a higher vision of original unity. But while Pearce is correct in pointing out the etymology of "appreciate," he does so at the expense of a more obvious and, I think, more valuable meaning.

"Appreciation" also implies an act of evaluation which ends favorably. It signifies a sensitive and proper awareness of the other. In a poem in which the self fears that he is nothing but a skeleton as a result of denying objective existence to the other, this interpretation of "appreciation" seems much more consistent. Stevens approaches that attitude to reality which Randall Jarrell, speaking of William Carlos Williams, calls "generosity" and Heidegger calls *Gelassenheit*.[24] This involves a willingness to accept the other for what it is and a refusal to attempt to impose human significance on something essentially foreign to the human. This is born out by what for Stevens is a strange insistence on the tactile qualities of existence: ". . . as if I left/ With something I could touch, touch every way." Throughout his poetry, whenever he sides with the reality part of the conflict with imagination, Stevens' sympathy for an immanental relation to the other appears. In this late poetry, however, it occurs in the process of rethinking the vision of "The Snow Man."

In "The Course of a Particular," for example, the value of the other's independent and meaningful existence is asserted despite that "in the final finding of the ear . . ./ . . . the cry concerns no one at all" (*P*, 367). In "As You Leave the Room," however, immanence and "The Snow Man" come to a more complex relationship. The poem describes the phenomenological effects on the self of a generous attitude toward reality and it does so with complete sympathy. Stevens, though, is too honest to allow this effect to stand unexamined. He concludes that this too is a fiction; it is only "as if" he acquired the sensation of touch which ends estrangement. What changes as a result of this reevaluation of some of his past fiction and of the phenomenon of immanence is only what is "unreal." "Nothing," which is the root of what-is, escapes unchanged; nothing even escapes this attempt to eliminate it. This recognition does not, however, imply a failure for Stevens. Although the "unreal" alone changes, man can know nothing more except the originless origin. To attempt anything "beyond" this would be to refuse the lesson of the listener's reduction in "The Snow Man" and countless other poems. It would be an attempt to live in bad faith by denying the fictional nature of even the most humanly valuable and sympathetic attitudes, like "generosity."

Chapter Six

# The Particularities
# of Tradition:
# History and Locale
# in *The Maximus Poems*


I

Until very recently Charles Olson's poetry has been consistently omitted from critical analyses of the "tradition" of American poetry as well as from critical attempts to define "Modern" poetry. Some of his fellow poets and former students have tried to impress upon the critical establishment the importance of Olson's achievement and of his goals, but for the most part these attempts have met with little success. The almost total silence surrounding Olson's work testifies both to the pervasive influence of the New Criticism among the current generation of critics as well as to the degree of Olson's difference from the American and Modern traditions which the New Criticism defines.

Indeed, in "A Retrospective Introduction" to *Modern Poetry and the Tradition,* written in 1965 for the rerelease of his text, Cleanth Brooks completely omits any mention of Olson's work. Brooks acknowledges that he should perhaps have given more attention to Williams and to Pound in his book to discover what separates their works from those of Eliot. He recognizes that Pound and Williams are the most important influences upon contemporary poetry. Yet, he resists Donald Hall's claim that these poets and their contemporary, postmodern heirs possess a new imagination (*MP,* xx). After quoting Hall's introduction to his

Charles Olson

anthology of 1963, *Contemporary American Poetry*,[1] Brooks claims that the structure of the poems of this new imagination is essentially the same as that of the Modern works he had described in earlier editions of *Modern Poetry and the Tradition:* "The poet juxtaposes two images, and hopes that the steel of the first will strike a spark from the flint of the second, and thus kindle the reader's imagination" (*MP,* xx). Brooks completely misunderstands the importance of Williams and Pound to contemporary poets: postmodern poets turn to *Paterson* and *The Cantos* to discover a less dehumanized way of writing poems in the world than, for example, the New Critical writing of the Fugitives. Brooks does not allow those elements of Williams' poems and of Pound's late *Cantos* which are contrary to the ironic, spatialized poetics of the New Criticism to emerge. His habituation to close verbal analysis, predicated upon a principle of ironic context, coerces poems like *Paterson* and *The Pisan Cantos* into the traditional mold of closed form, of ironically constructed aesthetic monads.

Despite his familiarity with Hall's anthology of postmodern American poetry, Brooks offers Robert Lowell's and Randall Jarrell's poems as evidence that "the poetry of the 1920s was not too narrowly based and that its principles did not inhibit fruitful development. Lowell and Jarrell fully assimilated the poetry that came to prominence in the 1920s and the critical theory derived from, and illustrated by, it" (*MP,* xxv). Brooks's ignorance of the poetics of "open form" which Olson's essay, "Projective Verse,"[2] asserts as a manifesto of postmodern poetry, not only causes him to disregard Olson, but to coerce the later poetry of Lowell, "Skunk Hour" and "For the Union Dead," for example, into the tighter forms of Lowell's earlier verse and to claim that Lowell's ability to order "intellectual wit" controls the late, irrational, "mad" poems of Roethke.

This brief examination of Brooks's late poetic assumptions suggests that he had not kept up with the poetic scene. Brooks's metaphysics and the methodology which arises out of it are not adequate to a poetry of open form which defines itself in opposition to the Modernist ideals of the concrete universal, ironic form, and autotelic structure out of which his own habits of reading emerge. Brooks's resistance to the innovations of Pound, Williams, and Olson in "A Retrospective Introduction" is indicative of Modern critical desires to retain—or construct—the continuity of "tradition." As the studies of Bate and Bloom in chapter one suggest, Modern critics have an existential and ontological stake in maintaining a union of texts, a "canon," whose imaginative order, unchanging structure, and objective status assure ontological security. When so rigidly conceived, the "tradition" is precisely the bulwark against natural process and history which Bate and Bloom perceive it to be. In this context, Brooks's coercion of Pound, Williams, the late Lowell, and the late Roethke into the New Critical "tradition" of "Modern," and notably, "American" poetry emerges not merely as critical blindness, but as a necessary evasion of discontinuity which the New Criticism's metaphysical stance, unmastered irony, requires. Change, disruption, process, and finitude are not only the characteristics of open form, but they are the defining traits of a discontinuous "tradition." However, they are also those marks of being-in-the-world which the New Critical impulse to godhead attempts to transcend.

I have argued in chapter four that the New Critical objection to open form requires that the Modern and American "traditions" largely omit the work of Whitman, Lawrence, and W.C. Williams. For example, Allen Tate's 1969 anthology of criticism, *Six American Poets from Emily Dickinson to the Present*,[3] not only credits Dickinson with being the first Modern American poet, but also completely ignores postmodern poets of open form.

In a similar way, Louis Martz, in *The Poem of the Mind*,[4] illuminates the Modernist poetic tradition as well as the nature of what Modern critics mean by an "American" tradition. Martz's meditative tradition begins with Southwell and Donne and an examination of the idea of the metaphysical imagination. His decision to "begin" the tradition with the metaphysical Donne does not need any explanation; it is quite explicitly connected to the admiration for Donne in both Eliot's criticism and that of the New Critics. Modernist critics return to Donne as the last figure whose imagination is ironic enough to represent the complexity of correspondences of the unified sensibility. Following T.S. Eliot, Martz argues that the "tradition" *dies* in England with the Restoration and Neoclassical revival of the eighteenth century. This argument also echoes that of Brooks in *Modern Poetry and the Tradition.* However, the "tradition" survives, in fact flourishes, according to Martz, in the poems of the American writer Edward Taylor who "has a place in literary history as the last heir of the great tradition of English meditative poetry."[5] As Martz's succeeding readings of American poets reveal, he quite clearly thinks of Taylor as the "beginning" of the American "tradition," which poets like Stevens, Williams, and Roethke maintain.

In order to assure the absolute continuity of the "tradition" which he is describing, Martz argues that there are no disruptive native American elements in Taylor's poetry. Unlike W.C. Williams, who condemns the Puritan poets for not being in *touch* with the land,[6] Martz insists that it is precisely this absence of the local which makes possible the preservation, the imitation[7] of the "tradition." Williams attacks Taylor's type of poetry for being "steely" and firm,[8] written by one of the "elect," from the perspective of unquestioned clarity and certainty which allows Puritan poets to ignore the dispersed "processes" of "nature" and "language" in which they create; Martz, on the other hand, defends this forgetting of the wilderness as the condition which keeps the meditative form from contamination by the reductive wit and decorum of the eighteenth century. In opposition to Williams' *In the American Grain,* Martz defines the American tradition as a purely formal achievement, an imitation of European forms, made possible precisely by Taylor's disinterest in the land and the particular details of his "locale." Martz's larger biases against the "geographical" and personal nature of open poems of process emerge from his definition of a meditative poem—a definition which establishes the direct descendence of his version of the tradition from the ironic New Critics: ". . . most of these essays deal with poetry of the interior life, where the mind, acutely aware of an outer world of drifting *unstable forms,* finds within itself the *power to create coherence and significance.*"[9]

Like the New Critics, Bate, and Bloom, Martz's poetics and analysis proceed from the assumption of a dualistic universe in which mind and its desired order are in painful conflict with a chaotic external world. His meditative "tradition" is a fiction blinded to its own fictional nature by the "natural attitude" of the Cartesian-Leibnizian inheritance. As a result of this entrapment within the onto–theological tradition, Martz perceives "art" to be an alternative to "life." He sees the creation of poems as a manifestation of that "will to art" which is an unchallenged assumption behind the poetics of T.E. Hulme and the aesthetics of Wilhelm Worringer.[10] The dualistic division of life and art which Martz manifests, and which clearly dominates the New Criticism and the works of Bate and Bloom, places man in opposition to nature, to whatever lies "outside" the mind. Furthermore, the will to art asserts the mental "power" over nature which allows man to dominate and control. It imposes order upon nature by transforming "life" into "art"; it creates closed artifacts, individual poems and "traditions" which the ironic mind can contemplate. The "meditative" poem is not only Gnostic in its attempt to impose order upon "chaos," but it participates in the same coercive tendency of mind which in technology leads to the despoiling of the environment.[11]

Martz, like Brooks in "A Retrospective Introduction," coerces the poetry of Williams, Roethke, and Stevens into this meditative mold. And, also like Brooks, he totally ignores the work of Charles Olson. The complete absence of Olson from Martz's criticism indicates that Olson's poems and criticism are so violently opposed to the entire mental set of the dualistic, coercive New Criticism and its "tradition" that they successfully resist any attempt to bring them within the "tradition." Olson's works illustrate what should be the primary insight of all historically aware, destructive criticism: poems do violence to their interpreters and potentially destroy methods of criticism which are used to "illuminate" them. Clearly, the complete omission of Olson's works by ironic critics of context suggests that they are both blind to the potentialities of the forms Olson creates and that they sense the potential danger to their own versions of criticism inherent in his poems.

The presence of Whitman, Williams, a deconstructed Stevens, and Charles Olson is either covered-over completely or distorted in received literary "histories" which *establish* the "American Tradition," particularly in Modern verse, because of the spatial, ironic, timeless set of habitual assumptions which is almost invariably *brought to* the poems and imposed upon them. The deconstructions of the genetic, dualistic, ironic, and Adamic fictions in previous chapters show that a critical methodology and literary history resting upon these fictions obscures alternative possibilities for interpretation and history. The traditional mentality which underlies criticism of American poetry protects the critics from the ontological insecurity they dread when confronted by a world which they see as inimicable to their wills and different from their desires. Most specifically, the tradition of Modern criticism avoids change and time by projecting monadic poetic structures and continuous literary traditions. Although in the 1960s, under the impact of both those poets whom the New Criticism ignores and those critical theories developed out of the phenomenology of interpretation, some American critics began to examine these habitual assumptions, most evaluations of the American tradition failed to consider the radically *anti-tradition-al* nature of poets like Whitman and Olson. The criticism of the 1960s makes especially clear precisely how habitually *present* the New Critical metaphysics and hermeneutics is—even among those who use it unconsciously—as *the* methodological approach to American poetry.

In an undistinguished but typical anthology of criticism, *American Poetry* (edited by Irvin Ehrenpreis), Louis D. Rubin, Jr. explicitly identifies the poetics of the Fugitive poets—Allen Tate, Robert Penn Warren, Donald Davidson, and John Crow

Ransom—with the critical theories of closure underlying the New Criticism:

> Among the chief Fugitives there was a commitment to form, an insistence upon the poem as existing within its language and on the page, with the responsibility for creating its own meaning, that contrasted sharply with the loose, undisciplined, formless experimentalism of so much little magazine verse of the period. What interested the Fugitives most was language, its properties, its concreteness; their poetry tended towards the tightly-seeded, packed line with the energy of the poem focused on the way in which images worked with and against other images to produce a kind of poetry, which however complex and even dense it might appear on quick reading, developed from beginning to end a controlled, cohesive meaning in which each image, each line, was part of the total movement of the poem. It is not surprising that Ransom, Tate, Warren, and their somewhat younger friend Cleanth Brooks were to prove the leading proponents of the critical development which Ransom was to christen the New Criticism.[12]

Rubin's own analysis of the Fugitives in "Four Southerners" quite appropriately pursues a New Critical approach to explicate the densities and complexities of the self-contained aesthetic monad.

The full significance of this essay, however, is not what it says or even how it says it, but rather its position within the anthology itself. With the exception of this article, the other pieces in *American Poetry* are arranged chronologically according to the dates of the poets treated. "Four Southerners" is presented first in the collection. It is presented as the normal way to read poems and as a defense of the kind of criticism and poems which made the New Criticism normative. In fact, a statement which closes the paragraph quoted above makes quite clear the privileged position which the Fugitive poetics and the New Criticism possess in relation to the rest of American poetry: "They taught a generation of students how to read." Within the anthology itself, the New Criticism determines the set of guiding assumptions which

Charles Olson

are brought to the readings, the interpretations in the rest of the anthology, and the "correct" way to read all poems as well.

Within such an unquestioned, "normative" context for criticism, Walter Sutton writes in "Criticism and Poetry" that Olson and his followers are failures:

> A persistent and typical weakness of these lines [from "The Kingfishers"] is the lack of a *shaping force* that can absorb "influences" by subordinating and *fusing* borrowed elements within the poet's own individual expression. There is instead a comparatively *relaxed* poetic line with many *unassimilated* details and echoes of the masters. Like many other poets of the third generation [of Modernism], Olson has committed himself to a revolutionary theory of organic form without having succeeded in carrying its principles into practice. [13]

The New Critical habit brings with it a picture of the eternal sameness of all poetry: form is defined by closure created by ironic context. As a methodology, it is trapped within the vicious circle of logic; its criteria are frozen and cannot develop in response to a poem. Therefore, all poems "misread" New Critically are either the same poem—i.e., the poem of irony—or, like Olson's, "failures." This commitment to method as an unquestioned assumption of reading is a privileged center which keeps the critic from becoming involved in the process of encounter with the text. It provides a ground, a certainty, which can only maintain the defense of the critic—the coercive Gnostic—if it is not exposed to works like Olson's, which threaten to destroy it. The fact that Harold Bloom's *Map of Misreading* is trapped within a similar circle indicates how many of the "opponents" of the New Criticism remain within the same metaphysical context as Brooks and Wimsatt. As I have pointed out in chapter one, Bloom must either admit the possibility of his method's inadequacy—and therefore the possibility that literature is not different from life, is not a bulwark against time and nature—or decide that literature has come to an end. In an apotheosis of the hubris of Modern criticism, he announces the death of poetry.

The examples of New Critical versions of the "tradition" could be multiplied extensively. Yet the result would always be the same, just as the "tradition" and "forms" which are made to appear in these New Critical texts are always identical. There is no substantial change registered between Brooks's version of the tradition in 1939 and Martz's in 1966. Tate's insistence upon closed form as *the* criteria for "Modern" poetry is the same in 1969 as it is in his essays in *The Kenyon Review*. Modern criticism has been writing the same story of Modern and American poetry for the past fifty years. And while there are some indications that things are changing—in those critics like de Man, Scott, Hillis Miller, Riddel, Hartman, and Spanos—a history of this Modern American poetry which would move the "tradition" off the "center" of New Critical form has yet to be written.

For example, Edward Hungerford's *Poets in Progress: Critical Prefaces to Ten Contemporary Americans* [14] omits all comment on Olson and is concerned with those poets who made their reputation during the period of the New Criticism's greatest authority—Lowell, Wilbur, Jarrell, and Merwin—and those like Robert Bly who can be seen to be, in many ways, the contemporary version of the New Critical poet. (Bly's 1962 collection, *Silence in the Snowy Fields,* reflects precisely the epiphanic, lyrical concerns of Tate's and Warren's poems, although with a more humane sense of the limits of linguistic complexity.)

Roy Harvey Pearce's *The Continuity of American Poetry* is certainly not an obviously New Critical book, yet, as some of my comments on Pearce's treatment of Stevens' poems indicate, Pearce's own orientation remains essentially *telos*-oriented, and, therefore, "traditional." His presiding metaphor of "continuity," with its genetic, organic, and *centered* connotations as well as his assumptions of the dualism of thought and world overwhelm his legitimately new insight into the importance of process and of the place of Whitman's poetry in any future description of the tradition of American and Modern poems. Once again, however, Olson is peculiarly absent and his absence is most obvious in a critical text devoted to an attempted over-coming of the New

Charles Olson

Critical reading of poems and to a restoration of critical attention
to the idea of poem as process. But Pearce's dualistic and genetic
assumptions, as well as his rhetoric of continuity, are inimicable
to Olson's monistic, nonlinear universe of world and word.

Along with the peculiar absence of Olson from Pearce's criticism, the blatant omission of a consideration of Olson from
Richard Howard's *Alone with America* is revealing. Certainly one
could expect to see Olson treated in an anthology which claims
to examine all those American poets who "have come into a
characteristic and—as I see it—consequential identity since the
time, say, of the Korean War." [15] Clearly, Howard does not recognize anything of consequence in Olson's work although
Olson's nearest friend, Robert Creely, is treated in some detail.
Once again, an examination of the principles underlying the
criticism in *Alone with America* reveals not only the presence of
the New Criticism, but the myth of the necessary continuity of
tradition.

Howard claims that six poets have arisen since Pearl Harbor
who have long been accepted "as types and at best as particulars
in our literary landscape: Berryman, Bishop, Jarrell, Lowell,
Roethke, and Wilbur." Howard goes on to say that the poets he
treats stand in a "dialectical relation" with these six "masters."
And although this relationship is arguable, he emphasizes that it
has *"endured."* Howard's insistence upon the continuity of the
American tradition, indeed, upon its homogeneity, arises out of
his own ontological need to have a strong, active tradition
grounding his attempts to write poems:

> if I intended to go on writing my own poetry, I discovered
> some years ago, there was a choice of *coming to terms* with the
> work of my contemporaries, my elders, my friends, or having
> no terms of my own to come to. . . . "If you cannot believe in
> the greatness of your own age and inheritance," Shaw wrote to
> Ellen Terry, "you will *fall into confusion of mind and contrariety of
> spirit."* This book is the *rescuing anatomy of such a belief;* the con-
> struction, piece by piece, of a *credendum*—articles of faith. [16]

[226]

Charles Olson

The reification of the tradition in a spatial image, an "anatomy," presents Howard with possibilities of order and methods of structure which prevent the direct, personal encounter with the confusion and dis-order that is the natural state of the present. In what he asserts as necessary to his own poetic act, Howard echoes the major Modernist critical version of the relationship of the Modern poet to his past. As in Bate, Bloom, and the New Critics, the past as an achieved aesthetic artifact is a defense against the dread of uncertainty and of the problematic involvement of man with his world that threatens to upset the ironic mastery of imagination over nature and time.

Indeed, the ironic consciousness which dominates so much Modern criticism appears in Howard's work in precisely the same form as it does in R.W.B. Lewis' interpretation of Whitman, i.e., the Adamic myth. Although Howard does suggest that contemporary poets "address themselves . . . to the process of experience rather than to its precepts," he asserts that they do this "in order to gain a universe not yet *manhandled.*" [17] Howard is completely correct in his suggestion that American poets are primarily activated in their art by a rebellion against the discursive forms of precept and proposition. However, this reaction categorizes the work of Eliot and Pound as well as that of Williams and Olson. Howard does not make the crucial distinctions which are necessary for his suggestion to become meaningful. He does not at any time raise the possibility of an American poetry which is not attempting to be Adamic in the naive, ironic sense of *returning* to some "new world," untouched, untamed, not yet "manhandled"; and he ignores poets like Whitman, Stevens, and Olson, who have a strong sense of the impossibility of such an Adamic enterprise as well as of its inauthenticity.

As I have argued in chapter four about Lewis' reading of Whitman, the critical insistence upon American poetry's supposed aspiration to Edenic states to name the world a-new is a variation on the New Critical, ironic consciousness. The myth of the new beginning is attractive because it frees the poet or reader

[227]

Charles Olson

from any sense of involvement in history, of any sense of responsibility, for, and of any restrictions imposed by, the past. As
Kierkegaard argues, the unmastered ironist's basic desire is to be
free to begin over again at any time. The Adamic myth presents
the poet-reader with a re-newed infinity of possibles, none of
which have been eliminated by actuality. The poet's ability to
choose, to create poems unencumbered by the world and the
past, is absolute in the Adamic state. Indeed, the Adamic myth is
another point of identity between the New Critics and their antagonists. For example, under the guise of the Freudian Scene of
Instruction, Harold Bloom remains in the major tradition of
American poetic criticism; he gnostically argues for the poet's
desire to return to that Adamic moment when he is his own father and is removed from the painful awareness of the limitations
imposed upon the poetic imagination aspiring to infinitude.[18]

Charles Olson's poetry and prose works insist upon a relationship between the poet and the past which denies the Adamic
myth. His concern for "origins," like Whitman's, is not a desire
to return to some timeless moment out of the world, in which
the poet's ability to create poems independently of history and
place is possible. Rather, Olson's sense of origins means an attempt to regain an awareness of man's temporal and geographical
nature in a world where poetry should only be written out of the
complex, deep historical relationship between a man and the
other objects within his world, his environment, his "field."

Yet the Modern, ironic, critical consciousness is completely
unsympathetic to Olson's enterprise even when aware of it. In
*Conceptions of Reality in Modern American Poetry,*[19] a late "revisionist" reading of Modern poetry, L.S. Dembo focuses not on
the image of man in the world in Olson's poetry, but on Olson's
supposed "idealization" of poetry and language. He accuses
Olson of writing "ideal poetry" in which he tries to project a
"vision" of his own "paideuma" as "polis," that is, "Plato's ideal
state, . . . in terms of pastoral images, such as the 'tansy,' a local
flower."[20] Dembo's study of the relation between American
poets and the "object" is influenced by Modern versions of the

[228]

image and symbolist theories of the pure poem. Throughout his book, he ascribes to Olson, as he does to other Modern American poets, the desire to somehow transfer the "object-nature" of the world directly to the body or shape of his poems. In other words, he continues the Modern critical enterprise of trying to solidify poems so that they become fixed, stable, and "aesthetic" objects.

Dembo's awareness of the poet's direct and intentional relation to the "thing" is uninformed by either the Whiteheadian or Heideggerean phenomenological orientations which would allow him to see a different, more "innocent," i.e. more reduced, relation between poem and object, a relation in which the poet reenacts his encounter with a being precisely to let the being's self-existence make a claim upon him and his language. The American poem, Olson's poem, is not trying to project something ideal, but rather to reenact something radically earthly, radically local, and radically temporal—i.e., a man's encounter with the particulars of his experience, his environment, and the history of his locale. This poetics is hardly an idealization; above all such poetry refuses to bracket—as sometimes Husserl does—an object's actual, temporal existence in the world. Olson's poetry proceeds from the radically fundamental existence of objects and leads to poems which share temporal being with other objects in the world.

Critical works which obscure the potential of such a poetics lead not only to the omission of Olson from accounts of Modern American poetry, but to completely distorted statements about his enterprise. For example, in "Lowell's Marble Meanings,"[21] Gabriel Pearson attacks Olson's theory of "open form" as "the counterpart of an ideology whose central concern is to detach American [poetry] from its European inheritance."[22] Pearson sees Olson's "Adamic myth" as the counterpart of the American technological assault upon nature and mankind. There is, in fact, a strongly coercive desire in the Adamic or ironic mentality, as we have seen in chapter three. Yet, to accuse Olson of siding with those elements of an American society which he disgustedly labels "pejorocracy" is a rash critical assertion and reveals Pearson's deep misunderstanding of Olson's project. Pearson is himself so thoroughly trapped within the Modern version of American poetry, which argues that the open poets—Whitman, Williams, Olson, and more recently Ammons—are Adamic, that, as a result, he cannot recognize that he is reading habitually. First, Pearson is looking for poetry of a certain New Critical type, which he finds in the early Lowell and does not in Olson. As a result, he condemns Olson. Secondly, he reads open American poetry through the Adamic myth of interpretation which surrounds those, like Whitman, whom New Critical theoreticians like Lewis have distorted to conform somewhat to New Critical readings and precepts. These two tendencies lead Pearson to an interesting contradiction: on the one hand, he attacks Olson for trying to get out of his society and out of his past and, on the other hand, he ridicules him for continuing that society's most coercive policies; and, furthermore, he praises Lowell's poetry for reducing the chaos of life in his society to aesthetic order, which effectively removes the artist and critics from that society. In other words, for Pearson, Olson's open forms invite societal coercion and approve it, while Lowell's aggressively closed forms provide an important ordered alternative to society.

Martin Dodsworth supports Pearson's Adamic reading and condemnation of Olson, but suggests some of the reasons why Olson's open forms cannot be received favorably by Modernist critics.[23] First of all, Olson's insistence upon man's geography and "man's existence as an object among objects" turns these poems away from " 'history,' the entangling web of relationships with others past and present with which we find ourselves willy-nilly engaged."[24] Secondly, Olson's poems and poetics do not deal with the current community of Modern society.[25] If both of these charges were true, they would seriously reduce the value of Olson's work. Since they are rather obviously not true and since they also emerge from the standard Adamic reading of open forms in American poetry, an examina-

tion of the motives behind Dodsworth's claims would be quite il-
luminating. To do this I must quote at some length:

> The hostility of his [Olson's] point of view to the human life
> and the poetic act as both fully committed to the sort of society
> we actually have is something that tends to reduce the scope
> and relevancy of his work. For the writing and reading of po-
> etry are both *social* acts: they take place in the context of history
> and the preconceptions of generations. Even in denying pre-
> conceptions poetry is engaged with a historical and social con-
> text that Olson prefers to miss out, or is actually incapable of
> offering us. He often reminds one of Whitman. . . . The poem
> is social act not merely in the sense that it is an act of com-
> munication . . . but also in that the way in which the message
> is taken is determined by the way in which the reader has
> previously understood poems and by the way in which poems
> have been read and valued in the centuries before the reader
> came across them.[26]

Despite the almost existential rhetoric of this quotation, Dodsworth's accusation that Olson does not involve himself in "history" means, in this context, that Olson's poems do not imitate
traditional forms and values. Thus, his poems do not satisfy the
present set of expectations regarding literature which underlie
both our society and our expectations in reading. Precisely because Olson refuses to imitate the tradition of the "they" world,
as Heidegger would put it, Dodsworth claims he is not historical. This strikes at the heart of Olson's project: his poems question and destroy the traditional elements which the crowd accepts
so that he can find, reveal, and evaluate alternative "traditions"
which are not merely accepted from others—from the historians
he refuses to trust as defenders of the present society—but which
he can see for himself in the Maya[27] or the writings of John
Smith.[28] The inability of Modern criticism to recognize this
aspect of Olson's poetry accounts most deeply for his absence
from the major accounts of the "history" of Modern poetry. Indeed, Olson destroys the entire idea of one reified, inherited

[231]

"tradition" upon which literary criticism works. His position is extreme: his ontology, his "epistemology," not only destroys the onto-theological "tradition," but it destroys the very means by which any "canon" can become static and passed on verbally as precept. Perhaps most radically, his poetry seems to suggest that the very idea of a "tradition" is made possible and is required by the Western tradition itself. His destruction of the proposition, of the "completed" linguistic form, along with his insistence upon taking a personal "look" at the facts, "results" in a "tradition" which is forever changing in response to the temporal being of those humans who examine it closely with no inherited preconceptions and values. The very word "tradition" is deconstructed by his poems and shown to be a mystified center of the logocentric "tradition."

One major obstacle in the face of a fuller appreciation of Olson lies in the common assumption made by his few defenders that his poetry and prose are an attempt to articulate a new vision, a new "tradition," a new polis which will replace the fallen "pejorocracy" which our civilization has become. In other words, for critics like Matthew Corrigan and L.S. Dembo,[29] Olson creates, projects, and *fixes* an alternative to the static, decayed world which we live in; he offers a morally more suitable, an imaginatively more generous "tradition" created out of his own "truer" reading of the past. While these critics are closer to Olson's spirit than those like Dodsworth and Pearson who do not see Olson's own involvement with society and the past, they are far from the crucial aspect of Olson's vision.

Modern critics have been looking for an alternative to the medieval world-view[30] of correspondences since the *Symbolistes*. They have sought strenuously for a unified world picture which would replace that lost with the demise of Christianity. Tate, Brooks, and Eliot, to mention only some, have turned to the Church as the answer. Yeats and Pound turned to varieties of fascism. But most usually, as I have been arguing throughout, Modern poets and critics hope that by reifying the works of the

[232]

imagination into some order which is permanent, poetry could be made to replace what security the Church had offered.

Corrigan and Dembo are working in the same critical tradition. They are willing to reduce radically Olson's sense of change, of natural and imaginative process to create for themselves out of his works a *new* center which will succumb to the same hardening and forgetfulness as that of the Renaissance. The spirit of Olson's work as well as the process of his poetry militates against the reestablishment of some fixed order. But they are not prepared to accept the radical sense of history and of "tradition" which lies in Olson's work. They are not prepared to live with the ongoing process of interpretation, of "seeing" for oneself, which Olson's sense of "history," and thus of "tradition," necessitates. Corrigan sees Olson as presenting "that something new and vital [which] is being formed out of the detritus of the present (to say nothing of the past), some new 'total, social future.' "[31] Dembo makes a similar argument in the special issue on Olson of *boundary 2* edited by Corrigan. According to Dembo—he is referring to Olson's "Maximus, to himself"— "Maximus' 'trade' (and therefore his identity) is the reconstruction of the polis with the tools of language, or in practical terms, the articulation of a vision of man's moral history and fate."[32] Dembo seems unaware of Olson's destruction of the term "vision" which does not allow his critics to use it in the traditional way Dembo does here. Dembo's use suggests some notion of transcendence just as in his essay on Olson in *Conceptions of Reality in Modern American Poetry,* he confuses Olson's use of "breath" with its traditional association with mysticism and spirit. Furthermore, Dembo's essay in *boundary 2* goes on to make Olson sound like an ironic, i.e., New Critical, poet who orders the chaotic patterns of life: "Maximus' burden is to fashion the Word (he is the 'Man in the Word') that will illuminate the pattern in human events."[33] Dembo, of course, makes a metaphysical assumption here by claiming that a pattern exists. He continues his use of metaphysical language by ascribing to

Charles Olson

Olson a plan to offer a permanent city, a new Jerusalem, a city of God on earth: "In this way he *seeks* to *fulfill* himself as a poet and to bring about the *new Gloucester* that is a *revitalization* of the *ideal forms* of the old"[34] (my italics). Dembo's unreconstructed use of the quest metaphor and the dualistic metaphor of "ideal-real" demonstrates how inadequate his own metaphysical structure is to reading Olson. Like Corrigan, he remains caught within Western teleological structures. To the extent that Dembo and Corrigan are caught, they are unaware of how total Olson's attack on the "pejorocracy" and its "tradition" *really,* as he would say, is.


II

J.B. Philip's refutation of Pearson and Dodsworth is a useful corrective to those who see Olson falling into some naive theory of original beginnings. Philip's essay, "Charles Olson Reconsidered," establishes, by a close analysis of "Maximus to Gloucester, Letter 27," that Olson's poetry is crucially involved both with society and the past: "What [Olson] is looking for is a method of revealing the detailed structure of a life in such a way as to understand the forces that act upon it, and the context, or lack of context, amidst which it proceeds. The poem is thus best seen as the central act within a wider critical process."[35] Yet Philip, too, insists that Olson is trying to project a new society, a new tradition which, free of the excesses and evils of the old, will function as the new center that is needed to replace the disintegrated past. Such readings of Olson are too comforting and too comfortable. They simplify Olson's work and, in their own ways, reify the process of his poetry into a new canon, a new, "better" artifact. Even so, Philip's analysis of Olson's involvement with society and history is obviously closer to Olson than any of the critics who charge Olson with egotism and eccentricity.

In *The Maximus Poems,* according to Philip, the process of

Charles Olson

criticizing the commercial, discursive, and exploitative American society "is obviously seen by Olson as the beginning of other, more positive ventures. . . . What he looks forward to is the re-ordering of American values." This reform will only be brought about by those who have come to know the "darkness" of con-temporary society by living in it and by trying to bring "light" to it: "It is there [in the darkness of that society] that an essential discrimination is learnt, and essential energies generated." From a confrontation with the darkness, Philip asserts, will emerge a "determination for change."[36] Despite his sense of the pressures of change in Olson, Philip describes the poetry in an un-de-stroyed language filled with metaphysical metaphors of dualism and transcendence: light and dark. Although Philip's insight into Olson's work is restricted by this critical language, his refutation of Pearson's and Dodsworth's claims makes it unnecessary to prove that Olson attacks the "pejorocracy" of Modern society and that he does examine his own relation to the past to find some alternative to the accepted "tradition." It is necessary, though, to go beyond Philip to examine what Olson finds to condemn in society and what he finds to praise in the past. Most importantly, it must be argued that Olson is perhaps the most radically interpretive poet of this century. That is, Olson insists upon a relation to the past and a "method" of encountering the past and nature which overthrows entirely the notion of "tradi-tion" and its concomitant ideas of *stasis,* continuity, and "objec-tive" criticism.

The earliest letters of *The Maximus Poems* are predominantly concerned with a presentation and destruction of society and the "tradition" upon which it rests. "The Songs of Maximus" and "Letter 3" are both of primary interest because of their concen-tration upon the misuse of language and the abuse of literature in the "pejorocracy." "The Songs of Maximus" seem to be more interesting as poetry, however, because of the clearer sense of movement in their lines and because of their fuller analyses of the failures of twentieth-century mass culture. "Letter 3" is marred by the rather generalized usage of the tansy flower as an alterna-

Charles Olson

tive to the crassness of the language abusers of Gloucester. Further, "Letter 3" is given over to prose statement so entirely that
it seems to violate Olson's own maxim that the line must conform to breath.

Both of these poems begin with a sense of the obscuring of
things in the world by language. "Song 1" of "The Songs of
Maximus" is perhaps the most complex statement criticizing the
"pejorocracy":

                    colored pictures
        of all things to eat: dirty
        postcards
                    And words, words, words
        all over everything
                        No eyes or ears left
        to do their own doings (all

        invaded, appropriated, outraged, all senses

        including the mind, that worker on what is
                                    And that other
            sense
        made to give even the most wretched, or any of us, wretched,
        that consolation (greased
                        lulled
        even the street-cars

        song
                                            (*MxP,* 13)

In typical Olson fashion, this poem begins in the middle of
things, in the process of thinking about, of writing the poem. It
avoids the full sentence of conventional verse as well as the end
stop line. Like Williams' and Pound's line, Olson's runs over to
maintain the sense of movement that the end-stop violates and to
draw attention, visually and aurally, to those "unimportant"
items of poetry which the iambic pentameter line normally obscures, e.g., "all" and "is." Drawing attention to "words" in
such a way seems to contradict the main complaint of the poem
that there are already too many words. But this seeming contra-

[236]

diction opens the poem up in an important way and insists upon an interpretation of that phrase "And words, words, words/ all over everything."

The Olsonian line draws attention to words as words precisely because the "pejorocracy" does not realize that all it sees and hears in its encounter with the world are "words." In existential language, one could say that the "they," the "crowd," substitutes inauthentically, like the ironic New Critics, a world of words for the actuality in which we live as free human beings. Indeed, Olson himself in "Human Universe," points out that, as a result of our history, of what we have chosen as our "tradition" (perhaps because of what has chosen us), we live in a "universe of discourse" (*SW*, 54). In other words, things can be hidden by words. The potential of words themselves to disclose is covered-up. The existence of beings in the world is obscured. Language is used inauthentically to present or maintain preformed, a prioristic versions of the objects in the world. The crowd in the "pejorocracy" deals with words in place of things, and, in fact, with a world of words and not with a "real" world at all.

It is not coincidental that the poem, which is essentially an attack on the misuse of language, opens up with a mention of pictures and advertising. Ads are "dirty postcards" because they seduce the populace into the falsely comforting, consuming, exploiting mentality of its society. More importantly, however, Olson's initial emphasis on "vision" in this poem on language is an attack on the reduction of language to "picture." In other words, in the context of Modern poetry's insistence upon the primacy of the visual image in verbal art, these opening lines are a critique of the ironic or image-making imagination. Even more broadly, as Sartre suggests in *Nausea* about the symbolists' use of language, the opening of this poem points out that the ironic, iconic, spatial use of language to project images is ultimately no different from the commercialized exploitation of language in ads and of nature in industry. In an intriguing reversal of Stephen Dedalus' assertion that imagistic language is not pornographic,

Charles Olson

Olson suggests that, like ads, images and symbols are pornographic because seductive. They turn the mind and the senses away from the dreadful world of objects and death toward a world of words. As Olson says in "Song 3" of "The Songs of Maximus," "the blessing/ that difficulties are once more" (*MxP*, 14). In other words, when the world is replaced by words—commercial or imagistic—"difficulty," which is the basic state of living in the world as one object among others, is obscured, and with it man's primary sense of his place in creation.

The anti-imagistic reading of the first lines is supported by the speaker's claim that eyes do not function in their own way any longer in our society. Language as discourse and as image displaces the immediate sensual perception of objects, which Heidegger calls *noein*, as the way to knowledge. The eyes only "see through" a web of words or they only see a series of images, constructed by others, interfering with the natural vision of things. The eye is potentially phenomenologically reduced; that is, the eye is capable of seeing the world free of the conceptions which discursive language imposes upon it and uninhibited by the intrusion of a verbally created, yet visually interfering, aesthetic artifact. In the "pejorocracy," however, the natural function of the eye is interrupted and a conscious, often violent process of stripping away the intruding "words" must take place before the eyes can function in their own way.

Of course, Walt Whitman makes precisely the same point in *Leaves of Grass* when he asserts that each and every American poet must see things for himself. Whitman welcomes poets who are not his imitators, but who will attend to the world more carefully than he has and, therefore, surpass him.[37] Pound and Williams insist upon similar phenomenologically reductive maxims: "Make it new!" and "No ideas but in things." Of course, Husserl's initial definition of phenomenology makes the same assertion: "Zu den Sachen Selbst," and even Heidegger, despits his hermeneutical emphasis, insists, in his own definition of phenomenology, upon allowing a thing to manifest itself from itself and in itself.[38]

Charles Olson

Olson, like these various phenomenologically oriented writers, does not insist that a poet see a thing in a *certain* way, but, rather, that he simply see. However, just how difficult it is to see becomes clear not only in *The Maximus Poems,* but in *The Special View of History,* where Olson explains that the "difficulty" of seeing results from the accumulation of a fraudulent scheme in the West for the last two thousand years. Olson discovers that seeing for oneself is authentic "history." Claiming the Greek historian Herodotus for his model, Olson says: "By history I mean to know, to really know" (*SVH,* 21). "History" is opposed to "discourse," which Socrates and the Greek philosophers invented. For Herodotus, according to Olson, " '*istorin* . . . appears to mean 'finding out for oneself,' instead of depending on hearsay" (*SVH,* 21). "Hearsay" is not merely the idle talk of the crowd in the "pejorocracy" but, as Olson makes clear in "Human Universe," it is an abuse of language which defines our entire tradition and, thus, inhibits our seeing:

> We stay unaware how two means of discourse the Greeks appear to have invented hugely intermit our participation in our experience, and so prevent discovery. They are what followed from Socrates' readiness to generalize, his willingness (from his own bias) to make a "universe" out of discourse. . . . With Aristotle, the two great means appear: logic and classification. And it is they that have so fastened themselves on habits of thought that action is interfered with, absolutely interfered with, I should say. (*SW,* 54–55)

Olson explains that the "universe" of discourse "is one of the first false faces of the law which I shall want to try to strike away" (*SW,* 54). Like Heidegger, he is aware of the violence needed to break down the traditional wall of habit which inhibits discovery. Olson's "goal" is to "dis-close"; like Heidegger, he tries to reveal what the discursive covers-over.

The tradition impedes the proper functioning of the human organism by cutting it off from the world. It is through the circuit of world-senses-imagination that creativity proceeds, that

[239]

dis-coveries are made. Language as discourse and image disrupts this circuit at every point. It obscures the world by re-presenting it in concepts and pictures; it frustrates the senses by denying them contact with objects in the world; and it rapes and coerces the mind:

> . . . all
> invaded, appropriated, outraged, all senses
> including the mind, that worker on what is

The mind and the senses are "greased/ lulled" by the veneer of words. They are made incapable of creative discovery. Man's potential for self-generation and action in the world is cut off: "And that other sense/ made to give even the most wretched, or any of us, wretched,/ that consolation. . . ." The combination of the sexual connotation of the world "outraged" and the suggested loss of potency in this last passage indicates the sterility and inactivity of the word-world of the pejorocracy.

When the circuit of world-senses-mind-action is complete, however, the poet can "disclose values" (*SW,* 63) which his community "could make use of" (*SW,* 63). Art created in the completion of this circuit is "kinetic," directly opposed to the static art of Stephen Dedalus and the New Critics. As such, kinetic art is an alternative to traditional metaphysics, which, according to Olson, is always "descriptive," i.e., "distanced" and "disinterested." Art is unique, different from metaphysics (and from the critical-poetic tradition defined by its language) because kinetic art alone can "get what you are after—so far as a human being goes, his life" (*SW,* 61). The New Criticism, of course, emphasizes an art which is not *interested* in life or the World but only in the Word. Such poetry cannot "get life." As Whitman's *Leaves of Grass* makes clear, only a poetry of process can re-produce a man and make him aware of his basically active, i.e., temporal, nature.

Olson argues that "There is only one thing you can do about the kinetic, reenact it." Throughout *The Maximus Poems,* he reproduces the actions of men, of lives—his own and those of

others, like John Smith. By doing so he gets through the veil of
words and images to the things themselves and thus breaks
through to the beginning of the circuit of creativity:

> art is the only twin life has—its only valid metaphysic. Art
> does not seek to describe but to enact. And if man is once more
> to possess intent in his life, and to take up the responsibility
> implicit in his life, he has to comprehend his own process as in-
> tact, from outside, by way of his skin, in, and by his own
> powers of conversion, out again. (*SW,* 61)

Man is to "re-gain" or "re-veal" his potential to act from "intent" and not from habit or "tradition." But Modern society,
based on a metaphysics of static description—through concept
and image—lulls the mind of man into a state of ease in which
his ability to act "intentionally" is abrogated. (I will return to a
discussion of intent in a later treatment of Olson's notion of
"care.")

Olson is clearly aware of what is lost in Modern society, but
is not as clearly certain of how to go about getting back the potentialities of acting in the world with conscious intent:

> And I am asked—ask myself (I, too, covered
> with the gurry of it) where
> shall we go from here, what can we do
> when even the public conveyances
> sing?
> > how can we go anywhere,
> even cross-town
> > > how get out of anywhere . . .
> > > > > *(MxP,* 13)

"Song 2" of "The Songs of Maximus" poses precisely the question of direction: which way to go to find an alternative, an
"anywhere" that is free of "the bodies/ all buried/ in shallow
graves?" (*MP,* 13).

As Olson quickly discovers, the *public* ways out are themselves taken over by the false singing of the electrically produced
song of the trolley cars. The poet is "covered" with the rot-

Charles Olson

tenness of the "pejorocracy" and needs to find a nonpublic, non-traditional way to go. For Whitman, the road to travel was easily found, since in America there was still quite a "newing." But one hundred years later, Whitman's heir, who wants desperately to travel, to begin making the connections with the world which will trigger the "circuit" of creation, must first un-earth a way to go.

"Song 3" suggests the two most important ways which Olson discovers. He goes back into himself, his family, his locale, and its history by first attending with some care to the specifics of the world around him:

>This morning of the small snow
>I count the blessings, the leak in the faucet
>which makes the sink time, the drop
>of the water on water as sweet
>as the Seth Thomas
>in the old kitchen
>my father stood in his drawers to wind (always
>he forgot the 30th day, as I don't want to remember
>the rent
>
>(MxP, 14)

Rather obviously, this song connects the specific initial encounter with an insignificant object in the world with a memory which it triggers. The circuit begins in this moment. The poet accepts the "energy," the emotional value of the falling water. The immediate data of the snow and water enter through the senses and encounter the poet's "inner energy . . . his dreams, for example, his thoughts, . . . his desires, sins, hopes, fears, faiths, loves" (SW, 60). The particulars of "external reality" contact the "inner energy" so proximally that the degree to which man and nature are one emerges quite clearly.

The "mind" immediately works upon "what is," the "inner" and "outer," the "one," and transforms the act of the moment into the language of the moment. In "Human Universe," Olson insists upon writing a poetry in which the language

[242]

Charles Olson

is "the act of the instant" and not "language as the act of thought about the instant" (*SW,* 54). The latter is at best discourse or the "suck of symbol" (*SW,* 61). Olson hopes to differentiate his poetry from Wordsworth's poetic intent to write from "emotion recollected in tranquility."[39] He wants to get the event down quickly before any of its energy is lost. His poems are like the Maya he admires so much: "O, they were hot for the world they lived in, these Maya, hot to get it down the way it was—the way it is, my fellow citizens" (*SW,* 66).

Olson's poems do not work reflexively, that is, they are not the records of events "recollected" and "described" in a later moment. The temporal–spatial distance from the initial energy of the moment's encounter and thought which is necessary for such tranquil "recollection" is the basis of the aesthetic distance which breaks the circuit Olson considers the basis of creativity. Delay cuts the poet off from the world and his sensual impressions of it and, thus, separates the mind from "what is." The imagination in recollection works only on what is contained in memory, "purified" of its immediacy, and, thus, "cool." The heat of the moment of discovery and encounter provides the violent energy needed to break down the hardened tradition which threatens to enclose all experience within its autotelically determined frame. The passage of time eases the strain on the poet's imagination in the process of experience and, after the experience is *all over,* when it is *completed,* and *finished,* when it can be *seen all at once* from the vantage point of the knowledge of the "end," it is more amenable to traditional forms and concepts. Recollection allows for an easier time of covering-up the discovery of the moment. In the moment of discovery, when all is *not clear* to the poet, when his knowledge is "incomplete," the authentic poet of process must be prepared to remain in doubt and uncertainty. He must possess "Negative Capability."[40]

Keats, of course, is a major source of Olson's awareness of the nature of the tradition as cover-up. Along with Heraclitus, whose fragments pepper Olson's work, Keats articulates the dissatisfaction of the poet of immediate process with the intellectual

[243]

Charles Olson

coercers of the "tradition," with those whose will to know is so powerful that, like Coleridge, they will let go the insight of the moment because of their "irritable reaching after fact and reason." In Olson's poems we can see the condemnation of those poets who create in recollection and those who do not possess negative capability. To create a poem about the act of the moment, by means of the greater "knowledge" provided by the awareness of the "whole" experience, is to coerce language and experience into forms which are not "true" to the "way it is." Olson sees a deep contradiction between the truth of the experience of the moment and any record or description of that event made afterwards. Olson realizes that truth is discovery, is what occurs in the process of opening-up the world in immediate experience. Language which in the moment reenacts the discovery is thus "truer" than language which records after the immediacy of the discovery cools. Olson's poems are ongoing disclosures with sudden changes in direction, abrupt discontinuities, frequent repetitions, and fragmented linguistic structures. As Olson argues in "Projective Verse," every kinetic poem must move unceasingly from one perception to the next without concern for logic or preconceived order. The only guideline is to "get down" the experience as it is and while it is "hot":

> ONE PERCEPTION MUST IMMEDIATELY AND DIRECTLY LEAD TO A FURTHER PERCEPTION. It means exactly what it says, is a matter of, at *all* points (even, I should say, of our management of daily reality as of the daily work) get on with it, keep moving, keep in, speed, the nerves, their speed, the perceptions, theirs, the acts, the split second acts, the whole business, keep it moving as fast as you can, citizen. And if you also set up as a poet, USE USE USE the process at all points, in any given poem always, always one perception must must must MOVE, INSTANTER, ON ANOTHER! (*SW*, 17)

The opening of "Song 3" of "The Songs of Maximus" is an example of the discontinuous nature of Olson's poetry of discovery. It begins the poem's movement, as Heidegger might say,

[244]

Charles Olson

along-a-way. There is a complete break with the language and problems of "Song 2." The "snow" and the "faucet" present themselves and they are immediately recorded. The poet breaks away from his meditation upon the weaknesses of the society and its language and is drawn to a world of things. These objects in turn spontaneously trigger the memory and love of Olson's "inner energy." And the circuit of action begins. In this moment, the poet has found his way. Yet, clearly, he does not know where he is going along this route. Following the presentation of the sink and clock whose measure and time contrast to the music and song of the pejorocracy, the poet's reverie of his father is itself disrupted. The path leads him to his childhood house, and lets him double back somewhat upon his earlier theme, the artificiality of our culture: the house in which there was love and energy now belongs to "Congoleum."

"Song 3" moves back to previous themes and images, but always by going forward to new ex-posures, new dis-coveries. Although Olson's poems often turn a quick look backward, they do not gather the past into themselves as they progress toward a future goal. A New Critical poem accretes meaning from interconnected patterns. The projective poem often changes direction with each discovery the poet makes on the way. But it never means a halt in the progress, an arrival at some end. Like Whitman, who, after his amazing poetic victory in the face of death in "Out of the Cradle," Olson never comes to a standstill; he never rests at a given point. His poems cannot stop in this way because they move to no *telos;* indeed, Olson's poems, as "reenactments" of life reveal that there is no end, no goal, no *telos.*

Following the brief "aside" on the "house," "Song 3" picks up on the fact that the dripping faucet does not work, does not do its job. At this point, the poem looks backward, but records the discovery of the poet who suddenly "sees" the potential significance of these mechanical failures:

> Or the plumbing,
> that it doesn't work, this I like, have even used paper clips

Charles Olson

as well as string to hold the ball up And flush it
with my hand

> But that the car doesn't, that no moving
> thing moves
without that song I'd void my ear of, the musickracket
of all ownership . . .

(MxP, 14)

Olson resists immediately transforming these details into any abstract assertion. The sudden shift of the poet's attention to the plumbing is an example of how his poems move rapidly from one perception to another. The abrupt turn to the broken car keeps the poem and poet, as well as the eye and mind of the reader, constantly in motion. Appropriately, the broken–down toilet is presented in fragments of sentences and images. No particular detail gains any privileged significance of symbol or allegory. Each part remains what it is, no more and no less. The "heat" of the immediate perception is transmitted by the fragmentary and hurried language which insistently violates the sentence and the formality of a "completed" thought. But quite typically, the abrupt transformation from the broken toilet to the malfunctioning car triggers the ideas of motion and noise. These notions, combined with the fact that the car is a means of conveyance, return the poem termporarily to the theme of the first two songs: the corruption of language in a commercial society. Language and capitalism are once again explicitly connected. The poet has found new evidence of this particular corruption. He has paradoxically "discovered" something he "already" "knew." Attention to detail, following the way wherever it leads him, brings Olson to the personal uncovering of evidence of the pejorocracy in one of the most common assumptions of our culture: the right to private ownership.

Yet, the poem does not pause over this "discovery," this concrete repetition of something already abstractly known. Despite the increase in awareness which comes with this passage, the poem is immediately diverted to a new perception:

[246]

Charles Olson

                    Holes
in my shoes, that's all right, my fly
gaping, me out
at the elbows, the blessing
                    that difficulties are once more
                                    (*MxP,* 14)

In *Being and Time,* Martin Heidegger argues that not until instruments begin to fail as such do we become aware of their independent existence and being. Analogously, as I have argued in chapter two, not until the "tradition" no longer works does it become evident that the "tradition" actually obscures rather than reveals. Olson in "Song 3" senses or dis-covers the same phenomenon. The smooth working of the "pejorocracy" lulls and greases the mind and senses so that the poet is not even aware that there are normal mental and sensual functions which are being denied him. But when the society and its support, its ground, that is, "tradition," begins to disintegrate, then its pernicious cover-up becomes clear.

The singing car and trolley of this poem indicate how completely the "pejorocracy" corrupts motion and direction. The electronic and mechnical Sirens obscure the risks and particularities—as well as the potential rewards—of traveling along a road marked by difficulties. Olson would "void [his] ear" of all this racket, all its noise and exploitation. And he finds as an alternative to this commercialization and ownership a poorer way. The closest details of his dress reveal to him how in his own being as a poet who refuses to submit to the "plentitude" of society he has an alternative present at hand. Like Lear who must strip off the trappings of his kingly role to see what lies closest to him—Cordelia's love and Goneril's hate—Olson must recognize in his own unaccommodated state "the blessing/ that difficulties are once more."

The way which must be taken to find that "anywhere" that has no shallow graves appears to be the poet's denial of any compromise with the crowd that surrounds him. Constant attention to his own position in the world and the details about him

Charles Olson

keep the poet on the path to some renewed dis-covery. The intrusion of the break-downs of the system makes him aware of its ontological and poetic inadequacies. But only his own vigilance, his own refusal to seek accommodation, provides the necessary disruption which keeps the poet on the way. "Difficulties" cannot be smoothed over. They draw the poet back to himself and his world. Most importantly, they compel the mind and senses to confront phenomena which have not *already* been digested and articulated in the language of the "they." Thus, difficulties are the means to dis-covery. They reveal the precariousness of man in the world and deny him the fiction of ease and comfort.

Following this discovery, Olson allows himself to summarize the value of his "vision." Yet even the seemingly "abstract" section of this poem grows out of a very specific and—to the poem and poet—new concrete detail. The general statements which "end" "Song 3" emerge from Olson's memory of and reading in *Gammer Gurton's Needle* and Ezra Pound's *Cantos:* [41]

> "In the midst of plenty, walk
> as close to
> bare
>           In the face of sweetness,
> piss
>               In the time of goodness,
> go side, go
> smashing, beat them, go as
> (as near as you can
>
> tear
>
> In the land of plenty, have
> nothing to do with it
>                       take the way of
> the lowest,
> including
> your legs, go
> contrary, go
>
> sing

                              (*MxP,* 14–15)

[248]

Charles Olson

The poem moves toward this articulation of a recurring theme. The "discovery" of the way of detail, of failed instruments, and of the importance of difficulties reaches its fullest statement and its most general significance in this passage.

"Song 3" moves from one detail and perception relentlessly to another. On the way, the poet opens up the existence and being of these things, not in their instrumentality, but in their thingness. At each encounter, the themes are basically the same; but they are repeated with an increase in the poet's awareness at each point. In the immediate elements of his life and history, the poet finds "evidence" for what is "really" true. As I have pointed out in chapter three about Kierkegaard's theory of the stages, temporal repetition—as opposed to New Critical "recollection"—always exposes greater degrees of awareness. Each "stage" of a repetition brings the poet closer to "voiding" himself of the "musickracket" of the "pejorocracy."

Basically, in poems like "Song 3," the poet's confrontation with details and particulars strips off layers of verbal interference maintained by both the tradition and our society. As a result of each "un-layering," the poet "sees" various things directly. In the larger context of *The Maximus Poems,* Olson destroys the images, concepts, and preconceptions which intrude between man and world and, thus, the poems allow the unity of man and nature to become apparent. Almost any Olson poem exemplifies his linguistic breakdown of the traditional privilege accorded the completed sentence. Further, most of his poems refuse to employ the "image" in the ironic senses of Modern literature and criticism. Most importantly, in Olson's *Maximus Poems,* as in "Song 3," things are not apprehended spatially, all at once, to provide static relief from change. Rather they insist upon process as *the* defining characteristic of life. They impose upon their readers the primordiality of time. By refusing to be completed, by breaking open the completed sentence, by denying creation via "recollection," they escape the "tradition," which reduces art to the formal completion of life and life's defense against disorder.

Olson's implicit attack on "recollection" results from his awareness of the fictional nature of the "tradition's" version of it-

[249]

self, of its "history." To give itself certainty and validity, the "tradition" assumes that its own "history" of itself is privileged. Yet, Olson is aware that it is impossible "to know what happened, even to oneself" (*SVH,* 19). In language reminiscent of Wallace Stevens, he writes: "At no point outside a fiction can one be sure" (*SVH,* 19). Like Kierkegaard, Olson knows that memory, "recollection," always lies because it oversimplifies. To order the past into comprehensible and understandable structures, the memory selectively removes from consciousness both points of ambiguity and any painful contradictions. "Recollection" explains the events "leading up to" the present, the "end," in order to make sense of their order and to clarify how "history" brings us to "where we are." Again, like both Stevens and Kierkegaard, Olson realizes that the attempt by "historians" to order the past is an aesthetic impulse, a desire to find a "certainty" which the events themselves in their unformed immediacy do not possess.

Thus, *The Maximus Poems,* quite consciously, disrupt the continuity of poetic "tradition," insofar as it is defined by "recollection" and "closed form." Like "The Songs of Maximus," *The Maximus Poems* undercut the "tradition's" claim to certainty not only by suggesting its "fictional" and therefore unprivileged, blinded nature, but by suggesting alternatives which the "tradition" omits in order to make itself work. It is in the latter that Olson differentiates himself from Wallace Stevens. Stevens feels we have no choice but to believe in a fiction since *everything* is a "fiction" and, to quote Heidegger's "What Is Metaphysics," "nothing else."[42] Olson, however, is similar to Heidegger in a different way. While, like Stevens, he disputes the "tradition's" distinction between "history" and "fiction," he agrees with Heidegger, and prefigures de Man, in claiming that there are mystified and demystified stances toward the world: "In other words there are TWO stances. Always are. It isn't a question of fiction versus knowing. 'Lies' are necessary in both—that is the HI-Magination" (*SVH,* 19). The "tradition" is mystified in its claim that its "history" of itself is "certain" and privileged. Olson, however, is "de-mystified" in realizing that there is truth and error in all "historical" claims.

The only "truth" Wallace Stevens seems prepared to admit in his deconstructions of the "tradition" is the nothingness which all language obscures. Olson, on the other hand, while admitting that all language lies, realizes that it is also potentially "authentic." A poetry of immediacy, which attempts to get the experience down while it is "hot," stands a greater chance of avoiding more of the traditional and habitual modes of language, which are inauthentic cover-ups, than does a poetry of "recollection" which is *for the most part,* "inauthentic."

*The Maximus Poems* reenact Olson's attack on the "tradition" and his awareness of its fictional nature by destroying its claims to "privilege" and the linguistic and "epistemological" structures upon which it rests. Olson's assault on Vincent Ferrini in "Letter 5" is paradigmatic of his destruction of the "tradition's" claims for itself.

The poem begins parenthetically: "(as, in summer, a newspaper, now, in spring, a magazine)" (*MxP,* 17). "Letter 5," like almost all of Olson's poems, refuses to begin "properly," from any "clear-cut" point of departure. Sartre's Roquentin realizes that when a reader opens a text of a work of art, he begins by paying attention to seemingly unimportant detail because, the reader knows from habit, the details always prove to be of use in moving the story along to its end. In other words, Roquentin explains how an author of a *fiction* chooses his beginning carefully with an eye to making it "fit" his predetermined "ending." "Letter 5," however, resists the kind of beginning which Roquentin finds in the "re-counting" (*raconter*) of a tale.[43] The details of the poem's opening are not only "unimportant" to its "end," but quite clearly are the thoughts of the moment which trigger the process of the poem. For example, the attack on Ferrini is immediately motivated by the appearance of the spring issue of the magazine he edits, *Four Winds.*

Indeed, before going on to criticize Ferrini directly, Olson follows his original thought where it leads him; he further particularizes the situation's "locale": "though how Gloucester will know what damage . . . only Brown's window . . . This quarterly/ will not be read" (*MxP*, 17). After a seemingly hackneyed, conventional meditation on the limits of literacy among the local people, Olson suddenly energizes the entire poem and moves it into the realm of the "tradition" and "history":

> Limits
> are what any of us
> are inside of
> (*MxP*, 17)

He makes a discovery of the basically spatio-temporal nature of all humans which obviates much of the limpness of the conventional assault of the people preceding it. And, indeed, his discovery brings Olson to his first direct attack on Ferrini, who, according to Olson, sentimentally praises and yet merely tolerates the people.

Like all of Olson's letters in *The Maximus Poems*, "Letter 5" destroys the traditional forms and expectations about fictional "beginnings" by expressing the immediate situation: the time, the place, and the "inner energy" of the poet. The beginning of this poem promises no final positivistic or symbolistic order, but instead offers to those who can follow only a way of moving through the immediate for the sake of important personal discoveries. This poem specifically introduces the theme of personal "situation," of personal "history," by insisting that all men are within limits. This discovery does not "grow" out of what precedes it. It is not a "logical consequence" nor part of a "mosaic" pattern. It is spontaneously offered as a "result" of the poet's encounter with the magazine and its locale, the city of Gloucester. As a "result" of this process of personal discovery, "Letter 5" is not amenable to the language of a literary tradition based on a poetry of "recollection." Olson's "discovery" cannot be seen as in any way being "aesthetically necessary." It is radically accidental and superfluous. It conforms to no preexistent order.

Charles Olson

Rather it emerges from the pressure of always moving from perception to perception and maintaining the "circuit" of "world-
senses-mind-object" which alone allows for creative discovery.

It is not necessary to show how this poem, like "The Songs
of Maximus," often doubles back, "repeating," not "recollecting," itself. The poem continually explores the same "situation"
and the same ideas, stripping away more and more elements
which inhibit disclosure. The structure of "repetition," which is
analogous to Kierkegaard's theory of stages which is discussed in
chapter three, is basic and generally unchanging in Olson's
poems. It always brings the poet through layers of the ordinary,
the familiar, until the closest details, like the commonplace of the
people's literary disinterest, are suddenly "energized" to disclose
something previously unnoticed in connection with them. The
sudden disclosure expands the poet's and reader's awareness of
the fundamental temporality of the situation.

Indeed, Olson's attack on Ferrini is based upon Ferrini's disinterest in the things which should be most familiar to him. Ferrini is of the "many" and not the "few" who have demystified
the tradition (*MxP,* 18). Olson looks for some "place" at which
he can meet Ferrini, but finally cannot find any because Ferrini
lacks a situation, any knowledge of his town's history and geography. He has made no attempt to ascertain things for himself, as
an authentic historian should, and, instead, perpetuates errors
about the town. Olson corrects Ferrini from first-hand knowledge on the events of the "C & R Construction Company"
(*MxP,* 21) and explains to him the details of the "first Race" in
1920 with "Bluenose" (*MxP,* 22). He admonishes Ferrini for
publishing an allegorical play on the sea in Gloucester:

> the shocking play you publish
> with God as the Master of
> a Ship! In Gloucester-town
> you publish it, where men
> have cause to know where god is
> when wooden ships or steel ships,

[253]

with sail or power,
are out on men's business
(*MxP*, 25)

Ferrini's inability to make his magazine, his "aesthetic object,"
reenact the life of his area results from his inability to see the
world around him. Ferrini, instead, sees books and experience
through the common eyes of other literary editors. Indeed,
Olson accuses him of pandering to other editors' taste for the
sake of publishing his own work:

what sticks out in this issue is verse
from at least four other editors
of literary magazines

do you think such scratch-me-back
gets by our eyes, the few of us there are
who read?
(*MxP*, 24)

The commercialization of language which Olson reviles in "The
Songs of Maximus" reappears in this denunciation of Ferrini. In
this repetition of the theme, however, Olson reveals a new context for such exploitation, namely, the dissociation from temporal and spatial "locale" which it requires.

Ferrini and his magazine live on the opinions and formulations of others:

your magazine might excuse itself
if it walked on those legs all live things walk on,
their own
(*MxP*, 24)

He imitates the accepted versions of things which the society
proffers. He divorces himself from the authentic history which
only personal, "walking," detailed attention to the locale and its
history can provide. Ferrini does not attend to those things
which are most proximate to any man of Gloucester:

It's no use.
There is no place we can meet.

Charles Olson

You have left Gloucester.
You are not there, you are anywhere
where there are little magazines
will publish you

(MxP, 25)

Olson frequently quotes Heraclitus to summarize his sense of man's alienation in the ordinary world of the "they": *"Man is estranged from that with which he is most familiar"* (*SVH*, 14). Ferrini is like Conant and Miles Standish and John Hawkins, almost willfully isolated from what is in his neighborhood. He is more comfortable, more "at-home," with what is "common-place" than with the difficult task of attempting to see beyond the "ordinary" to the things which are covered-up.

In *The Special View of History*, Olson claims that authentic history, i.e., the history Herodotus practices, is "the one way to restore the familiar to us" (29). But authentic history requires the ability to stand in doubt, in mystery. Keats, of course, is the paradigm of this potential for Olson. To the degree that an account, a reenactment, is not fiction, that is, to the extent that poetic language is "authentic" and "dis-closive," it must be able to endure a corresponding degree of error, uncertainty, and mystery. The authentic historian does not attempt to close off all variations and permutations by "explaining" all possibilities in aesthetic order. In "Canto XIII," Ezra Pound, speaking through the figure of Kung, suggests that in the past historians did not try to close all the gaps in their explanatory constructs. They more honestly accepted the "presence" of mystery, i.e., the absence of any account which "makes sense":

> And Kung said " Wan ruled with moderation,
> > In his day the State was well kept,
> And even I can remember
> A day when the historians left blanks in their writings,
> I mean for things they didn't know,
> But that time seems to be passing."[44]

The driving urge of the West is to close off the gaps of mystery by expanding "knowledge":

[255]

Charles Olson

> By history I mean to know, to really know. The rhyme is still
> "mystery." We can't stand it. Nothing must be left undone.
> We have to run up against the wall. There is nothing which
> happens to us which we don't have the right to know what
> the—— goes on. Even to know that one can't know. Which is
> the hooker.
>
> (SVH, 20–21)

This knowledge of "mystery" means more than merely ac-
knowledging the "limits" of the spatio-temporal situation which,
as "Letter 5" points out, we all live in. It implies an essentially
ontological truth about the nature of man's being and his language. Man possesses the ability to reveal and cover-up because
of his essentially temporal understanding. As my discussion of
Heidegger in chapter two points out, each and every disclosure,
i.e., each and every truth, emerges out of and exists simultaneously in error. This constant presence of "error" is an unre-
movable mystery. Keats, of course, represents the same idea by
the phrase, "Penetralium of mystery," and the ability to stand in
the face of it by "Negative Capability." Thus, according to "Letter 5," the "tradition," through imitation and "recollection" of
the common-places of the "they" world, not only obscures the
familiar and artificially separates man from the world—this is the
Cartesian-Leibnizian dualistic heritage—but it obscures the very
existence of the "mystery" until, in a moment of breakdown
within the tradition, the mysterious, the necessarily inexplicable,
reasserts its right to attention.

   In *The Maximus Poems,* Olson not only insists upon the attention to the ordinary as a way of making discoveries, but also
upon the necessity for recognizing the error or mystery in objects
and experiences as well. For example, in "Letter 20," his account
of the fisherman Shea is presented as a conscious fiction:

> The story
> you could never get straight,
> it was only,
> as always
>
> (MxP, 91)

Charles Olson

But Olson insists on the value of presenting the "history" of this
man and the events aboard ship:

> It is not the substance of a man's fault,
> it is the shape of it
> is what lives with him, is what shows
>
> in his eyes (in our eyes
>
> (*MxP,* 91)

The ascertainable, certain detail is not the crucial matter, but
rather, attending to the human effects of a situation, discovering
what lies exposed without attempting to coerce some complete
and therefore misleading "recounting" of the event to the surface. Olson is satisfied with what appears; he does not let the fine
insight of Shea's appearance escape him because as Keats says of
Coleridge, he is "incapable of remaining content with half
knowledge." [45]

Yet, Olson actively "walks" through the material at hand to
see what he can discover. "Letter 15," for example, corrects the
factual information concerning Nathaniel Bowditch, a Gloucester
sailor, that "Maximus to Gloucester" mistakenly presents.
Olson, in the earlier poem, reported Bowditch's story as it was
recounted by Bowditch's son. In fact, the earlier version of the
Bowditch story is the version "which we were all raised to believe" (*MxP,* 67). But, as a result of more careful "historical" examination, "The whole tale, as we have had it, from his son,
goes by the board" (*MxP,* 67).

Just as within individual letters, Olson returns, within the
entire volume, to previously treated themes and topics in order
to open them up and to strip away from himself false "re-count-
ings" which block his perception of the details. The Bowditch
episode is a case in point, but it is only part of a general strategy
upon which *The Maximus Poems* rests. A fuller analysis of this
area must be delayed until one more aspect of Olson's attack on
the "tradition" is made clear.

In "Maximus, to himself," (Letter 12), Olson complains: "I
have had to learn the simplest things/ last. Which made for dif-

Charles Olson

ficulties" (*MxP*, 52). This is a poem emerging out of the poet's own sense of failure in his enterprise and, as such, is analogous to Whitman's "Out of the Cradle" and "As I Ebb'd with the Ocean of Life." In each of these poems, the poet senses that the major obstacle he has been trying to overcome in order to write the kind of poetry he intends—for Whitman this obstacle is always death and suffering—perhaps has finally overcome him. These are all poems of the poet's "dejection."

For Olson, the blocking agent is the tradition in which he has grown up:

> that we grow up many
> And the single
> is not easily
> known
>
> (*MxP*, 52)

Estranged from even what is closest to him, Olson struggles to overcome the fragmentation of the "self" and the separation from the world which the "tradition" creates. The "single" which he hopes to know is not only the individual things which the "they" world obscures through its language and habits, but also the "single" world in which man and other beings are all "objects" in one nature. Just as Ferrini cuts himself off from Gloucester, the "tradition" cuts Olson off from his potential for being in contact with things and being aware of his place in a monistic world.

Olson senses that he has not done the world or nature's business. Unlike those who have acted directly in one of these contexts, Olson has dealt with language all along:

> I have made dialogues,
> have discussed ancient texts,
> have thrown what light I could, offered
> what pleasures
> doceat allows
>
> But the known?
> This, I have had to be given,

[258]

Charles Olson

a life, love, and from one man
the world.

> Tokens.
> But sitting here
> I look out as a wind
> and water man, testing
> And missing
> some proof.
>                     (*MxP*, 52–53)

To be "given" the world and life is no better than to deal merely
with words; it is to remain caught by a "tradition" which does
not want a man to look for himself. Olson has been shown that
the "world" on the other side of language is accessible. But such
knowledge is not yet personal or authentically "historical"
enough. It comes from another's eyes. Early in *The Maximus
Poems,* in a passage which echoes Johannes Climacus' attack on
the Hegelians in *Fear and Trembling* and Whitman's advice to the
American poet to "no longer take things at second or third
hand," Olson scorns the possibility of the transference of such
knowledge from one person to another:

> . . . . tell you? ha! who
> can tell another how
> to manage the swimming?
>
> he was right: people
>
> don't change. They only stand more
> revealed. I,
> likewise

>                 (*MxP*, 5)

In "Maximus, to himself," Olson realizes that despite his efforts which may have come too late, he has fallen into the
"habit" of accepting the world from others. He has not managed
to get beyond words, "ancient texts." The way is open to him,
but he must continue to "reveal" himself, to travel further along
into the particulars which alone will break down the "many"

[259]

Charles Olson

which hide the "single." In Whitmanesque tones, Olson surveys
the "vistas" before him and declares the continuation of his
project:

> It is undone business
> I speak of, this morning,
> with the sea
> stretching out
> from my feet
>
>                    (*MxP,* 53)

The recurrent sibilant of this passage reinforces the impulse
Olson has to "speak" of his position. Rather than listening to the
words of others, Maximus, to break through, to dis–cover, must
journey outward into that sea, the source of creation and death,
in the language of his own voice. "Ancient texts" are no longer
enough material for uncovering; the voice of the poet must expand itself to match the stretching sea.

Men cannot be *taught* how to "swim," how to discover,
how to travel because the transmission of such "information" is
essentially falsifying. In "Human Universe," as we have already
seen, Olson points out that logic and discourse have so worked
abstractions and concepts as well as Platonic ideals into our language that the fact of language as the speech of an individual has
been buried (*SW,* 53–54). Borrowed language, just like borrowed forms, "cool" the experience of the "object's" pressure on
the self. Harold Bloom, we recall, believes in the possibility of a
"tradition" which "works," i.e., which preserves and carries-
over the essential discoveries of one generation to another. Heidegger, of course, argues that the verbal means for carrying over
such learning is itself the means of covering-up, of being inauthentic. The assertion, the concept, the sentence, the "idea" are
all simplifications and reifications. Olson's position in "Human
Universe" is similar to Heidegger's:

> What makes most acts—of living and of writing—unsatisfac-
> tory, is that the person and/or the writer satisfy themselves that
> they can only make a form (what they say or do, or a story, a

[260]

poem, whatever) by selecting from the full content some face of it, or plane, some part. And at just this point, by just this act, they fall back on the dodges of discourse, and immediately, they lose me, I am no longer engaged, this is not what I know is the going-on (and of which going-on I, as well as they, want some illumination, and so, some pleasure). It comes out a demonstration, a separating out, an act of classification, and so, a stopping, and all that I know is, it is not there, it has turned false. For any of us, at any instant, are juxtaposed to any experience, even an overwhelming single one, on several more planes than the arbitrary and discursive which we inherit can declare. (*SW*, 55)

The inauthenticity of the "tradition" and its basic language structures arises precisely from the potential for "stopping." While Heidegger in *Being and Time* attacks the traditional logocentric concept of the assertion to reveal a more primordial structure of temporality in Dasein and Being, Olson destroys the two basic conceptions of Western language which "freeze" experience, and adopts as the basis of his own poetics the "heretical" view of nominalism.

Olson realizes in "Maximus, to himself," that by having the "known" given to him, that is, through the revelations others make to him in language, he remains cut off from the things in the world by "words." The particular is preceded by a universal when disclosure occurs through the linguistic communication of another. To get to the thing, Olson concludes, the poet must not only confront things from a phenomenologically reduced stance in which all presuppositions have been thrown aside, but with an awareness that as long as language itself, nouns and verbs, precedes the thing in itself, as it is claimed to do in Western "realistic" and "conceptual" linguistic theories, the thing is inevitably obscured by a "representation."

In this matter, Olson is closer to Berengar of Tours and Roscellinus or William of Occam than he is even to Pound, Williams, or Husserl.[46] And his position is much more radical and precise than is Williams' claim that there are "No ideas but in

[261]

things!" In "Tyrian Business," Olson echoes Parmenides on language:

> There may be no more names than there are objects
> There can be no more verbs than there are actions
>
> (*MxP,* 36)

Though L.S. Dembo, in "Olson's *Maximus* and the Way to Knowledge,"[47] describes the nominalistic function of the language in this poem, he does not bother to put Olson's adoption of this extreme position into any context *vis-à-vis* the tradition. Furthermore, Olson, according to Dembo, uses the nominalistic theory of language to achieve an idealist position. Dembo seems unaware of the historical antipathy between nominalism and idealism as well as of Olson's own dislike of Plato.

Nominalism *as a doctrine* originated among heretics and sceptics, those who doubted the validity and certainty of the inherited Christian tradition. Logically and philosophically, nominalism emerges from the firm belief that there are no universals, but only discrete facts. Of course, Parmenides recognizes that thinking and speaking are the same thing, and nominalists convert his recognition into an often heretical attack on the established "realistic" and "conceptualist" theories of language, epistemology, and ontology. While it would be possible to discriminate among the various important nominalists in the past and to point out that William of Occam's nominalism appeared at the same time as the empirical movement in the West, such an expanded treatment would be tangential here. From the most immediate point of view of this study of Olson, what stands out about the nominalists is their insistent opposition to the success of the "traditional" conceptualizations of language inherited from Plato.

"Realism," of course, describes Plato's theory that the "real" is the most abstract and general. Ascribing primary "reality" to *ideas* leads to the linguistic position that particulars are perceivable and understandable, indeed, only "ex-pressible," by virtue of the prior existence of the universal. In a similar manner, the "conceptualist" theory of language argues that perception is not possible without the prior existence of "concepts," i.e.,

[262]

"ideas" which dwell in the mind of the beholder and no longer, as in Plato, in some spiritual realm. The nominalist position on universals is that they are simply "names" existing after the facts of the particulars. Of course, by extension, such a position denies Gnostic faith in any spiritual order or "other world." It also denies the validity of any theory of correspondences by which the particular and worldly gain meaning only by participating in the hierarchical chain of ascendencies to the One.

The New Critics, of course, insist that there is a driving impulse in art toward "concrete universality." Ransom and Wimsatt are both preoccupied with the possibility of seeing such figures as the house in *Howard's End* and the lighthouse in *To the Lighthouse* as abstract and general embodiments of the "shape" which all art strives to assume.[48] The New Critics are suspicious of the possibility of linguistic universals because linear uses of language are tainted with scientism. Yet they hope to gain entry to the same spiritual and general realm as the "realists" and "conceptualists" by means of "art" rather than "logic." However, the same aprioristic epistemology and the same atemporal ontology underlie both the New Critics' goal, the "concrete universal" of closed form, and the "ideal" vision of the "realists."

By insisting upon the Parmenidean vision of the equivalence of thought and speech, Olson breaks out of the limitations of the traditional notion of universals. His language is, as a result, more directly connected both to the beings of the world about him and to his own encounters with them. Both "realism" and "conceptualism" break the "circuit" of creation by interposing "words" between the "eye" and the "world." Nominalism lets the poet get to the fundamental perception with which Wallace Stevens "opens" "An Ordinary Evening in New Haven":

> The eye's plain vision is a thing apart,
> The vulgate of experience.
>
> (*P,* 331)

Dembo's reading of "Tyrian Business" shows clearly the effort needed to break through to a functioning nominalist perception of the world. The attempt often "results" in fragments and aban-

Charles Olson

doned starts (*MxP*, 36). But when the poet can achieve such nominalistic perception, the circuit of creation is started:

> the flowering plum
> out the front door window
> sends whiteness
> inside my house
>               (*MxP*, 41)

Perception is restored as a movement which takes place "from the outside in" and the process of language and thought begins simultaneously with the appearance of the thing which gives the poet the noun he needs to speak. Furthermore, the insistent claim of the thing to be itself and to be the sole means of presenting language prevents the poet from transforming the particular into a universal or symbol:

>                           I, dazzled
>     as one is, until one discovers
>     there is no other issue than
>     the moment of
>                 the pleasure of
>                         this plum,
>
>     these things
>     which don't carry their end any further than
>     their reality in
>     themselves
>                       (*MxP*, 42)

"The eye's plain vision" reclaims the linguistic potentiality to discover the world. It destroys the interference of "words" and lets the poet "discover" the "pleasure" of the moment caught, as Keats would say, from the "Penetralium of mystery."

Indeed, the "discovery" of the mediated identity of words and things, of thought and speech, not only can activate the creative process, but can call a halt to it. It can "disrupt" the linguistic impulse to demand renewed attention to itself. It will not allow the particular to be forgotten in the working of language:

[264]

Charles Olson

(And I buzz,
as the bee does,
who's missed
the plum tree,
and gone and got himself caught
in my window

And the whirring of whose wings
blots out the rattle of
my machine)

(*MxP*, 44)

Essentially, then, Olson's attack on the existent "tradition" centers on the way in which traditional, habitual forms of language, and indeed, the tradition's own conceptions of the nature of language, blind men and poets to the priority of things in the world and man's place in the world as one object among many. His nominalist linguistic position, along with his insistence upon the "circuit" of perception, leads him to create poems (the order of the elements in this sentence could be reversed and be no less "true" of Olson) which begin from the immediate situation, the attention to the particulars which not only define that situation, but which give him the language needed to move on. The major effect of the Olson poem is precisely one of movement, of shifting rapidly from one perception to the other and thereby making the reader aware of the temporal nature of the poet in his encounter with his situation. Quite appropriately, it is out of this insistence upon personal experience and motion that the major figures of Olson's *Maximus Poems* emerge, as well as his insight into the very nature of "traditions" as equally personal, moving phenomena.

III

As I have mentioned above at the conclusion of my discussion of the "tradition," "imitation," and "recollection," there is a general strategy upon which *The Maximus Poems* seem to rest: the reenactment of the only authentic "tradition" available to the

[265]

Charles Olson

truly destructive, nominalistic poet. In *Causal Mythology,* Olson, along with Robert Duncan (who was in the audience at Berkeley the day Olson delivered this talk), makes the clear programmatic statement that whatever a poet uses of his situation, whatever becomes part of his experience, whatever he tries to get down "hot" is, in fact, the only "tradition" we can have. Olson and Duncan must be quoted at some length on this. Olson's response is triggered by a question as to why he goes outside our culture for his myths:

> I don't believe in cultures myself. . . . I believe there is simply ourselves, and where we are has a particularity which we'd better use because that's about all we got. Otherwise we're running around looking for somebody else's stuff. . . . Truth lies solely in what you do with it. And that means *you.* I don't think there's any such thing as a creature of culture.
>
> I think we live so totally in an accultured time that the reason why we're all here that care and write is to put an end to that whole thing. Put an end to nation, put an end to culture, put an end to divisions of all sorts. . . . We have our picture of the world and *that's* the creation. . . .
>
> ROBERT DUNCAN:
>
> Charles, I think I can swing back to—that as poets we have to find the term that stands for what we have known that's there. And it might go all the way back to, I mean I certainly, this last one goes back to the place you found where it is. You know.
>
> CHARLES OLSON:
>
> Yeah. That's right.
>
> ROBERT DUNCAN:
>
> Now you don't care if you found it yesterday. You found it there. So you have to go there.
>
> CHARLES OLSON:
>
> That's right.
>
> ROBERT DUNCAN:
>
> And you recognize that, you read through miles and you recognize that this thing's it.
>
> CHARLES OLSON:
>
> Yeah. That's all. And believe you me I know everyone has their own recognitions. . . . I find that what we call my-

[266]

Charles Olson

thology is the inclusion of all this that you're speaking of. The *recognition*. And I don't believe that there is a single person in this room that doesn't have the opportunity—the absolute place and thing that's theirs. I mean places and things that are theirs. . . . I don't believe that everyone of us isn't absolutely *specific*. And *has* his specificity. . . . The *reductive* is what I'm proposing. I don't think you can get your recognitions by going out. I think they come by going—from within. (*CM,* 35–37)

Olson's definition of "mythology" as the inclusion of all personal recognitions is specifically that kind of "tradition" which a destructive poet can have. The emphasis that should be drawn from this dialogue between Olson and Duncan must be placed on the process of finding, of "recognizing" the familiar and specific through the reduction. "Re-cognizing" does not, of course, mean for Olson a process of recollecting or representing, as it does for traditional epistemologists from Plato to Kant, or as it does to "hermeneuticists" like Betti and E.D. Hirsch. Rather, Olson's use in *The Maximus Poems* of the local and specific items of Gloucester *reenacts* the process of finding "the term that stands for what we have known is there." They are the "map" of his "picture of the world."

Although terms like "map" and "picture," which Olson uses throughout his works, are borrowed from the spatial, ironic imagination, Olson's insistence upon the process and movement necessary to the discovery of the details in the map helps to retrieve a forgotten sense of temporal discovery in such language. William Spanos has argued that Pound's use of the word *"periploi"* is a key to seeing the changed vision of "Post-modern" poetry. Unlike the Modern "iconic" or "ironic" poet, Pound and Olson do not hope to see the whole world laid out spatially on a map seen from above; they do not try to see the universe on a plane. Rather, Pound and Olson try to regain the older method of map-making which grows directly out of motion, dis-covery, and encountering the unknown. Pound calls this process of charting a coast line, *periplum*.[49]

In "On First Looking out through Juan de la Cosa's Eyes,"

Charles Olson

Olson distinguishes between Behaim, a German cartographer whose globe left a blank space between the Azores and Japan, and de la Cosa, Columbus' mapmaker. Behaim, basing his own maps upon the reports of others and the established tradition that by sailing West one could reach the East, "created" out of ignorance, out of hearsay, and not discovery and, therefore, he perpetuated error. La Cosa, on the other hand, knows from immediate experience as a voyager of the presence of the unexpected and unexplored New World which his maps record:

> But before La Cosa, nobody
> could have
> a mappemunde
> *(MxP, 77)*

La Cosa is a sailor who "reenacts" the process of his discovery in the maps, the *periploi,* which he draws as he goes along the coast of lands. One of Olson's typical figures is, of course, the fisherman who, like la Cosa, participates in the same process of disclosure:

> (As men, my town, my two towns
> talk, talked of Gades, talk
> of Cash's
>
> drew, on a table, in spelt,
> with a finger, in beer, a
> portulans
> *(MxP, 77)*

"Portulans" is a method of making early coastal maps by tracing the course followed by the ship.[50] Just as the poet in "The Songs of Maximus" moves along from one perception to another making an outline of his journey, through the entire *Maximus Poems,* Olson "draws" a "map," a "portulans" of his "recognitions." In this presentation of what has in various moments triggered the creative energy, the poet "constellates" *(MxP, 59)* his "recognitions." In other words, having destroyed the "tradition" and having exposed how any "tradition," as well as the idea of "tra-

Charles Olson

dition," is a cover-up, a "cooling" of the immediate and a dimi-
nution of language to realism or conceptualism, Olson reveals his
own "tradition," his own "mythology," which is the record of
how he got to where he is. In "Maximus, to Gloucester, Letter
II," Olson articulates precisely this idea:

> That a man's life
> (his, anyway)
> is what there is
> that tradition is
>
> at least is where I find it,
> how I got to
> what I say
> (*MxP*, 48)

"Tradition" is precisely for Olson not only "what there is" and
"where I find it," but, perhaps most importantly, the way in
which "I got to what I say." Thus, "tradition" becomes in Olson
not only the personal record of a poet's life and discoveries, but it
is also a *disclosure of the potentiality for disclosure* which lies within
the attempt to define the self and to articulate what, as Duncan
says, "we have known is there."

In "Maximus, at Tyre and at Boston," Olson explains that
the attempt to find the "single" in the "many," which pains him
so much in "Maximus, to himself," becomes successful in reenacting the discovery of this "tradition" or "mythology." At the
end of this poem, Olson writes:

> that we are only
> as we find out we are
> (*MxP*, 95)

This theme of drawing the single out from behind the veil of
"words" in the "pejorocracy," from beneath the layers of habit
and presupposition, recurs often in this volume of poems. But in
"Stiffening, in the Master Founders' Wills," the destructive process of stripping away the old "tradition" becomes explicitly
identified with the "map" of the poetic discovery of the new,
personal, destructive "tradition":

[269]

Charles Olson

> We pick
>
> a private way
> among debris
> of common
> wealths—Public
> fact as sure
>
> as dimensions stay
> personal. And one desire,
> that the soul
> be naked
> at the end  ·
>
> of time
>
> (*MxP*, 132)

The explicit connection of the "private way" with the "debris" of nations and common worlds, i.e., commonly held beliefs and "cultures," reinforces the general identification of the destruction of the Western "tradition" in the poems with the project of being "stripped" naked of that "they" world.

Certainly, then, as I suggested in the introductory critical remarks of this chapter, those who look at Olson for the establishment of a new "tradition," or like Dembo, a new ideal "polis" on earth, are mistaken. Olson suggests most clearly that any "tradition" which is held in common, which is used to "transfer" the knowledge of "how to swim" closes off realms of investigation and obscures the potential for all people to "map" their own myth or "tradition." What Olson is providing for poetry in this context is not the reduction of the past "to nullity," to quote Heidegger's important caution once again, but rather a way of encountering whatever is part of the "locale," that is, a way of going to wherever and whatever the poet needs in order to express what he knows immediately to be the case. In other words, such a poetics means that each and every poet must stand in a destructive, interpretive relation to what precedes him in art as well as in a reductive relation to the societal structures which surround him and cut him off from the things most familiar to

[270]

him. *"The Tradition"* cannot be *fixed* as any canon of works or even any canon of interpretations. There are as many "traditions" as there are authentic poets of destruction who look with their eyes at the world about them and who imitate Herodotus as historian and try to find things out for themselves.

The relation among poets of this type is radically discontinuous. Their works cannot be placed in a static set of patterns nor can they be described by metaphors of continuity and development. Olson's poetics and poetry, although highly allusive, and, therefore, seemingly "traditional," is exactly unlike the kind of poetry which Bate and Bloom hope to see written. They see no alternative for the poet but writing in an accepted, previously given order of texts. It is precisely the "freedom" from any definitive "tradition" which prevents any feelings of anxiety in Olson about his relation to the past. Furthermore, Olson's poetry is unlike the Gnostic insistence of both Bate and Bloom that the poet escape flux and uncertainty through the imitation of a canon. Indeed, Olson's liberty from the burden of the past comes from his insistence that the poet must stand in a destructive, not an imitative, relation to the past, with the result that the past is seen in all its uncertainties, ambiguities, and contradictions, and not in the formal certainty of an aesthetic fiction.

The primary figures of Olson's *Maximus Poems* are derived from the historical past of the immediate region of Gloucester, from documents, stories, i.e., "oral" tradition, and other more "exotic" sources—for example, the pre-Socratics, the Maya, and the Phoenicians. Central to the figures Olson draws from his geographical locale are the fishermen of Gloucester, the artists and workingmen of the "polis," and, from New England's past, the recurring figure of John Smith. Heraclitus and Parmenides appear in quotations of their fragments, and their ontological and linguistic insights lie behind much of the theme and method of the volume. The Maya are likewise present as an alternative to Western culture and as an example of an entire people who apparently lived in a phenomenologically reduced relation to their world. John Smith, along with some few other people from

Charles Olson

New England's early history, are men in whose lives Olson finds "evidence" for the destructive, stripped relation to the world he thinks is necessary to poetry, and they represent the potentialities which the official American "history" has covered-up. Perhaps the most "central" figure in the volume is Maximus of Tyre, who, it seems, is neither a mask for the poet nor a metaphor, but rather another of those "terms" which Olson finds in his "travels" for the particular qualities of teacher and historian he hoped to articulate.

Although each of these figures "means" something different every time it recurs because of the changing place on the map of Olson's voyage, they are all united by the fact that they trigger Olson's creative circuit. They all present possibilities which he is trying to find beneath the "words" of the "pejorocracy." His personal "tradition" or "mythology," in which he "re-enacts" certain disclosures as particular discoveries for what he "already" knows, is also an example of what the "tradition" of the West and of America especially has covered-up.

Many of the early *Maximus Poems* repeat the theme of the "polis" and of the "few" whose "eyes" are sufficient to establish a "polis." Earlier in this chapter, I have argued against L.S. Dembo's reading of Olson's "polis" as an idealization of the city and suggested that for Olson, the "polis" "represents" the re-disclosed potential for using the senses in a phenomenologically reduced way. Understood in this latter way, the "polis" is one of the major figures of *The Maximus Poems*. Indeed, it is potentially such an energy-charged trope that it could be seen metonymically as figure for the whole enterprise of the volume.

"Polis" is primarily defined by the potential to use the senses authentically, to set the circuit of creation into motion, "by going," as Olson says in *Causal Mythology,* "from within." In "Letter 3," for example, Olson opposes those "who use words cheap" (*MxP,* 9) to those few whose rootedness in their locale demands a nominalistic and authentic use of language. In one of the clearest instances of Olson's casting off any illusion that Max-

[272]

imus of Tyre has been adopted as a mask, he addresses himself, in his own voice, to the people of the polis:

> I speak to any of you, not to you all, to no group, not to you
>     as citizens
> as my Tyrian might have. Polis now
> is a few, is a coherence not even yet new (the island of this city
> is a mainland now of who? who can say who are
> citizens?
>
> Only a man or a girl who hear a word
> and that word meant to mean not a single thing the least more
>     than
> what it does mean (not at all to sell any one anything, to keep
>     them anywhere,
> not even
> in this rare place
>
> (MxP, 11)

Olson cannot be a teacher like Maximus of Tyre in these matters.
He does not believe in the transference of personal knowledge of
this type. He can only speak to the initiated; hence, the charge by
his critics that his poetry is "elitist." Indeed, it must be. It can ultimately only be heard by those who are prepared already. It can
only be understood by those who have experienced the breakdown and the lie of the tradition and have made the phenomenologically destructive effort to free their senses and their minds.
As my discussion of "Letter 9" points out, the reduced mind recognizes that things have no end beyond themselves; likewise, the
minds of those who "form" the "polis" realize that words,
emerging out of things and not ideas or concepts, do not go
beyond themselves and the objects they disclose.

   "Letter 5" is a major example of Olson's use of the "polis"
as the potential for authentic encounter with the world. In opposition to Ferrini, whose commitment is to imitation and the
common world of the "they," the "polis" is radically personal
and immediate in its perceptions. Olson addresses Ferrini to

Charles Olson

point out those (such as Helen Stein, a painter[51]) who do authentically what he does inauthentically:

> Helen Stein's eyes, and those others, Gloucester, who look,
>    who can still look,
> look right straight down into yr [Ferrini's] pages, into the
>    pages of this sheet you've had the nerve
> (no different from their nerve)
> to put upon the public street


> It is not the many but the few who care
> who keep alive what you set out to do:
> to offer Gloucester poems and stories
> the High School Flicker's not the end of

(MxP, 18)

This passage introduces a major element in the Postmodern poetic and suggests a thematic linkage between Olson and Heidegger. In *Being and Time,* as William V. Spanos argues, the intentional relation of Dasein to his world is defined as "care"
(*Sorge*).[52] Heidegger's term is not being imposed upon Olson in
any way. Indeed, in this same poem, the poet goes on to repeat
the notion of "care" as an alternative to the traditional way of
confronting the world as a series of assumed "givens."

In a passage which helps to disclose the interaction in Olson's "tradition" between the "polis" and the Portugese fishermen of Gloucester, Olson reveals the fisherman's ability
to *see* details so finely and distinctly that he could "dis–cover"
from the sand on a stick of butter what sort of base lay at the
bottom of the ocean at any given point. Carl Olsen possesses the
potential for portulans, i.e., the ability to discover and record
immediately, because of his uninhibited vision; in other words,
he has "care":

> a peak of the ocean's floor he knew so well (the care
> he gave his trade, his listening

Charles Olson

as knowing as a halibut knows its grounds (as Olsen knows
those grounds)

(*MxP*, 19)

In fact, it is precisely "care" which Ferrini lacks in his journal,
*Four Winds:* "You see I can't get away from the old measure of
care: how your magazine don't raise me" (*MxP*, 22).

In *Icon and Time,* Spanos develops the distinction between
authenticity and inauthenticity, that is, the "traditional" world of
the "they" and the personal, immediate, "historical" world of
the "discoverer," by an analysis of the state of being "care-less":

> Broadly this mode of comportment involves . . . a kind of
> "concern" that will, in fact, neutralize care: a *care-less,* a *disinterested,* perception of the world of things and other human beings
> as objects present-at-hand (*Vorhandene*) inside a super-object, so
> to speak: a perception that spatializes the nothingness of finitude, that draws a bounding line around time, to allow man to
> plunder the living earth.[53]

We not only recognize in Spanos' description of the "care-less"
world the "pejorocracy" which Olson attacks so viciously in *The
Maximus Poems,* but in the important notion of "dis-interest" as
the aesthetic equivalent of "care-lessness," we can see the entire
complex of the New Criticism, irony, "recollection," and "imitation." Indeed, the continuity of the literary tradition as such is
possible only if the poet and critic is dis-interested in the "objects" he "studies." Furthermore, a poetry created from a relation to the "tradition," by "imitation," requires the author's
"dis-interest" in the world and acceptance of a life covered over
with "words, words, words."

As Spanos points out, "care" is always "care for" something, or for the world as a whole, when it is authentic. "Care
for" the world, however, does not mean only a resolution not to
coerce, exploit, or ignore the world for the sake of a "universe of
discourse." "Care for" reveals the potentiality of Dasein, to use
Heidegger's terms, for opening up the world around Dasein, to
expand the "horizon" of meaning. In other words, Dasein as a

[275]

Charles Olson

care-ful human being is a "discoverer"; in Olson's figures, he is a walker, a fisherman, a portulans-maker, a poet who breaks down traditional forms and who re-enacts an experience of discovery while it is hot.

Olson's major figures all open up the realm of meaning and of experience by approaching the world with that *intention,* by being "care-ful." Although John Smith is the major example of the concerned man in *The Maximus Poems,* other figures appear whom Olson "plots" because they help him as poet open up his world in a similar way. In the early poems, the various people who are aware of their potential to discover make up the "polis." Usually, they are important because they can still "see." Of course, poetically, "sight" is metonymy for the larger process of coming to the world stripped, "revealed," to be able carefully to expand the realm of meaning. Yet, very specifically, Olson discloses that the faculty of "touch" is of primary importance as a way of proceeding on a voyage of discovery, of coming to know "things."

"Letter 7," for example, refers to the carpenter William Stevens, the painter Marsden Hartley, whose paintings of hands are important to Olson, and to the sailor Jake, whose own hands were like those Hartley painted. "Hands," of course, is a metonym for "touch," for the potential to create, "to make things" (*MxP,* 31). The carpenter and the shipwright, Al Gorman, had to attend to details and be precise. The existence of their creations required it:

> Only: no latitude, any more than any, elite. The exactness
> caulking, or "play", calls for, those millimeters
>
> No where in man is there room for carelessness
> Or those arrogations I gave him the costume of
>
> (As hands are put to the eyes' commands
> > (*MxP,* 32)

Charles Olson

Of course, Olson's account of these hands and their creations is a substitute for the authentic poet's own circuit of creation. The eyes which see cannot execute, cannot create.

Hartley certainly intends his paintings of hands to comment on the nature of his own artistic processes. Olson takes his paintings in this way. The last section of "Letter 7" testifies to Hartley's observant eye and the success of his own creative hands. Olson measures the "reality" of the paintings against the details of a fisherman's hands in Gloucester:

> (I only knew one such other pair of hands as Hartley's. Jake, his name
> was, mate aboard the Lafond's gill netters.
> When I knew him
> his nails
> were all gone, peeled away from the brine they'd been in all the days of
> his life.
> Hartley's fingers gave this sense of soaking, the ends as stubbed
> as Jake's, and each finger so thick and independent of the other, his own
> hands were like gloves.
> But not cloth. They stayed such salt rock as Jake's
> were—or as marshmallow is, if the trope will stand, as Hartley's hands
> did stand, they were so much (each finger) their own lives' acts
> (*MxP*, 34)

In this complicated passage, the hands Hartley paints become identified with his own and, of course, with Jake's. The comparison to Jake's hands is not only a test of Harley's success in his art, but testifies to the kind of art that he created and, by implication, that Olson hopes to present. Jake's hands are important because they are a living testimony to his direct, un-lettered encounter with the environment upon which he depends and which he knows intimately by touch. Hartley is not only observant enough to register Jake's hands, as Olson is, but is careful

[277]

Charles Olson

enough to direct his own hands to great "exactness" in creating
the reenactment of his experience. "Care" is not merely the
proper attitude toward objects in the world, but most importantly, is the only authentic stance toward the creative circuit. In
effect, the authentic person is potentially capable of expanding
the horizon of meaning only through the "careful" completion of
the artistic process. Olson's "care" is not a passive stance in the
face of nature—even "after" the violent act of stripping off the
tradition. It is an attempt to reenact the experience of the active
voyager or walker in his locale.

Capt. John Smith assumes almost "archetypal" status in this
context in *The Maximus Poems*. However, just as in *The Cantos*
Pound's concern for Malatesta and Jefferson is with the concrete
particulars of their individual lives, Olson's care for Smith is presented as evidence of the potential for such careful living which
the "tradition" has hidden. In "Maximus, to Gloucester, Letter
II," Olson presents Smith as precisely the kind of personal, immediate voyager who makes "portulans" of his discoveries and
who "names" the new worlds he finds. "Tragabigzandah"[54] was
Smith's name for Cape Ann:

"TragabigZAND-ah" (more Capt. Shrimpe
from the loudness of him, quondam Drummer,
than the Admiral of New England Smith proudly
took himself to be, rightly, who sounded
her bays, ran her coast, and wrote down
Algonquin so scrupulously Massachusetts
And I know who lived where I lived
before the small-pox took them all away
and the Pilgrims
had such an easy time of it
to land

What further wowed us was
he had a swooning Turkish Princess
in his arms:
                    Historie
come bang into the midst of

our game! Actors,

[278]

Charles Olson

where I have learned another sort of
play
                    (*MxP*, 49)

This section of the poem opens by presenting the reader and the poet with an "alternative" to the official version of the geography. This section also introduces another recurrent theme: the opposition of the authentic Smith and the inauthentic Pilgrims, Massachusetts Bay Company, and Miles Standish. Smith, like Olson, struggles with the agents of the pejorocracy who profit from other men's searches of the coast:

    sd Smith (refused
as navigator by
the Pilgrims, Standish
chosen instead)
            (*MxP*, 69)


    they put Smith down
as, and hire a Standish
to do corporative
murder: keep things clean,
by campaigns

    drop bombs.
            (*MxP*, 125)

The American tradition is officially continuous, and Olson sees patterns of repetition in it. The impersonality of airplane bombings covers-up the horror of the napalming in Vietnam. The "pejorocracy" preserves itself and continues on from Standish to the exploiters of the Modern world. But there is also a "polis," a few whose "careful" eyes and hands do not allow them to participate in this "tradition," but who are shunted aside by its particular societal manifestation—as Smith was displaced by Standish.

    Smith's sight led to action in the world and to creation in words. In "Maximus, to Gloucester," Olson quotes Smith's poem, "The Sea Marke" in its entirety. The poem cautions sailors to sound the coast well, carefully, as they approach and leave the land of New England. In G.F. Butterick's annotated

[279]

guide, Olson reportedly comments on this poem of Smith's:
"Why I sing John Smith is this, that the geographic, the sudden land of the place, is in there, not described, not local, not
represented."[55] Failure to sound with care leads, of course, to
shipwreck.

In "Some Good News," Olson explains that Smith remained out of the consciousness of America because the "tradition" was cool:

> Smith,
>
> as Sam Grant after,
> was futile
>
> until the place
> and time burned
> with the same heat as
> the man
>
> (*MxP*, 123)

In other words, Olson's own intense desire to disclose, his recognition of the potential for man to expand the horizon makes it
possible for him to retrieve Smith from the "tradition" which
had covered him up and obscured him in a few conventional historical clichés. Olson's discovery of Smith as a term for naming
what Olson himself *"really* knows" about things in the world
makes Smith "burn" with the same kind of energy he possessed
in his acts.

Olson's retrieval of Smith is an example of how a destructive
poet can expand meaning in the world by exposing something or
someone lost in the "words" of the tradition. The past is not
merely used by the poet for subjective purposes in this way;
rather, the equation with the energy of the person from the past,
Smith, is a necessary condition for Olson's discovery of him.
Furthermore, Olson's own energetic discovery of "Smith" as a
name for "what he knows" requires a negatively capable relation
to the past which allows Olson to be open to the possible energizing of the imagination from any possible direction.

Certainly the ironic consciousness of the New Criticism can-

Charles Olson

not be expected to understand the poetic enterprise of *The Maximus Poems*. The openness of the poets of process to the potential disclosure of meaning and being in realms not sanctioned by the literary-historical canon upsets the definite "sea lanes" of the New Critical mind. "Portulans" is radically uncertain, direct, and interested. It is often, as it was for Smith, a matter of life and death, a matter of being reduced to the natural being which Dasein is as being-in-the-world. Most importantly, the New Criticism cannot respond to a poetry in which energy is of importance. Energy needs to be experienced to be understood and not merely watched from a distance. The disinterest of the New Critics compels them to miss completely the very affective areas in which Olson's poetry is most successful. The New Critics stand back to examine his "words" and fail to feel or to "see" the process by which the poet and poem are reenacting the experience which energizes the poet. The New Critics, expecting a poetry of "recollection," cannot encounter a "poetry of world" which demands an immediate response. They do not *care* to stand directly in the face of life's discoveries.

Whitman, Stevens, and Olson along with others like Lawrence, Williams, and Robert Duncan, have been successfully ignored for their radically antitraditional stances. Olson's programmatic attack on the grounds underlying the study of literature in America for the most part makes him, if not the best of these poets, by far the most volatile from the literary establishment's perspective. I hope that the impact of his poetry and that of the others I have mentioned will disclose to critics the need to move away from the traditional assumptions they habitually make and into a realm of greater uncertainty where the act of reading is defined by its instability and risk.

# Notes

Chapter 1: Literary History and Literary Interpretation: Toward a Theory of Poetic Destruction

    1. Martin Heidegger, "Die Zeit des Weltbildes," *Holzwege,* 4th ed. (Frankfurt am Main: Vittorio Klosterman, 1965), pp. 81–82; for a comment on the iconic or spatial characteristics of "worldview," which I call "periodization," in terms of the New Critics, cf. also William V. Spanos, "Heidegger's Phenomenology of Time: Hermeneutics as Discovery," Paper no. 2, University Seminar in Postmodernism, SUNY/Binghamton, 3/19/75, p. 20.
    2. These titles will recur repeatedly in my text; I will refer to them in parentheses by these abbreviations: *The Burden of the Past* (Cambridge, Mass.: The Belknap Press of Harvard University Press, 1970), *BP; The Anxiety of Influence* (New York: Oxford University Press, 1973), *AI; A Map of Misreading* (New York: Oxford University Press, 1975), *MM; Poetry and Repression* (New Haven and London: Yale University Press, 1976), *PR; Wallace Stevens: The Poems of Our Climate* (Ithaca and London: Cornell University Press, 1977), *WS; Blindness and Insight* (New York: Oxford University Press, 1971), *BI;* "Nietzsche's Theory of Rhetoric," *Symposium,* 28 (1974), pp. 33–51, NTR; "Genesis and Genealogy in Nietzsche's *The Birth of Tragedy,*" *Diacritics,* 2 (1972), pp. 44–53, GGN. I have chosen to deal with these relatively early texts of Paul de Man because they afford me the greatest hermeneutic possibility for moving in the direction of a poetics of destruction. While I find de Man's other essays valuable and fascinating, they are not as important to my project here. It is also true that in his most recent work, de Man has moved entirely away from any type of historical thinking or understanding of literature. In fact, in "Shelley Disfigured," a paper given in the Fall of 1978 at Columbia University, de Man made quite clear that he sees literary and historical languages as alien from each other. Since I have no wish or need to enter into the latest version of this fray, I recommend readers see: J. Hillis Miller, "Tradition and Difference," *Diacritics,* 2 (1972), pp. 6–10; Miller "The Critic as Host," *Critical Inquiry,* 3 (1977), pp. 439–47; M.H. Abrams, "The Deconstructive Angel," *Critical Inquiry,* 3 (1977), pp. 425–38; Edward W. Said, "The Problem of Textuality: Two Exemplary Positions," *Critical Inquiry,* 4 (1978), pp. 673–714; and Said, "Political and Historical Ideas in Contemporary American 'Left' Criticism," *boundary 2,* 7 (1979), which discusses the restricted nature of de Man's antihistorical criticism. I am

indebted for some of my ideas on Bloom to Daniel O'Hara, "The Romance of Interpretation: A 'Postmodern' Critical Style," *boundary 2,* 8 (1980).

3. See *Being and Time,* trans. John Macquarrie and Edward Robinson (New York: Harper and Row, 1962), pp. 26f, 193, 362ff. This is only one of many references which I shall make to the hermeneutic circle and the problem of interpretation in this and subsequent chapters.

4. Like Paul de Man, I differentiate between myth and fiction by recognizing the writer's belief in a story or narrative as "true" as the defining characteristic of myth, whereas "fiction," as in Wallace Stevens, is offered as such and with no claim to the direct expression of immediate truth.

5. See Steven Crites, "Pseudonymous Authorship as Art and Act," *Kierkegaard,* ed. Josiah Thompson (New York: Doubleday, 1972), see esp. pages 210–15, subtitled "Aesthetic Rest vs. Existential Movement."

6. Kierkegaard, of course, lashes out constantly against the Hegelian movement of "Mediation" because it is only a logical process of "reconciling," of "harmonizing." It is the basis of the Hegelian dialectic, and, as such, the cornerstone of Hegel's completely static, ahistorical system. Perhaps the most powerful attacks on mediation occur in *The Concept of Dread,* trans. Walter Lowrie (Princeton: Princeton University Press, 1957), pp. 10–12, where mediation provides the basis for logical "motion," i.e., the reconciliation of opposites in logic, but not in actuality; and in *Concluding Unscientific Postscript,* trans. David F. Swenson and Walter Lowrie (Princeton: Princeton University Press, 1941), pp. 335f, 355, 373–75. In terms of Hegel's system of history, mediation is the mechanism for assuring the inevitable development of world events along a certain dialectical path. Kierkegaard counters this structure with his own analysis of freedom and of human history which, as he says of repetition, "recollects forward," that is, it reviews past events with an eye toward fulfilling the possibilities they reveal in the present for the human being's future and possible renewal. For a further discussion of this idea see my next essay on Heideggerean repetition as well as Spanos, pp. 24–34; see also Stephen Crites, "Pseudonymous Authorship as Art and as Act," pp. 215–19, for a discussion of "repetition" as the movement of possibility occurring within the actuality of human time.

7. See Kierkegaard's *Fear and Trembling,* trans. Walter Lowrie (Princeton: Princeton University Press, 1941) and my third chapter, "Cleanth Brooks and Modern Irony: A Kierkegaardian Critique."

8. *The Myth of the Eternal Return,* trans. Willard R. Trask (Princeton: Princeton University Press, 1971), pp. 29 and 76.

9. For an alternative view of the potentialities of oral poetry and the oral tradition, one which is not objectified or spatialized see Spanos, who argues precisely that the oral impulse destroys the *logos* as a timeless form, the Word, because it is etymologically identifiable with discourse as discovery. I develop the idea of discourse as a loosening-up of tradition, as its destruction, in fact, in my next chapter. Bloom's Kabbalistic theory of oral tradition is close to that of the poet Jerome Rothenberg, whose orality is designed to "re-collect," to "re-cover," the objectified mythic system of primitive cultures in a way intended to overcome the anxiety of everyday-being-toward-death. See Antin, "A Correspondence with William Spanos," *boundary 2,* 3 (1975), pp. 595–652.

10. *Qu'est-ce que le structuralisme?* (Paris: Editions du Seuil, 1968).

11. In *Being and Time,* Heidegger describes Dasein's being "as the sole authentic for-the-sake-of-which." Dasein's "orientation" in the face of entities within the world is to let

those things be. This extends to the understanding of an intentional act; see pp. 117–21.

12. I adopt this word "game" from Jacques Derrida's essay, "Structure, Sign and Play in the Discourse of the Human Sciences," *Writing and Difference*, trans. Alan Bass (Chicago: University of Chicago Press, 1978), pp. 278–93. Since critical language cannot rest solidly upon an unquestioned transcendent center or ground, it becomes, as a sign system, subject to the play of endless substitutions and permutations. The indeterminateness of these games of transformation abrogates the ontological security of logocentrism which the certainty of centered scientific structures provides: "And on the basis of this certitude," Derrida writes, "anxiety can be mastered, for anxiety is invariably the result of a certain mode of being implicated in the game, of being caught by the game, of being as it were at stake in the game from the outset."

13. There are important relationships between Derrida's term, *"la différance,"* and Paul de Man's awareness of the necessary binary opposition of truth and error, consciousness and unconsciousness, blindness and insight. I cannot, however, develop these fully here because such an analysis would take me far afield. Derrida's peculiarly suggestive term combining the senses of "differing" and "deferring" ultimately is concerned with the possibility of difference within the space of representation. Nonetheless, I shall use Derrida's term to suggest the irreconcilable and violent "differences" which de Man finds at the heart of every critical utterance as well as at the "center" of literary interpretation and literature itself. Jacques Derrida, "Differance," *Speech and Phenomena and Other Essays on Husserl's Theory of Signs,* trans. David B. Allison (Evanston: Northwestern University Press, 1973), pp. 129–60.

14. I borrow the term "foci" from Richard Klein's analysis of de Man, "The Blindness of Hyperboles: the Ellipses of Insight," *Diacritics,* 3 (1973), pp. 33–44.

15. I use this term with the full sense of Heidegger's development of the structure of understanding in *Being and Time*. A fuller discussion of *Verstehen* as a means or process of disclosure primordially constituting the world follows in my next chapter.

16. Walt Whitman's poetic theory of indirection is somewhat analogous to both de Man's and Rousseau's use of the term. Essentially, for de Man, indirection involves the recognition that language is necessarily misinterpreted and that, as a result, successful communication needs to circumvent this potentiality of all language by employing it against itself. De Man's deconstruction of Rousseau's "indirect" use of language is paradigmatic: "The *Discours sur l'origine de l'inégalité* and the *Essai sur l'origine des langues* are texts whose discursive assertions account for their rhetorical mode. What is being said about the nature of language makes it unavoidable that the texts should be written in the form of a fictionally diachronic narrative or, if one prefers to call it so, of an allegory. The allegorical mode is accounted for in the description of all language as figural and in the necessarily diachronic structure of the reflection that reveals this insight. The text goes beyond this, however, for as it accounts for its own mode of writing, it states at the same time the necessity of making this statement itself an indirect, figural way that knows it will be misunderstood by being taken literally. Accounting for the 'rhetoricity' of its own mode, the text also postulates the necessity of its own misreading. . . . It tells the story, the allegory of its own misunderstanding . . ." (*BI,* 135–36).

# Notes for pages 52–69

Chapter 2. Heidegger's Phenomenological Destruction: A Theory of Poetic Interpretation

1. For an example of how this might be done to post-New-Critical writing, see Paul A. Bové, "The Poetics of Coercion: An Interpretation of Literary Competence," *boundary 2*, 5 (1976), pp. 263–84 which destroys Culler's adoption of a structuralist model.

2. "The Dissociation of Sensibility," *The Romantic Image* (New York: Random House, 1957), pp. 138–61. I refer to this essay because Kermode clearly develops the idea of "tradition" as a variant of the myth of the Fall which I have discussed in chapter one and which I will discuss in terms of the New Criticism and Walt Whitman in the two succeeding chapters. See also, John Fekete, *The Critical Twilight* (London: Routledge & Kegan Paul, 1977), pp. 24–5.

3. Martin Heidegger, *Being and Time,* trans. John Macquarrie and Edward Robinson (New York: Harper and Row, 1962); this book will be cited parenthetically in my text as *BT.*

4. Evanston: Northwestern University Press, 1967, p. 137. Hereafter, this book will be cited in my text as *AD.*

5. See, for example, Werner Brock *Existence and Being* (Chicago: Henry Regnery Co., 1949); Michael Gelven, *A Commentary on Heidegger's Being and Time* (New York: Harper and Row, 1970), hereafter cited as *C;* Beda Alleman, *Hölderlin und Heidegger* (Zürich: Atlantic Verlag, 1954), esp. "Geschichte und Historie," pp. 68–80; Thomas Langan, *The Meaning of Heidegger* (New York: Columbia University Press, 1954), hereafter cited as *MH;* Vincent Vycinas, *Earth and Gods* (The Hague: Martinus Nijhoff, 1961); John N. Deely, *The Tradition Via Heidegger* (The Hague: Martinus Nijhoff, 1971).

6. See *AD,* pp. 45, 56, 58, 130–37; also, William V. Spanos, "Heidegger's Phenomenology of Time," p. 5.

7. See Spanos, "Heidegger's Phenomenology of Time," pp. 7–10, 34–36; see also David Antin in his "Correspondence" with Spanos and Robert Kroetsch, pp. 595–652.

8. See as only one example among many, Jacques Derrida's deconstruction of Rousset's *Forme et Signification,* "Force and Signification," in *Writing and Difference,* esp. p. 17 where he deconstructs Rousset's use of geometric metaphors of figure and movement, space and duration, in the latter's reading of Corneille and Marivaux among others. Derrida argues that "metaphor is not innocent." He reveals how the geometric metaphors not only "mobilize all the resources and attention of the author, but [how] an entire teleology of Corneille's progress is coordinated to it."

9. Ed. Ann Charters (Berkeley: Oyez, 1970), p. 21. Olson argues that all authentic history disappeared with Herodotus until this century because "an enormous fallacy called discourse, invented by Socrates, drove science, myth, history *and* poetry away from the center, substituting in imagination's and faith's place politics, government, athletics and metaphysics." I do not intend this quotation to deny Olson's own insistence on returning voice to poetry to rejuvenate it, but only to indicate the possibility of inauthentic speech, of inauthentic orality. Coincidentally, Antin offers—and Spanos and Kroetsch partially accept—Socrates as an alternative to Homer, who, somehow, becomes the paradigm of the *writing* poet. See *boundary 2*, 3 (1975). For a complete exposition of Olson's commitment to the oral see "Human Universe," *Selected Writings,* ed. Robert Creeley (New York: New Directions, 1966), pp. 53–54. See also Joseph Riddel, "An 'American' Poe-

tics?," *boundary 2*, 8 (1979), for a further discussion of the metaphoricity of American poetry from Poe to Olson.

10. "Projective Verse," *Selected Writings*, p. 23.

11. See note four above as well as Charles M. Sherover, *Heidegger, Kant and Time* (Bloomington: Indiana University Press, 1971).

12. "Re-thinking Metaphysics," *Heidegger and the Quest for Truth*, ed. Manfred S. Frings (Chicago: Quadrangle Books, 1968), pp. 107–8.

13. *Selected Essays* (New York: Harcourt, Brace and World, 1964), pp. 4–5.

14. Schrag, p. 108.

15. Trans. James S. Churchill (Bloomington: Indiana University Press, 1962), p. 207, hereafter cited as *KPM*.

16. "Heidegger, Kierkegaard, and the Hermeneutic Circle: Towards a Postmodern Theory of Interpretation," *boundary 2*, 4 (1976), pp. 455–88. Reprinted in *Martin Heidegger and the Question of Literature: Towards A Postmodern Literary Hermeneutics*, ed. William V. Spanos (Bloomington: Indiana University Press, 1979).

17. *Introduction to Metaphysics*, trans. Ralph Manheim (New Haven: Yale University Press, 1959), p. 39.

18. Evanston: Northwestern University Press, 1971, p. xxxi.

## Chapter 3: Cleanth Brooks and Modern Irony: A Kierkegaardian Critique

1. Among Scott's many books and articles, see especially *The Broken Center: Studies in the Theological Horizon of Modern Literature* (New Haven: Yale University Press, 1966); *Negative Capability: Studies in the New Literature and the Religious Situation* (New Haven: Yale University Press, 1969). In this context, Miller's most important text is, of course, *Poets of Reality* (Cambridge: Harvard University Press, 1965). For Kermode, see *The Romantic Image* (New York: Random House, 1964), especially his attack on the modern myth of the dissociation of sensibility; Kermode's *The Sense of an Ending* (New York: Oxford University Press, 1967) is a highly individual approach to the problem of fictional form and his speculations on openness are immediately relevant to much of what I will say later about Kierkegaard and Yeats. Until the appearance of his forthcoming book, *Icon and Time*, readers must look to periodical articles for Spanos' theories of Postmodernism and critical discourse. For the first version of his destruction of the New Criticism, see "Modern Literary Criticism and the Spatialization of Time: An Existential Critique," *JAAC*, 29 (1970), 87–104; "Modern Drama and the Aristotelian Tradition: The Formal Imperatives of Absurd Time," *Contemporary Literature*, 12 (1971), 345–72; and for what is perhaps his most explicit published statement to date on this entire area as it affects fictional form and the temporal experience of reading, see "The Detective and the Boundary: Some Notes on the Postmodern Literary Imagination," *boundary 2*, 1 (1972), 147–68. The results of Spanos' most recent work in this area can be found in "Postmodern Literature and the Hermeneutic Crisis," *USQR* 34 (1979), pp. 119–31. On the displacement of the *"verbal icon"* and the *"concrete universal"* from the ideologies of contemporary poetics and criticism, see Charles Altieri, "From Symbolist Thought to Immanence: The Ground of Postmodern American Poetics," *boundary 2*, 1 (1973), 605–41.

2. In "A Retrospective Introduction," Brooks recognizes that he and Eliot chose to ignore Whitman and Williams at their own risk and that these are now the poets who in-

terest contemporary authors and critics. *Modern Poetry and the Tradition* (New York: Oxford University Press, 1965), p. viii. I will refer to Brooks's work in my text by the following abbreviations: *Modern Poetry and the Tradition, MP; The Well Wrought Urn* (New York: Harcourt, Brace and World, 1947), *Urn;* "Irony and 'Ironic' Poetry" *College English,* 9 (1948), 231–37, IIP.

3. I shall follow Kierkegaard's terminology in *The Concept of Irony,* trans. Lee M. Capel (Bloomington: Indiana University Press, 1968), and use "Absolute Freedom" to refer to the dream of the ironist to be above all restrictions upon his imagination's desires as he wanders through an infinitude of possibilities where his "freedom" from being in the world results in no freedom at all. "Authentic freedom," on the other hand, refers to the ability and willingness to accept and to act in immediate actuality in order to give content and substance to life so that freedom becomes not abstract possibility but an authentic interrelationship with the world.

4. "Intensive Manifolds," *Speculations,* ed. Herbert Read (New York: Harcourt, Brace, 1924), pp. 173–214. Henri Bergson, *Time and Free Will,* trans. F.L. Pogdon (New York: Harper and Row, 1960), p. 103.

5. Bergson, pp. 101–3.

6. Quoted in MP, p. 96, from Tate's "Humanism and Naturalism," *Reactionary Essays* (New York: Charles Scribner's Sons, 1936), pp. 126–47. Modernism's attack on humanism as a substitute for religion centers, as in this essay, upon the former's inability to develop a sense of "concrete tradition" (p. 135). Particularly, humanism associated itself with deterministic history, causality, abstraction, and "moral fascism" (p. 144). It believed in a dualism and did not try to establish a unity of experience, which the ironist and the symbolist want as a means of denying the pernicious effects of their economic actuality upon their imagination. In *Nausea,* the symbolist and ironic Roquentin develops the idea that the humanists are as Fascistic as the bourgeois of Beauville. In "The Humanism of Irving Babbitt," T.S. Eliot describes many of the criticisms of the humanistic position which Tate extends in this essay. See Eliot, *Selected Essays* (New York: Harcourt, Brace, and World, 1964), pp. 419–28.

7. I adopt this word "caught" for this context from the first stanza of Yeats's "Sailing to Byzantium" because the persona of that poem experiences and expresses just the horror of death and entrapment which the ironist fears most. *The Collected Poems of W.B. Yeats* (New York: Macmillan, 1956), p. 191. I will return to a discussion of this poem in a different context.

8. T.S. Eliot, in "The Metaphysical Poets," *Selected Essays,* p. 247, differentiates between the "mind" of Donne and Herbert and the "mind" of Tennyson and Browning, or as Brooks would see it, between the ironic consciousness and the bourgeois, positivistic consciousness: "A thought to Donne was an experience; it modified his sensibility. When a poet's mind is perfectly equipped for its work, it is constantly amalgamating disparate experience; the ordinary man's experience is chaotic, irregular, fragmentary. The latter falls in love, or reads Spinoza, and these two experiences have nothing to do with each other, or with the noise of the typewriter or the smell of cooking; in the mind of the poet these experiences are always forming new wholes."

9. As far as I can tell, Eliot first used this famous phrase in his "Introduction" to the translation of the *Anabasis* of St. John Perse (New York: Harcourt, Brace, 1949). Although Eliot's phrase, because of its epigrammatic authority, has become part of our insistent modernist legacy, Eliot was by no means alone in his claims for a uniquely poetic

means of knowledge and linguistic ordering. Hart Crane is the one of all the many other poets and critics whose formulation, in 1926, of the modern denigration of logical form and precise linguistic signification is closest to the position of Eliot and Brooks. In a letter to Harriet Monroe, "explicating" the difficulties of "At Melville's Tomb," Crane writes of what he calls the "logic of metaphor": "as a poet I may very possibly be more interested in the so-called illogical impingements of the connotations of words on the consciousness (and their combinations and interplay in metaphor on this basis) than I am interested in the preservation of their logically rigid significations at the cost of limiting my subject matter and perceptions involved in the poem. . . . Its paradox, of course, is that its apparent illogic operates so logically in conjunction with its context in the poem as to establish its claim to another logic." *The Complete Poems and Selected Letters and Prose of Hart Crane,* ed. Brom Weber (Garden City: Doubleday, 1966), pp. 234–35. I am grateful to Philip Dow, who, following the presentation of part of this chapter at SUNY/Binghamton in the spring of 1975, reminded me of this letter.

10. In a symposium on Romanticism at Yale University, Brooks continued to be loyal to some of his original and fundamental ideas: the yoking together by violence of Coleridge and Donne, i.e., the esemplastic imagination and the metaphysical conceit. "Coleridge as a Metaphysical Poet," *Romanticism: Vistas, Instances, Continuities,* ed. David Thorburn and Geoffrey Hartman (Ithaca: Cornell University Press, 1973), pp. 134–54.

11. See Edward Said's *Beginnings: Intention and Method* (New York: Basic Books, 1975). Said's interpretation of the crucial role which beginnings play in the project of developing literary meaning points out another area of critical importance which the New Critics ignore because of their emphasis on nontemporal aspects of literature. Perhaps most importantly, Said's book adds considerably to the already growing sense that Brooks, Wimsatt, and the others oversimplified the importance of intentionality—which is, of course, as the phenomenologists point out, a temporal category. As Said puts it: "The beginning . . . is the first step in the intentional production of meaning" (p. 5).

12. *The Concept of Irony,* p. 269. This book will be cited in my text as *CI.*

13. "The Critical Monism of Cleanth Brooks," *Critics and Criticism,* ed. R.S. Crane (Chicago: University of Chicago Press, 1952), pp. 83–107.

14. Quoted in *MP,* 99, from "Religion and the Old South," *Collected Essays of Allan Tate* (Denver: A. Swallow, 1959), pp. 317, 319. The purpose of this essay is to help the Southern mind develop a "private, self-contained, and essentially spiritual life" (p. 322) so that utility and mechanism will not only lead toward a partial appreciation and realization of life but also to a nonutilitarian, nonabstract, total contemplation of objects, facts, details, lives, as *images.* Tate's emphasis is on the totalization of experience as opposed to the fragmentation of the Western technocrats.

15. Joseph Frank, *The Widening Gyre* (New Brunswick: Rutgers University Press, 1963), p. 9, see pp. 55–59. W.V. Spanos first pointed out to me the confusion which exists in the discussion of Modernism as a result of Frank's use of "spatialization" in a way seemingly so different from Hulme and Bergson's earlier usage. For Hulme, spatialization always takes the form of the "extensive manifold" and never of the aesthetic monad: "The process of explanation is always a process of unfolding. A tangled mass is unfolded flat so that you can see all of its parts separated out, and any tangle which can be separated out in this way must of course be an extensive manifold" (*Speculations,* 177). Frank's book will be referred to as *WG.*

16. See Mircea Eliade, *The Myth of the Eternal Return,* trans. Willard R. Trask (Princeton: Princeton University Press, 1971), pp. 123ff; *Myth and Reality,* trans. Willard R. Trask (New York: Harper and Row, 1968), pp. 34, 72–74, 77ff.

17. See *Myth and Reality,* pp. 49ff; *The Myth of the Eternal Return,* pp. 100–1.

18. Like Stephen Dedalus, I too "use the word arrest" to indicate the pervasive nature of Modernism's denial of time through aesthetic form. For an explication of Stephen's "aesthetic" along these lines, see Spanos, "Modern Literary Criticism," 96–98.

19. See Spanos, "Modern Literary Criticism," p. 89.

20. Brooks borrows this idea of "balanced tensions" from I.A. Richards, *Principles of Literary Criticism* (London: Routledge and Kegan Paul, 1924), pp. 107ff.

21. Princeton: Princeton University Press, 1971, pp. 62, 135.

22. *The New Apologists for Poetry* (Minneapolis: University of Minnesota Press, 1956), pp. 125ff, 132, 135–39.

23. "A Definition of Aesthetic Experience," *Creation and Discovery* (New York: Noonday Press, 1955), p. 95.

24. Spanos, "Modern Literary Criticism," p. 87.

25. *Blindness and Insight,* pp. 102–11.

26. "The Angelic Imagination," *Collected Essays,* pp. 432–54.

27. See Kermode, *The Romantic Image,* and Graham Hough, *Images and Experience* (Lincoln: University of Nebraska Press, 1960); three older texts seemingly no longer of importance testify to the modern critical preoccupation with the Image: Glenn Hughes, *Imagism and the Imagists* (Stanford: Stanford University Press, 1931); Martin Gilkes, *A Key to Modern Poetry* (London: Blackie, 1938); Stanley Coffman, *Imagism, a Chapter for the History of Modern Poetry* (Norman: University of Oklahoma Press, 1951).

28. James Joyce, *A Portrait of the Artist as a Young Man* (New York: Viking, 1964), pp. 204–16.

29. Søren Kierkegaard, *Repetition,* trans. Walter Lowrie (New York: Harper and Row, 1964). In crucial statements on metaphysical "dis-interest," Kierkegaard points out that all systems founder in their completeness and consistency on the author's "interest," i.e., on the personal involvement and human participation in what is at stake in an act of thought or creation. In other words, what Kierkegaard argues in his opposition to metaphysics can be extended to Stephen's "aesthetic": it emerges from an existential involvement in the immediate situation and is designed to deal with the pains and horrors of that situation under the guise of *disinterest.*

30. "The Noble Rider and the Sound of Words," *The Necessary Angel* (New York: Random House, 1951), pp. 1–36. For some evidence that Stevens is not the kind of ironist I have been discussing, see Joseph Riddel, "Interpreting Stevens: An Essay on Poetry and Thinking," *boundary 2,* 1 (1972), 79–97 and chapter four as well.

31. Trans. James S. Churchill (Bloomington: Indiana University Press, 1962), hereafter cited as *KPM.*

32. *The Collected Poems,* p. 192.

33. I am, of course, not using "drama" here to mean a pattern of resolved stresses, as both Brooks and Kierkegaard's Constantine Constantius mean it. In a more Aristotelian sense, I use it to mean an imitation of an action appropriate to the "character" or persona who speaks the "part." As I hope my comments on the poem point out, the "patterns" in this poem can never be resolved, and therefore the poem can be "dramatic" only insofar as, "beginning" nowhere and "going" nowhere, it represents a human attempt to come

Notes for pages 121–130

to grips with an imaginative stance which seems desirable to the persona confronted by death and finitude.

34. *The Man and the Masks* (New York: E.P. Dutton, 1948), see esp. pp. 171–76.

35. New York: Macmillan, 1965. Yeats attempts to explore the complex psychology of masks and roles, particularly in the exquisite chapter "The Tragic Generation," pp. 185–233. See also Daniel O'Hara's unpublished dissertation, "Under the Watch—Mender's Eye: The Simplifying Image of the Creator in Yeats's *Autobiography*," Temple University, 1976.

36. Kermode, *Romantic Image*, passim. W.V. Spanos has often tried to convince me that, when seen spatially, Yeats's poems do look just like a dry image. This is an argument he repeats in the manuscript of his forthcoming book, *Icon and Time*. "Hard" and "dry" are words used by Hulme and Pound to contrast their imagist ideal to the wet, soft messiness of Romantic poetry. In *Nausea,* of course, Sartre adds another dimension to this modern contrast by using viscous metaphors in Roquentin's attempted descriptions of the absurd, of nothingness. Trans. Lloyd Alexander (New York: New Directions, 1964), pp. 7–9, 24, 125–35.

37. I am indebted throughout this discussion to Spanos' attempts to articulate a "temporal hermeneutics" for literary criticism.

38. "On *The Sound and the Fury:* Time in the Work of William Faulkner," *Literary Essays,* trans. Annette Michelson (New York: Philosophical Library, 1957), p. 79. See Edith Kern's commentary on the significance of this reversal of the New Critical priority of text and metaphysics. *Existential Thought and Fictional Technique* (New Haven: Yale University Press, 1970), pp. 86–87. Alan Wilde has contributed an important series of articles on the differences between High Modern, Late Modern, and Postmodern writing. His work overlaps mine at times but ultimately presents a different point of view. See especially, "Barthelme Unfair to Kierkegaard: Some Thoughts on Modern and Postmodern Irony," *boundary 2,* 5 (1976), 45–70; "Modernism and the Aesthetics of Crisis," *Contemporary Literature,* 20 (1979), 13–49; and "Irony in the Postmodern Age," *boundary 2,* 9 (1980).

39. "Pseudonymous Authorship as Art and Act," pp. 205–15, 222–29.

40. Trans. Walter Lowrie (Princeton: Princeton University Press, 1968), p. 146.

41. Trans. David Swenson (Princeton: Princeton University Press, 1941), p. 188, see p. 528; hereafter cited as *CUP.*

42. *Repetition,* pp. 58ff.

43. Trans. Walter Lowrie (New York: Schocken Books, 1967), pp. 21–93.

44. See note 16 above and Hulme's illustration of how "ex-plan-ation" is a spatialization. See also Paul A. Bové, "The Penitentiary of Reflection: Søren Kierkegaard and Critical Activity," *boundary 2,* 8, no. 3 (1980).

45. See Crites, "Pseudonymous Authorship," 229ff.

46. For an examination of the implications of the type of existential form under consideration here as it affects drama, see Spanos, "Modern Drama and the Aristotelian Tradition." Both *Symboliste* (or ironic) and Positivistic (or well-made) forms are created to make audience and author feel "at home" in an essentially "uncanny" (*unheimlich*) world.

47. For a reading of the postmodern landscape in American poetics from a different but parallel perspective, see Charles Altieri, "From Symbolist Thought to Immanence."

48. *Stages on Life's Way,* p. 26.

Notes for pages 131–132

Chapter 4. *Leaves of Grass* and the Center: Free Play or Transcendence

1. *The Continuity of American Poetry* (Princeton: Princeton University Press, 1961), pp. 69–82, 164–173; "Whitman and Our Hope for Poetry," *Historicism Once More* (Princeton: Princeton University Press, 1969), pp. 327–50. The crucial importance of Pearce's essays is that they demonstrate conclusively that Whitman's poetry is essentially a representation of process. In fact, for the purposes of this chapter, Pearce's analysis stands in place of any further presentation of the way in which individual poems move "processionally," creating on the way of the imaginative journey. For a discussion of some of the limits of Pearce's work see Paul Bové, "The World and Earth of William Carlos Williams: Paterson as a 'Long Poem,' " *Genre,* 11, no. 4 (1978), 575–96.

The New Critical opinion of Whitman's work is not even generally articulated. Indeed, one could conclude from the paucity of reference to *Leaves of Grass* in the major works of the first generation of the New Critics that Whitman did not even enter their consciousness. See Allen Tate, *Collected Essays* (Denver: A. Swallow, 1959), which contains two passing references to Whitman; John Crowe Ransom, *The New Criticism* (Norfolk, Conn.: New Directions, 1941) in which Ransom mentions Whitman once in a discussion of Winters' condemnation of the poet; Ransom agrees that Whitman is too "diffuse" (p. 236); W.K. Wimsatt, *Verbal Icon* (Louisville: University of Kentucky Press, 1954), which mentions Whitman's work only once as an example of Romantic looseness (p. 227). The following New Critical texts on Modern poetry, written almost exclusively by Americans, make no mention of Whitman at all: Allen Tate, *The Hovering Fly* (Freeport, N.Y.: Books for Libraries Press, 1968); Tate, *The Literary Correspondence of Donald Davidson and Allen Tate,* ed. John Fain and Thomas Young (Athens: University of Georgia Press, 1974); John Crowe Ransom, *Beating the Bushes* (New York: New Directions, 1972); Ransom ed., *The Kenyon Critics* (Cleveland: World Publishers, 1951); Austin Warren, *Connections* (Ann Arbor: University of Michigan Press, 1970); and I.A. Richards, *Practical Criticism* (New York: Harcourt, Brace, 1929).

For a fuller discussion of the nature of the tradition of American poetry as established by the New Criticism in the more immediate context of an attempt to destroy that tradition see the opening section of my sixth chapter, on Charles Olson.

2. Chicago: University of Chicago Press, 1955, p. 52; hereafter this book will be cited in my text as *AA.* For a discussion of the New Criticism as neo-Kantian, see Frank Lentricchia, "The Place of Cleanth Brooks," *JAAC,* 29 (1970), pp. 235–51. Although Lentricchia concludes that Brooks's neo-Kantianism leads to a contextualist and not a formalist theory of poetry, his description of this "contextualism," when seen in the light of my recent discussion of Brooks (chapter three), could be used to lend support to my attack on the primary Kantian aesthetic principle, namely, ironic distance or disinterest: "the poem [as Brooks sees it] is not an escape from experience into the purities of aesthetic form, but an *illumination* of a rich and *complex* world that we normally deny ourselves the *pleasure of contemplating* because of the blinding classificatory drive of the propositional discourse that mediates the world for us day in and day out" (p. 245; my italics). Lentricchia is unaware of how Brooks's language of presence informs the entire discussion of ironic form and how it denies actuality to achieve the pleasure of contemplation.

3. *The Continuity of American Poetry,* p. 75.

4. W.C. Williams, "An Essay on *Leaves of Grass,*" *Leaves of Grass,* ed. Scully Brad-

ley and Harold W. Blodgett (New York: W.W. Norton, 1973), pp. 903–12. This Norton Critical Edition is a reproduction of the Standard Readers' Edition of *Leaves of Grass,* by the same editors (New York: New York University Press, 1965). I will refer to the poems and Prefaces of *Leaves of Grass* in this critical edition in my text in parentheses as (*LG*). Robert Duncan, "A Poem Beginning with a Line by Pindar," *The Opening of the Field* (New York: Grove Press, 1960), pp. 63–64, and "Changing Perspectives in Reading Whitman," *The Artistic Legacy of Walt Whitman,* ed. Edwin Haviland Miller (New York: New York University Press, 1970), pp. 127–52; Stanley Burnshaw, *The Seamless Web* (New York: George Braziller, 1970), pp. 205, 214, 225; John Vernon, "Language and Body in Modern Poetry," *University Seminar in Postmodernism,* Paper no. 1, 1974, SUNY/ Binghamton, pp. 8–9.

5. I borrow the snake metaphor from Vernon (pp. 5, 15) who has transferred the Adamic myth to the broader field of contemporary poetry which he labels "naked poetry," borrowing the term from "At First She Came to me Pure," by Jiminiz, trans. Robert Bly. See John Vernon, *Poetry and the Body* (Urbana: University of Illinois Press, 1979).

6. *Historicism Once More,* p. 331.

7. Ibid., p. 335.

8. Ibid., p. 335.

9. See also Charles Feidelson, Jr., *Symbolism and American Literature* (Chicago: University of Chicago Press, 1955), pp. 16–26, who claims for Whitman precisely the "absolute freedom" from actuality which the ironist or symbolist desires: "But empirical fact and rational form had no hold on Whitman and Emerson" (p. 16). Feidelson regards Whitman's poems "ironically," spatially, in Spanos' term, "from the end" to show how they transcend the world to establish the priority of the creative—i.e., infinite—imagination. But when Whitman "fails," according to Feidelson, it is because he has "deprived himself of an external standpoint," (p. 27) i.e., because he has not hovered above actuality and perceived "reality" from one unified perspective.

10. For a paradigmatic interpretation of Whitman's desire for the "central man," as well as for an attempt mistakenly to establish an American tradition along the lines of poetic aspiration to such an ideal synthesis, see Harold Bloom, "The Central Man: Emerson, Whitman, Wallace Stevens," *The Ringers in the Tower: Studies in Romantic Tradition* (Chicago: University of Chicago Press, 1971), pp. 217–34, and "Emerson and Whitman: The American Sublime," *PR,* pp. 235–66.

11. See note 18 of my third chapter.

12. In the context of John Vernon's discussion of the possibility of "naked poetry," some attention should be payed to the desire to be "unclothed" as part of the Adamic myth, which I see as essentially an attempt to get out of time by denying both the "presence" of the past and its futurity.

13. For a fuller discussion of these terms as the center of Bloom's critical enterprise, see chapter one, pp. 7–31.

14. See W.V. Spanos, "Heidegger's Phenomenology of Time," pp. 24–34; see also my discussion of Kierkegaard's mastered irony as an attack on the aesthetic model in my previous chapter. I.A. Richards is, of course, the model here. See *Principles of Literary Criticism* (London: Routledge & Kegan Paul, 1967), pp. 139–43.

15. On the coercive aspects of "sight," see Michael Foucault *Discipline and Punish,* trans. Alan Sheridan (New York: Pantheon Books, 1977) esp. pp. 195–229.

16. See Derrida, "La différance," pp. 57–66, which include his discussion of Hei-

# Notes for pages 147–170

degger's use of "trace" in "Der Spruch des Anaximander," *Holzwege* (Frankfurt: Vittorio Klostermann, 1950), pp. 296–343. This idea of "trace" underlies de Man's own theory that all insight of critical language appears in "much more tentative utterances" (*BI*, 102) just as the broader ideas of the ontological difference and *la différance* encompass his structure of blindness–insight.

17. "The Nature of Language," *On the Way to Language*, trans. Peter Hertz and Joan Stambough (New York: Harper and Row, 1971), pp. 60ff.

18. *Writing and Difference*, pp. 278–79.

19. See chapter 1, above.

20. W.V. Spanos, "The Detective and the Boundary: Some Notes on the Postmodern Literary Imagination," pp. 151–58.

21. Derrida, p. 279.

22. Ibid., p. 292.

23. *The Poem of the Mind* (New York: Oxford University Press, 1966), p. 85.

24. *Thoreau and Whitman* (Seattle: University of Washington Press, 1961), p. 47.

25. *The Cycle of American Literature* (New York: Macmillan, 1955), p. 79.

26. Metzger, p. 47.

27. See "Vauvenargues," *Interior Distance*, trans. Elliott Coleman (Ann Arbor: University of Michigan Press, 1964), esp. pp. 31, 43ff.

28. William Wordsworth, "Ode: Intimations of Immortality from Recollections of Early Childhood," *Poetical Works*, ed. Thomas Hutchinson, rvsd. Ernest de Selincourt (New York: Oxford University Press, 1969), pp. 460–62; hereafter cited in my text by line number. In *Wordsworth: Language as Counter-Spirit* (New Haven: Yale University Press, 1977), Frances Fergeson presents a radically deconstructive Wordsworth. But this is not Whitman's "Wordsworth," that is, not the "Wordsworth" my hermeneutics is concerned with.

29. Plato, *Phaedo*, trans. F.J. Church (New York: Bobbs-Merrill, 1951), pp. 3–30.

30. Ibid., p. 25.

31. Derrida, p. 279.

32. Derrida argues that the very concept of a centerless structure is seemingly absurd. Yet, the breakdown of all languages of presence results in precisely this absurdity: "structures" which are "built around" not a fixed and definite point of origin, but instead about a "function" or changing relationship among parts. In other words, in a de-centered structure like Whitman's *Leaves of Grass*, the "place" of the center in traditional structures is taken by a series of changing processes at the very heart of the entire structural manifold. This insight is exactly the crucial one in Derrida's work. De-centering a structure does not mean its inevitable collapse, rather it means that there is no point of stasis, of fixity, or of transcendence which is not involved in the processes of change or subject to the questioning of human doubt. Instead, there is constant interchange among parts, a constant shifting of the "shape" of the structure. I follow Derrida and call this "structurality." In the critical enterprise, such de-centering means that the relative "positions" and "moments" of the text and the reader are all fluctuating so that neither "subject" nor "object" has any completely privileged stature. Perspective is dissolved.

33. Cyclic repetition in Whitman is much closer to that of Kierkegaard and Heidegger than it is to the mythic atemporal repetition which Eliade describes in primitive cultures and which I have discussed in the context of Modern irony in chapter two. The earlier discussion of the "phoenix" figure in this chapter must be seen in the same light as the

temporal repetition of "Crossing Brooklyn Ferry." Both of these poems grow out of the crucial passage ending the 1855 "Preface" quoted above which insists on the absolute restlessness of following the Whitmanic poet through his new worlds.

34. "The Dream of Descartes," *Studies in Human Time*, trans. Elliott Coleman (Baltimore: The Johns Hopkins Press, 1956), p. 57. Poulet defines the *totum simul* as "the concept of a timeless instant in which everything can be apprehended at once."

35. See Daniel T. O'Hara's brilliant discussions of the romance imagination's structures of the sublime in "The Temptations of the Scholar: Walter Pater's Imaginary Portraits," *Destructing the Novel: Essays in Contemporary Criticism*, ed. Leonard Orr (Troy, New York: Whitston, 1979).

## Chapter 5: Fiction, Risk, and Deconstruction: The Poetry of Wallace Stevens

1. Wallace Stevens, *Opus Posthumous*, ed. Samuel French Morse (New York: Alfred A. Knopf, 1957), p. 169. Hereafter cited in my text as *OP*.

2. "The Modern Age (3): Wallace Stevens and the Ultimate Poem," *The Continuity of American Poetry*, pp. 376–419: "Wallace Stevens: The Last Lesson of the Master," *Historicism Once More*, pp. 261–93. I choose Pearce because, although he tries to escape the ahistorical tendencies of the traditional New Critical bias, he comes to conclusions about Stevens which are similar to the New Critically influenced analyses of the poet's work.

3. *The Continuity of American Poetry*, p. 381.

4. *Historicism Once More*, p. 293.

5. *The Act of the Mind*, eds. Roy Harvey Pearce and J. Hillis Miller (Baltimore: The Johns Hopkins Press, 1963), p. 3. The emphasis is mine.

6. See note 3, chapter 3.

7. "Interpreting Stevens: An Essay on Poetry and Thinking," pp. 82–83.

8. *On Extended Wings* (Cambridge: Harvard University Press, 1969), p. 5.

9. Riddel, p. 91. Riddel's review article is a radical revision of his own earlier position on Stevens. In *The Clairvoyant Eye*, Riddel is extremely traditional in his New Critical *explications* of the poems. His language in that book is also the mystified language of the ontotheological tradition he follows Heidegger and Derrida in "destroying." (Baton Rouge: Louisiana State University Press, 1965).

10. Ibid., p. 85.

11. Ibid., p. 86. This is not a position Riddel would take now. For he is supremely aware of the metaphoricity of all writing. Of his many essays, see "An 'American' Metaphorics?", *boundary 2*, 7 (1979).

12. *The Palm at the End of the Mind*, ed. Holly Stevens (New York: Random House, 1972), p. 54. Hereafter cited in my text as *P*. I have chosen to work with this text rather than *The Collected Poems* not only because it presents Stevens' major poems in chronological order, but also because it contains many of the poems Stevens wrote after the publication of *The Collected Poems* which before had been available only in *Opus Posthumous*.

The treatment of "The Snow Man" presented in this chapter began to emerge in a seminar at SUNY/Binghamton in Modern American Poetry conducted by William Spanos. In a discussion of the Husserlian reduction in his forthcoming *Icon and Time*, Spanos makes less extended use of the destructive reading of this poem. See section II,

"The Crisis of Philosophy and the Phenomenological Reduction," in Chapter II, "Husserl's Phenomenology and the Return to Origins."

13. *The Prelude, Poetical Works*, p. 586. Hereafter cited in my text by book and line number.

14. M.H. Abrams, *Natural Supernaturalism* (New York: Norton, 1971), p. 79. Hereafter cited in my text as *NS*. I study Abrams' readings of these poems and not the poems themselves to suggest how one poem often destroys not another poem, but the "ordinary," i.e. "traditional," understanding of that poem. In other words, in showing how "The Comedian as the Letter C" destroys Wordsworth and Shelley, I am actually suggesting that the Stevens poem may be *really* only confronting what the habitual readings of those earlier poems have allowed readers to see in them. This idea of poetic interpretation of other poems is a complicated business. When one poem destroys another, a critic cannot always be sure if there is a direct reference to the earlier poem in the later or merely an implicit destruction of the previous interpretations of the earlier poem; usually, there is some of both.

15. *The Excursion, The Poetical Works*, pp. 603–13.

16. *Poetical Works*, ed. Thomas Hutchinson, corrected by G.M. Matthews (New York: Oxford University Press, 1970), pp. 14–15.

17. See Bové, "The Poetics of Coercion," pp. 278–82.

18. Vendler, p. 20.

19. Ibid., p. 14.

20. Ibid., p. 52.

21. Trans. Annette Lavers and Colin Smith (Boston: Beacon Press, 1968), pp. 1–6.

22. Martz, p. 17.

23. "Stevens: The Last Lesson of the Master," p. 282.

24. "Introduction," *Selected Poems of William Carlos Williams* (New York: New Directions, 1949), pp. i–xix, passim. The importance of Heidegger's term *Gelassenheit* for the study of modern literature was first recognized and developed by Nathan Scott. See "The Literary Imagination in a Time of Dearth," *Negative Capability*, pp. 59–88; *The Wild Prayer of Longing* (New Haven: Yale University Press, 1971).

## Chapter 6: The Particularities of Tradition: History and Locale in *The Maximus Poems*

1. Donald Hall, ed., *Contemporary American Poetry* (Baltimore: Penguin Books, 1963). Three recent books have appeared which alter somewhat my claims that the Modern critical academy has not heard Olson's poetry. Since these texts appeared too late for me to take the specifics of their readings into account, I can only say that their general theses more or less lend support to my position on Olson. Also, I cannot deal in any detail with the remnants of "New Criticism" in their readings—something I would have to do to include them in the general discussion of criticism which opens this chapter. See Sherman Paul, *Olson's Push* (Baton Rouge: Louisiana State University Press, 1978); Robert von Halberg, *Charles Olson: The Scholar's Art* (Cambridge: Harvard University Press, 1978); Paul Christensen, *Charles Olson: Call Him Ishmael* (Austin: University of Texas Press, 1979).

2. This essay and many of Olson's poems were prominently presented in a well-known and influential anthology which Brooks should have known: Donald M. Allen, ed., *The New American Poetry* (New York: Grove Press, 1960).

3. Minneapolis: University of Minnesota Press, 1969, pp. 3ff.

4. New York: Oxford University Press, 1966.

5. Martz, pp. 78–79.

6. *In the American Grain* (New York: New Directions, 1956), pp. 81–104; see Martz, p. 79 for his comment on Williams; see also my later discussion of "touch" in Olson's *Maximus Poems.*

7. See my discussion of the concept of "imitation" in Bate and Bloom in my first chapter as well as my later discussion of Olson's anti-imitative poetics.

8. See my discussion of hard, closed form in chapter three. Williams is probably alluding to T.E. Hulme's definition of Modern poetry which so influenced the New Critics. For a further analysis of this trope, see Spanos, "Modern Literary Criticism and the Spatialization of Time," which has been expanded and revised in the light of phenomenological destruction in the first chapter of *Icon and Time.*

9. Martz, "Preface," p. ix. My italics.

10. See Spanos, *Icon and Time,* chapter one, for an elaboration of this dualistic heritage in Modernism, as well as my first chapter, where I disucss this mystified dualistic rhetoric.

11. See note 8, chapter three, for an examination of the fascistic tendencies of literary humanism.

12. "Four Southerners," *American Poetry,* ed. Irvin Ehrenpreis (New York: St. Martin's Press, 1965), pp. 13–14.

13. *American Poetry,* p. 191. My italics.

14. Northwestern University Press, 1962.

15. New York: Atheneum, 1972, p. x.

16. Howard, pp. xi–xii. All but the last italics are mine.

17. Ibid., p. xiii.

18. See section II, chapter one above.

19. "Postscript: *Charles Olson and Robert Duncan;* The Mystique of Speech and Rhythm" (Berkeley and Los Angeles: University of California Press, 1966), pp. 208–19.

20. Dembo, p. 213; for some sense of the inadequacy of Dembo's formulation of Olson's enterprise see Olson's attack on Plato in "Human Universe," *Selected Writings,* ed. Robert Creeley (New York: New Directions, 1966), p. 55. This essay will hereafter be cited in my text as *HU.*

21. *The Survival of Poetry,* ed. Martin Dodsworth (London: Faber and Faber, 1970), pp. 56–96. In light of my discussion of the ironic stance and Spanos' analysis of spatial form in Modern literature, Pearson's title is revealing. Pearson is a doctrinaire New Critic, who insists that even Lowell's late poetry is formally chiseled and ironic: "But the casual address of the [late] poetry should not deceive us. Each poem is in fact braced by a rigorous logic. Even where it does not display it, it reaches towards a formal rhetoric that predetermines the poem's shape and destination. Each poem is brought round unmistakenly *by* the poet, whose agency the poem declares, to a predestined closure. The poem always exists somewhat after some fact, idea or event; it is not itself a fact, an idea, or an event. It affirms some order which is its ground of being" (p. 80). Pearson denies

what he sees in the late poems in favor of what they do "not display." He habitually reads poems ironically, spatially, i.e., as objects perceived "all-at-once" which must, therefore, be written with an end in mind from the beginning, an end which will close off the entire poem. Such a poetics is radically unlike that in Olson's poems, which often break-off in process and seem to forget their initial direction.

22. Pearson, p. 77. Pearson confuses open form with technological coercion, when, as Sartre shows in *Nausea* and as Olson points out in "Human Universe," it is both the "proposition" and what Olson calls the "suck of symbol" which are the linguistic equivalents of capitalism, imperialism, and technological exploitation.

23. "Introduction: The Survival of Poetry," *The Survival of Poetry*, pp. 11–36.

24. Dodsworth, p. 25.

25. Ibid.

26. Ibid., pp. 28–29.

27. See "Mayan Letters," *Selected Writings*, pp. 69–130.

28. Smith is referred to throughout *The Maximus Poems* as one of the alternative men of American "history" who was not interested in exploitation, but in the process of discovering what exists in the New World. *The Maximus Poems* (New York: Jargon/Corinth Books, 1960), esp. pp. 124ff. Hereafter these poems will be referred to in my text as *MxP*. I will also use the following abbreviations: *The Special View of History*, ed. Ann Charters (Berkeley: Oyex, 1970), *SVH*; *Causal Mythology*, ed. Donald Allen (San Francisco: Four Seasons Foundation, 1969), *CM*; *Selected Writings*, ed. Robert Creeley (New York: New Directions, 1966), *SW*.

29. Matthew Corrigan, "Materials for a Nexus," *boundary 2*, 2 (1973–74), pp. 201–28; L.S. Dembo, "Olson's *Maximus* and the Way to Knowledge," ibid., pp. 279–90.

30. See the opening discussion of chapter two above, as well as note 1 of the same chapter.

31. Corrigan, p. 202.

32. Dembo, p. 288.

33. Ibid.

34. Ibid., pp. 288–89.

35. *Journal of American Studies*, 5 (1971), pp. 304–5.

36. Philips, p. 296.

37. See chapter four.

38. See chapter two.

39. This famous phrase of Wordsworth's comes, of course, from the "Preface to the Lyrical Ballads": "I have said that poetry is the spontaneous overflow of powerful feelings; it takes its origin from emotion recollected in tranquility." While the first half of this quotation seems to contradict the second and to suggest that Olson misunderstands Wordsworth, the full development of this idea makes clear that Wordsworth understood the newly generated emotion to be free of all unsettling and painful elements: "all these [rhyme, meter, ordinary language] imperceptibly make up a complex feeling of delight, which is of the most important use in tempering the painful feeling always found intermingled with powerful descriptions of the deeper passions." *Poetical Works*, ed. Thomas Hutchinson, rvsd. Ernest de Selincourt (New York: Oxford University Press, 1969), p. 740.

40. *The Letters of John Keats*, ed. Hyder Edward Rollins (Cambridge: Harvard University Press, 1958), vol. 1, p. 193.

41. C.F. Butterick, "An Annotated Guide to *The Maximus Poems* of Charles Olson," unpublished dissertation (1970), p. 13. See also, Butterick, *A Guide to the Maximus Poems of Charles Olson* (Berkeley: University of California Press, 1978). Since this expanded version of Butterick's dissertation appeared after I completed this chapter, I continue to refer to the original dissertation. The arrangement of Butterick's text facilitates any cross-reference between the two versions.

42. *Existence and Being,* trans. Werner Brock (Chicago: Henry Regnery, 1949), pp. 327–29.

43. *Nausea,* pp. 37–40.

44. *The Cantos of Ezra Pound* (New York: New Directions, 1970), p. 60.

45. *The Letters of John Keats,* p. 194.

46. On "traditional" versions of nominalism, see Meyrick Heath Carre, *Realists and Nominalists* (New York: Oxford University Press, 1946); Rolf A. Eberle, *Nominalistic Systems* (Dodrecht: Reidel, 1970); Heike Augustinus Oberman, *The Harvest of Medieval Theology* (Cambridge: Harvard University Press, 1963).

47. See Dembo, "Olson's *Maximus* and the Way to Knowledge," p. 283.

48. See esp. W.K. Wimsatt, "The Concrete Universal," *The Verbal Icon* (Lexington: University of Kentucky Press, 1954), pp. 69–84.

49. See *Icon and Time,* chapter two, "Heidegger's Phenomenology of Time: Hermeneutics as Discovery," University Seminar on Postmodernism. SUNY/Binghamton.

50. Butterick, p. 75.

51. Ibid., p. 16.

52. See Spanos, "Heidegger's Phenomenology of Time: Hermeneutics as Discovery," pp. 7–10.

53. Spanos, p. 9.

54. Butterick, p. 47.

55. Ibid., p. 69.

# Index

# Index

# Index

217-27, 270-71; for Bloom, 14; for de Man, 40-43, 47; for Whitman, 146-47

Martz, Louis, 157, 177, 225; *The Poem of the Mind,* 219-21

Miller, J. Hillis, 95, 225, 283*n*2, 287*n*1

Milton, John, xiii, 11; *Paradise Lost,* 14

Modernism, xi, 7, 45, 52, 69, 85, 89, 94, 96, 119, 131, 153, 155, 207, 217-21, 224-25; critical, x-xii, 26-27, 222; de Man on, 38-39; challenge to criticism, 49-50, 52; Brooks' modernism, 97-99; and irony, 106-7, 110, 112, 123, 130; angelism, 114-15; and Whitman, 163; and Stevens, 183-85

New Criticism, ix, xi-xiii, xv-xvi, 1, 23, 25-26, 29, 49-50, 52-53, 62, 79, 90, 92, 98, 110, 112-13, 117, 119, 123, 130-32, 134-36, 138, 143, 148, 177-78, 182-84, 217-28, 230, 233, 237, 240, 245, 249, 263, 275, 280-81, 292*n*1

Nietzsche, Friedrich, 1, 16, 22, 38-42, 45, 50, 53, 64, 86, 116, 153, 155-57, 183; *The Birth of Tragedy,* 38, 155; *Use and Abuse of History,* 39

Olson, Charles, x, xii, xv-xvi, 85, 89, 92, 95-96, 132, 164, 178-79, 217-81; *Maximus Poems,* xi, xiv, 234-35, 239-40, 249-52, 256-57, 259, 265, 267-68, 271-72, 275-76, 278, 281; *Special View of History,* 69, 239, 250, 255-56; "Projective Verse," 218, 244; Dembo on, 228-29, 233-34, 262-63; field, 228-29; open form, 229-30, 245-46, 249; tradition, 232-35, 239-40, 250-51, 258-61; 265, 268-71, 279-81; Philip on, 234-35; pejorocracy, 234-40, 246-47; "Maximus to Gloucester, Letter 27," 234; "Songs of Maximus," 235-36, 238, 241-42, 244-49, 254; language, 237-38, 240, 246-47, 251, 258-59, 261-65; *Human Universe,* 237, 239, 242-43, 260-61; history, 239, 255-57, 271-72, 278-79; art and metaphysics, 240-41; negative capability, 243-44, 255-57, 280; Vincent Ferrini, 251-55, 258, 273-75; "Letter 5," 251-56, 273-75; repe-

tition, 253, 279; "Letter 20," 256-57; "Letter 15," 257; "Letter 12," 257-61; "Tyrian Business," 262-65; *Casual Mythology,* 266-67, 272; periplum, 267-68; "On First Looking out through Juan de la Cosa's Eyes," 267-68; "Maximus to Gloucester, Letter II," 269, 278-79; "Maximus, at Tyre and at Boston," 269-70; polis, 272-74, 279; "Letter 9," 273; care, 274-81; "Letter 7," 276-77; "Some Good News," 280

Pearce, Roy Harvey, ix, 131-32, 134, 182-83, 198, 207, 214, 226, 292*n*1; *Historicism Once More,* 133; *The Continuity of American Poetry,* 225

Plath, Sylvia, 96

Pound, Ezra, 98, 132, 134, 217-19, 227, 232, 236, 238, 261, 267; "In a Station of the Metro," 96; "A Pact," 131; *Cantos,* 218, 248, 255, 278

Pynchon, Thomas, 51, 85, 130; attacked by Bloom, 20-22; *Gravity's Rainbow,* 21; *V,* 21

Ransom, John Crowe, xii, 49, 94, 96, 222-23, 263, 292

Repetition, 11-12, 16, 90; as destructive re-reading, xvi-xvii; ongoing interpretation, 88; and mastered irony, 189; recollection, 243, 249-50; Olson, 253, 279

Richards, I.A., 184

Ricoeur, Paul, 31

Riddel, Joseph, 183-86, 188, 198, 201, 203, 286*n*9, 295*n*9

Romanticism, 37, 52, 149, 160, 182-83, 195-99, 203, 205, 207, 213-14

Rousseau, Jean-Jacques, 43-47, 142-43, 156-57, 178

Said, Edward W., 283*n*2; *Beginnings,* 289*n*11

Sartre, Jean-Paul, 73, 123-24, 130, 191; *Nausea,* 237, 251

Shelley, Percy Bysshe, 198; *Alastor,* 195-97

Spanos, William V., 88, 96, 113, 115, 225, 267, 283*n*1, 284*n*9, 286*n*7, 287*n*16, 287*n*1; *Icon and Time,* 72, 275, 287*n*1, 291*n*36, 293*n*14, 295*n*12, 299*n*49

# Index